ROMANTICISM
AND
FEMINISM

ROMANTICISM
AND
FEMINISM

EDITED BY

ANNE K. MELLOR

INDIANA UNIVERSITY PRESS
Bloomington and Indianapolis

We are grateful to the Editors for permission to reprint portions of
Jane Aaron's essay which originally appeared in *Prose Studies*.

Manufactured in the United States of America

Library of Congress Cataloging-in-Publication Data

Romanticism and feminism.

Includes index.
1. English literature—19th century—History and
criticism.   2. Romanticism—Great Britain.   3. Feminism
and literature—Great Britain—History—19th century.
4. Women and literature—Great Britain—History—19th
century.   5. English literature—Women authors—History
and criticism.   6. Women in literature.   I. Mellor,
Anne Kostelanetz.
PR469.F44R66   1988   820'.9'145   87-45406
ISBN 0-253-35083-2
ISBN 0-253-20462-3 (pbk.)
3 4 5 98 97 96 95

CONTENTS

I.
Introduction

ON ROMANTICISM AND FEMINISM

Anne K. Mellor

This volume of essays, together with the recent books of Mary Poovey, Mary Jacobus, and Margaret Homans,[1] marks the coming of age of a feminist criticism of the major texts of the English Romantic period. These essays developed out of the first sessions of the Modern Language Association Convention devoted entirely to the problem of the English Romantic poets and women, the sessions presented in December 1985 under the auspices of the Late Eighteenth-Century and Romantic Divisions as well as the Wordsworth/Coleridge Association and the Byron Society. This origin explains both the variety of theoretical approaches and the absence of essays on such major Romantic figures as Blake, Coleridge, and Percy Shelley. One might argue, however, that the writers discussed here— William and Dorothy Wordsworth, Byron, Keats, Scott, Wollstonecraft, Mary Lamb, Mary Shelley—are central to any discussion of the problem of gender in English Romantic writing and criticism, since the particularly prominent status of their work helped construct even as it represented their society's attitudes toward sexual difference.

It might be useful to situate these essays within two relevant contexts, methodologically within the development of a feminist literary criticism in America, England, and France over the last decade and historically within the context of the three canonical Romantic writers not otherwise discussed in this volume—Blake, Coleridge, and Percy Shelley. In the last ten years two distinct modes of feminist literary criticism have appeared, which Toril Moi in her useful survey *Sexual/Textual Politics: Feminist Literary Theory* (1985) has called Anglo-American Feminist Criticism and French Feminist Theory, taking Anglo-American and French not as national demarcations but as intellectual traditions in which individual critics work. The Anglo-American tradition is based on the perception that the social construction of gender originates in biological sexual difference but at the same time goes far beyond innate sex differences in its development of an ideological gender-system. This tradition assumes both that women have physical experiences that men cannot share (menstruation, pregnancy, childbirth, lactation, menopause) and, more importantly, that their perceptions of the world are shaped by the differential sex-roles that Western societies have historically enforced upon women and men.

Feminist critics working in this Anglo-American tradition have developed a method that Elaine Showalter has christened "gynocriticism,"[2] a working hypothesis that women both write and read differently from men. The role of the critic is to define these differences, locating them both in the particular biographical experiences of the writers and readers and in the more general cultural ideology that conditions both the behavior patterns and the modes of discourse available to men and women. These critics have followed Virginia Woolf's assertion in *A Room of One's Own* that "we think back through our mothers if we are women" and have argued that there is a distinctive female literary tradition with its characteristic themes and forms. Sandra Gilbert and Susan Gubar in *The Madwoman in the Attic* (1979) defined one dimension of this tradition as the articulation of a female anger at the oppressions of patriarchy, an anger that—if repressed or turned back against the woman—could also produce female masochism, depression, and madness, as in Charlotte Brontë's *Jane Eyre* or Charlotte Perkins Gilman's *The Yellow Wallpaper*. Other feminist critics have stressed the more positive aspects of this tradition. Paralleling Carol Gilligan's recent study of the differences between "female" and "male" modes of ethical thinking, they have emphasized the degree to which such female-authored texts as Jane Austen's *Mansfield Park* or George Eliot's *Middlemarch* celebrate the values of community, cooperation, and self-sacrifice over those of individual achievement and uphold what Gilligan would call a "female ethic of care" as opposed to a "male ethic of justice."[3] Or they have analyzed the ways in which texts written by women critique the dominant gender ideology of their time, showing that both the women authors and their female characters present a more complex concept of female experience and capacities than those defined by the patriarchal doctrine of the separate spheres.

Even as they have tried to regain contact with a uniquely female culture through the archival retrieval of writings by women, these Anglo-American critics have also pointed up the ways in which that experience was often articulated in noncanonical forms, in the genres of letters, diaries, and the less prestigious short story and silver-fork or mass-produced novel. Drawing on the linguistic studies of Wendy Martyna, Robin Lakoff, and Mary Ritchie Key, several have explored Virginia Woolf's insight that men and women writers typically use different styles, plots, syntaxes, and vocabularies.

As readers of literary texts, Anglo-American feminist critics have become, in Judith Fetterley's phrase, "resisting readers."[4] They have directly challenged the sexist assumptions implicit in both the canonical texts of English and American literature and in the traditional body of criticism of those texts. They have pointed up the subtle ways in which texts manipulate readers into acquiescence and even pleasure with existing sex-role expectations; at the same time, they have highlighted those male- as well as female-authored texts that subversively explore alternative modes of sexual identity and experience. Perhaps I should add that Anglo-American feminist criticism has included male as well as female literary critics; as Sandra Harding has argued in her critique of "feminist standpoint theory,"[5] men can adopt a feminist critical perspective as easily as women have in the past adopted a masculinist perspective.

Implicit in Anglo-American feminist literary criticism is a practical politics. Much of this criticism, especially in England, has grown out of a self-conscious socialist program, an effort to identify the sources of sexual, racial, and class oppression and to work toward their elimination. Since the personal is the political, a discussion of the private female experiences articulated in literary texts often produces in the reading critic a sense of shared injustice that must be rectified, by changing both individual life-styles and collective institutions. Gynocriticism has thus directly addressed the modes of production prevailing in both academic and publishing institutions, arguing for a more equitable representation of women writers and critics in the curriculum, the staff and faculty, the student body, and the publishing programs of both university and trade presses.

In contrast, the tradition of French feminist theory is more philosophically oriented. It originated in the attempt to call into question, even deny, the validity of the binary mode of thinking that has characterized philosophical discourse since the ancient Greeks. The dualism inherent in Western thought, whether conceived in terms of the Greek opposition between techne/physis, or the Cartesian mind/body split, or the Kantian subject/object (ding-an-sich), or the Hegelian dialectic of thesis/antithesis, or—most crucially for feminist theorists—the difference of male/female, enforced a cultural practice that could only produce the repression and exploitation of the Other, be it the other class, the other race, the other sex. French philosophers and psychoanalysts have insisted that one can eliminate social oppression only by first eliminating binary rational thinking. In particular, French feminist theorists have insisted that the cultural practice of troping the female as the Other, as that which is opposed to mind/subject/techne, must be radically altered.

In order to undermine dualistic thought-modes and cultural systems, French feminist theorists have argued that the Other—the female—must be resituated, not in opposition but within. The woman must become not an object but a process, an opening up into the unconscious, an activity that Alice Jardine has called "gynesis."[6] Once polarity and balance are destroyed, one can explore new thought-modes (the "post-modernist" project) and deconstruct old systems into a liberating chaos, flux, or playfulness, a jouissance. Hence, Derrida has undermined the Kantian dualism by eliminating the ding-an-sich, arguing that there is only an "absence" at the center of linguistic referentiality; Lacan has insisted that the question "what do women want?" (in the sense both of desire and lack) radically undermines binary linguistic constructions of personal identity; and Julia Kristeva has asserted that language must return to the chora, to the semiotic babble or originary communication experienced between mothers and infants.

In the context of this deconstructive approach, existing modes of linguistic communication can only be regarded as the oppressive domination
of the Name of the Father, of a hegemonic patriarchal discourse. Within
this phallogocentric writing, the female exists only as the absent or silenced
other. For a woman to write in such a language, then, is tantamount to a
denial of the female; hence Margaret Homans, in her recent *Bearing the
Word,* has argued that when a woman writer uses figurative language
(under the Nom de Pere), she participates in the death of the female. The
alternative proposed by French feminist theorists is the construction of a
new language of the female or other, an *écriture féminine,* which deliberately
ruptures binary systems of synchronic and diachronic oppositions, of syntax, vocabulary, and genre. Monique Wittig's *Les Guérillères* (1969) and the
writings of Luce Irigaray and Hélène Cixous are notable recent attempts to
decenter existing linguistic structures and to open a space for the female to
emerge in discourse.

Since the French feminist project is both more theoretical and more
radical than the Anglo-American project and calls for no less than the
deconstruction of all existing systems and institutions of cultural authority,
it has been criticized for lacking a pragmatic political program. French
theorists would respond of course that such Anglo-American political practices as affirmative action and comparable worth initiatives take place only
within existing oppressive capitalist institutions and render those institutions ever more powerful by enabling them to coopt resistance. This debate
is not settled in the essays included in this volume, but it informs some of
their underlying strategies.

Not surprisingly, the bulk of the essays included here work within the
assumptions of the Anglo-American tradition. Some offer an analysis and
critique of the ideological gender-system that conditioned the linguistic
strategies of major Romantic writers, as in Marlon B. Ross's description of
the masculinist concept of the self promoted by Wordsworth or Nancy
Goslee's study of Scott's stereotypical portraits of women. Kurt
Heinzelman, writing from both a Marxist and a feminist perspective, argues that the sexual division of labor in the Wordsworth household encoded a domesticated system of gender. Working within the French
feminist tradition, Karen Swann explores Keats's silencing of the female in
"La Belle Dame sans Merci" as an inherent convention of the Western
romance. Others show the extent to which male Romantic writers felt
threatened by the rigid gender definitions of the early nineteenth century
and attempted to appropriate to themselves the attributes of the female, as
in Alan Richardson's study of the Romantic poets' self-conscious embrac-
ings of the emotions, irrationality, and dreams, or Sonia Hofkosh's analysis
of the ways in which Byron and Keats feminized themselves in relation to a
masculine marketplace.

The essays in the second half of the volume engage in the project of
recovering the silenced voices of the female writers of the period. Susan
Wolfson tracks Dorothy Wordsworth's response to her brother's poetics,

Jane Aaron analyzes Mary Lamb's contradictory effort simultaneously to protest against her economic sufferings and to protect her precarious position within a patriarchal system of labor and discourse, and Stuart Curran provides an overview of what women poets were saying in the late eighteenth century. The concluding essays focus on the writings of two of the leading women writers of the period. By rereading both the concepts of romance and motherhood in Mary Wollstonecraft's fiction, Laurie Langbauer, like Karen Swann, calls into question the viability of conventional genre. My own essay suggests that in *Frankenstein* Mary Shelley unearthed the voice of mother nature in order to condemn both Frankenstein's scientific project and the system of gender-oppression it represents. All these essays implicitly challenge the received notion of the Romantic canon as the "Big Six" (Blake, Wordsworth, Coleridge, Byron, Shelley, Keats) by drawing attention to the wealth and significance of the literary production that occurred outside of the limited corpus of these particular male poets.

It is worth reflecting further on this particularly narrowly defined Romantic canon and on the values such canon-formation implicitly upholds. Marlon B. Ross and Alan Richardson argue that the Romantic ego was both potently male, engaged in figurative battles of conquest and possession, and at the same time capable of incorporating into itself whatever attributes of the female it desired to possess. In effect, the sublime Romantic ego defined itself as god the father, the creator of that language "which rules with Daedal harmony a throng / Of thoughts, and forms, which else senseless and shapeless were."[7] This concept of the poet-savior is as central to Blake, Coleridge, and Shelley as to the poets discussed in this volume. Blake everywhere insisted that the artistic imagination is god, while at the same time defining the ultimate fourfold human form divine as male; the female is but an "emanation" of this fourfold Man.[8] Coleridge, however, conceived of the primary imagination, the "echo of the Infinite I Am," as androgynous. In "The Eolian Harp," the lute that tropes the poetic or secondary imagination is first presented as phallic, "Placed length-ways in the clasping casement," and then as female, "Like some coy maid half yielding to her lover." But this androgynous imagination is appropriated by a male poet and rejected by the reproving female, the woman wailing for her demon lover. For Coleridge, the androgynous male is the source of divine creativity, giving birth to the mighty fountain of the river Alph in "Kubla Khan" in an image that is simultaneously ejaculative and parturitive. In contrast, the potentially androgynous female is an image of horror, figured in the Uba Thaluba of Coleridge's nightmares, in the Life-in-Death of "The Ancient Mariner," and in the lamia-like Geraldine of "Christabel."

Percy Shelley carried to an extreme this dual strategy of deifying the male ego even as it cannibalized the attributes of the female. In his *Essay on Love*, he defined the beloved female as the antitype of the male, "a miniature as it were of our entire self, yet deprived of all that we condemn or despise, the ideal prototype of every thing excellent or lovely that we are capable of conceiving as belonging to the nature of man."[9] The image of the beloved

woman as the perhaps unattainable reflection and completion of the male
ego recurs obsessively in Percy Shelley's poetry, from the veiled maidens of
"Alastor" and "The Witch of Atlas" and the fleeting glimpses of Intellectual
Beauty to the radiantly revealed Asia of "Prometheus Unbound." This
narcissistic dimension of Percy Shelley's thought, unmasked in his wife's
portraits of Victor Frankenstein and Adrian in *The Last Man,* led him to
conceive the heroic Cythna in *The Revolt of Islam* only as a feminine form of
her dead lover Laon, as the renamed Laone.

The critical canonization of only six of the literally hundreds of male and
female writers of the early nineteenth century reflects certain assumptions
deeply imbedded in our political culture. These six male poets have been
heralded because they endorsed a concept of the self as a power that gains
control over and gives significance to nature, a nature troped in their
writings as female. They thus legitimized the continued repression of
women and at the same time gave credence to the historically emerging
capitalist belief in the primacy of the individual over the group. Moreover,
as poets rather than prose-writers, they upheld a hierarchical ordering of
the arts inherited from the eighteenth-century Enlightenment, a hierarchy
that reinforced the elite who had access to Latin, Greek, and the classics of
the past, in other words, those males wealthy enough to gain an education
at private schools and universities. The language of the common man and
woman is found not in the poems of Wordsworth but in the tracts, ballads,
broadsides, and penny-dreadfuls of the street, a vernacular discourse that
literary critics of the Romantic period have until very recently ignored.

In the future, a feminist as well as a new historical criticism of the
Romantic period in England must challenge these traditional prejudices
and undertake the intellectual enquiry already well underway in other
fields of English and American literary criticism, the opening and reshaping of the literary canon. We must read with renewed attention and appre-
ciation the hundreds of female and male writers working in the early
nineteenth century, all those novelists, essayists, journalists, diarists, and
letter-writers who had narratives to tell other than those plotted as "natural
supernaturalism" or "the romantic sublime" or "romantic irony." In these
forgotten or wrongly dismissed writings, we may find stories of equal or
greater significance than those told by Blake, Wordsworth, Coleridge, Byron, Percy Shelley, and Keats, tales of parenting and motherhood, of male
and female friendship, of sexual and racial and class oppression, of anger
and desire and unrecompensed loss and jouissance, above all, tales of *shared*
rather than solitary experience.

NOTES

1. Mary Poovey, *The Proper Lady and the Woman Writer: Ideology as Style in the Works
of Mary Wollstonecraft, Mary Shelley and Jane Austen* (Chicago: University of Chicago

Press, 1984); Mary Jacobus, *Reading Woman: Essays in Feminist Criticism* (New York: Columbia University Press, 1986); Margaret Homans, *Women Writers and Poetic Identity: Dorothy Wordsworth, Emily Brontë, and Emily Dickinson* (Princeton: Princeton University Press, 1980) and *Bearing the Word: Language and Female Experience in Nineteenth-Century Women's Writing* (Chicago: University of Chicago Press, 1986).

2. Elaine Showalter, "Towards a Feminist Poetics," in *Women Writing and Writing about Women,* ed. Mary Jacobus (London: Croom Helm, 1979), pp. 22–44.

3. Carol Gilligan, *In a Different Voice: Psychological Theory and Women's Development* (Cambridge, Mass.: Harvard University Press, 1982).

4. Judith Fetterley, *The Resisting Reader: A Feminist Approach to American Fiction* (Bloomington: Indiana University Press, 1978).

5. Sandra Harding, "The Instability of the Analytical Categories of Feminist Theory," *Signs* 11 (1986): 645–64; see also Nancy Hartsock, "The Feminist Standpoint: Developing the Ground for a Specifically Feminist Historical Materialism," in *Discovering Reality: Feminist Perspectives on Epistemology, Metaphysics, Methodology and Philosophy of Science,* ed. Sandra Harding and Merrill B. Hintikka (Dordrecht: D. Reidel, 1983).

6. Alice A. Jardine, *Gynesis: Configurations of Woman and Modernity* (Ithaca: Cornell University Press, 1985).

7. Percy Shelley, *Poems of Shelley,* ed. Thomas Hutchinson (Oxford: Oxford University Press, 1907): *Prometheus Unbound,* act 4, lines 416–17.

8. Anne K. Mellor, "Blake's Portrayal of Women," *Blake: An Illustrated Quarterly* (1982–83): 148–55.

9. Percy Shelley, *Shelley's Prose or The Trumpet of a Prophecy,* ed. David Lee Clark (Albuquerque: University of New Mexico Press, 1954), p. 170.

II.
Silencing the Female

ROMANTICISM AND THE COLONIZATION OF THE FEMININE

Alan Richardson

Feminist revaluations of late eighteenth- and early nineteenth-century literary history have tended to concentrate on the difficulties facing women writers as producers within a predominantly male tradition. Male hegemony over publishing, reviewing, education left only the novel readily open to woman writers, and even that with conditions; the novelistic conventions and accepted literary language of the time were themselves implicated in patriarchal ideology, less possibilities that a woman could exploit than strictures that she had to work against or subvert.[1] As poets, women were patently excluded from the "masculine tradition" persuasively delineated by Margaret Homans, within which women featured not as active, creative subjects but as passive, quasi-natural objects, "objectified as the other" and made "property" by the male subject.[2]

Homans's account, and those modeled on it,[3] obscure, however, a more insidious form of appropriation characteristic of the Romantic and "pre-Romantic" literary tradition. While men remain very much in control of this tradition, its characterization as simply "masculine" has drawn critical attention away from a tendency of great interest for feminist theory. After reviewing the recent gender theories of Nancy Chodorow among others, Coppélia Kahn has directed critical attention to the "shadowy region" of "male identification with the mother" and its "influence on perceptions and depictions of women in patriarchal texts."[4] I will argue that, in moving from an "Age of Reason" to an "Age of Feeling," male writers drew on memories and fantasies of identification with the mother in order to colonize the conventionally feminine domain of sensibility.

In *The Reproduction of Mothering* Chodorow has shown how the conventional association of woman with emotion and sympathy arises from the structure of the traditional family. Because early (pre-oedipal) experiences of human contact center on the mother, and because the (oedipal) transition from this period encourages girls to maintain their identification with the mother while boys reject her in favor of the father, "different relational capacities for boys and girls" develop. "Girls emerge from this period with a basis for 'empathy' built into their primary definition of self in a way that

13

boys do not. Girls emerge with a stronger basis for experiencing another's needs or feelings as their own."[5] Boys, on the other hand, learn to define themselves "in terms of denial of relation and connection (and denial of femininity)"; in the difficult process of achieving separation from the mother, the boy "rejects and devalues women and whatever he considers to be feminine in the social world."[6]

The devaluation of the feminine predicated by Chodorow's argument is particularly vehement in the English Augustan period; women, considered sensible but not reasonable, were all but denied status as human, that is, rational, beings. For "manly," ultra-patriarchal figures like Samuel Johnson and Lord Chesterfield, women can at best parody men—a "woman's preaching is like a dog's walking on his hinder legs"—and even then only for brief intervals: women "are only children of a larger growth; they have an entertaining tattle, and sometimes wit; but for solid reasoning, good sense, I never knew in my life one that had it, or who reasoned or acted consequentially for four-and-twenty hours together."[7] Pope, upholding his age's valorization of reason along with men's monopoly upon it, could describe the ideal woman in his *Epistle to a Lady* only as a "Contradiction": "Heav'n, when it strives to polish all it can / Its last best work, but forms a softer Man!"[8] The gendered division of reason and passion, with the degradation of women it entails, serves as a target for Mary Wollstonecraft throughout the second *Vindication;* women were granted primacy in the "culture of the heart," she held, only to have their "scanty . . . portion of rationality" begrudged or withheld.[9]

A similar, though subtler, depreciation of the feminine informs the ideology of the Victorian period, in line with Chodorow's contention that male devaluation of women and "relationality" fits well with and is encouraged by advanced industrial capitalism.[10] But during the intervening period, corresponding to what literary historians call the "ages" of Sensibility and Romanticism, the patriarchal tradition was qualified by a widespread revaluation of the feminine, of the emotions, and of relationality. The change in cultural attitudes, which in some ways corresponds to the interregnum of "affective individualism" that Lawrence Stone places between two periods of patriarchal ascendence in his schema of English social history,[11] seems to follow less from economic conditions than from developments in moral philosophy and esthetics. With reason under attack by both empiricists in England and idealists on the Continent, sympathy in ethics and empathy in art criticism emerged as central values.[12] And the feminine was in turn recuperated as a locus for such conventionally "womanly" capacities. Chateaubriand found "la societé des femmes" crucial to the rise of the new Romantic sensibility: "Elles ont dans leur existence un certain abandon qu'elles font passer dans la nôtre; elles rendent nôtre caractère d'homme moins decidé; et nos passions, amollies par le mélange des leurs, prennant à la fois quelques chose d'incertain et de tendre."[13] It is not coincidental that Chodorow's definition of feminine empathy—"experiencing another's needs or feelings as one's own"—recalls both Keats's "negative capability" and the notion of sympathy central to Shelley's *Defence of Poetry:* "A man, to be greatly good, must imagine intensely and comprehensively; he must put himself in the place of another and of many others; the pains and pleasures of his species must become his own."[14] The Man of Feeling found himself every bit as much a contradiction in terms as Pope's ideal (and therefore rational, and therefore male) woman. And as a result he developed strategies—bequeathed in turn to the Romantic poets—for encroaching on the outlands to which women had been banished.

Perhaps because the gendered opposition of reason and emotion is, for considerations delineated by Chodorow, so deeply embedded in Western culture, Romantic writers could not simply claim emotional intensity and intuition as male prerogatives. Instead, where male writers had relegated sympathy and sensibility to their mothers, wives, and sisters, they now sought to reclaim "feminine" qualities through incorporating something of these same figures. The primary foundation for such fantasies of incorporation was sought in memories and depictions of early infancy, when the (male) child initially includes aspects of the mother, especially the breast, in his developing self-conception. Throughout the pre-oedipal period the boundary between infant and mother remains unstable in the psyche of the child, who moves between "fusion, separation, and refusion" with the mother, introjecting maternal qualities and achieving a separate identity only gradually and with difficulty.[15]

The strategies for absorbing feminine qualities developed by Sensibility and Romantic writers all seem to proceed from early experiences of and fantasies about the mother's body. Blake, in *The Book of Urizen,* sees the "female form" as composed of "blood, milk and tears";[16] as externalized expressions, or gifts, of the mother's body, milk and tears gain a great deal of significance for male writers throughout the period. Sometimes the two are interchangeable. Sir Richard Steele, an early sentimental writer, describes in an essay in *The Tatler* how he "imbibed" (drank in) his feminine sensibility through early witnessing his mother's tears (at his father's death):

> There was a Dignity in her Grief amidst all the Wildness of her Transport, which, methought, struck me with an Instinct of Sorrow, which, before I was sensible of what it was to grieve, seized my very Soul, and has made Pity the Weakness of my heart ever since . . . having been so frequently overwhelmed by her Tears before I knew the Cause of any Affliction, or could draw Defences from my own Judgement, I imbibed Commiseration, Remorse and an unmanly Gentleness of Mind.[17]

The mother here exemplifies emotion, compassion, the irrational; the small child, yet to develop "defences of Judgement" (or ego-defenses), internalizes the mother's tears. Rousseau, who idealizes feminine sensibility throughout his works, traces the roots of his own "caractère effeminé" to the tearful sessions with which, during his early childhood, he and his father mourned his mother's death; tears link Jean-Jacques to the absent mother as they linked Steele to the present mother.[18] Such "unmanly" tears become the badge of sensibility: one thinks of Werther's regular fits of weeping, of Mackenzie's prodigiously tearful Man of Feeling, of Yorick's handkerchief "steeped too much already to be of use" when he weeps for Maria in *The Sentimental Journey*[19]—all figures whose effeminacy is closely interwoven with their compassionate sensibility. Throughout Romantic literature tears function as an icon of the male's sympathetic powers, sometimes signifying his restoration through a moment of unforced compassion, as when Blake's Los draws on childhood experiences of relatedness for a redemptive movement of empathy:

> Also Los sick & terrified beheld the Furnaces of Death
> And must have died, but the Divine Savior descended
> Among the infant loves & affections, and the Divine Vision wept
> Like evening dew on every herb upon the breathing ground.[20]

Even Julien Sorel (whom Mme. de Renal at first takes for "une jeune fille deguisée") recovers his humanity in several redemptive fits of tears.[21]

Wordsworth locates the source of his sensibility—and tears—in childhood experiences shared with not his mother but his sister:

> The Blessing of my later years
> Was with me when a boy:
> She gave me eyes, she gave me ears;
> And humble cares, and delicate fears;
> A heart, the fountain of sweet tears;
> And love, and thought, and joy.[22]

Here the Romantic poet's incorporation of feminine qualities approaches a metaphoric heart transplant. In *The Prelude*, Wordsworth similarly apostrophizes his sister in gratitude "for all the early tenderness / Which I from thee imbibed"; as the verb implies, Dorothy functions in the poetry largely as a displaced version of the absent mother.[23] Directly before the apostrophe to Dorothy, Wordsworth celebrates the essential maternity of the fully imaginative man:

> he whose soul has risen
> Up to the height of feeling intellect
> Shall want no humbler tenderness, his heart
> Be tender as a nursing mother's heart;
> Of female softness shall his life be full,
> Of little loves and delicate desires,
> Mild interests and gentlest sympathies.

And in the sonnet "1801" Wordsworth makes clear that femininity is no less central to politics than to poetics:

> I grieved for Buonaparté, with a vain
> And an unthinking grief! The tenderest mood

> Of that Man's mind—what can it be? what food
> Fed his first hopes? what knowledge could *he* gain?
> 'Tis not in battles that from youth we train
> The Governor who must be wise and good,
> And temper with the sternness of the brain
> Thoughts motherly, and meek as womanhood.
> Wisdom doth live with children round her knees.

The good patriarch must himself grow matriarchal; a ruthless figure like Napoleon must have been early deprived, Wordsworth implies, of the milk of human kindness.

Wordsworth describes the food of his own first hopes early in *The Prelude*, when the child develops his affective capacities through both nursing and a metonymic psychic equivalent:

> blest the Babe,
> Nursed in his Mother's arms, who sinks to sleep
> Rocked on his Mother's breast; who with his soul
> Drinks in the feelings of his Mother's eye![24]

The image of nursing recurs throughout Romantic literature precisely because it graphically represents the male child's absorption of his mother's sympathetic faculty even as his primary affective bond is established. Byron develops a figure in *Childe Harold* which, like Wordsworth's, combines soul-feeding with breast-feeding:

> Full swells the deep pure fountain of young life,
> Where *on* the heart and *from* the heart we took
> Our first and sweetest nurture.[25]

And earlier in the same poem his poet-persona claims in a rather extreme metaphor to have maintained the relation into adult life, displacing the mother with mother nature:

> Dear Nature is the kindest mother still,
> Though always changing, in her aspect mild;
> From her bare bosom let me take my fill,
> Her never wean'd, tho' not her favour'd child.

As with Steele's and Wordsworth's adoption of the verb "imbibe," the figure of nursing can be rarefied or transcendentalized, and the mother can appear as a lover or sister; the male's absorption of feminine characteristics, however, remains constant. In a vision of Diana, a figure at once maternal and erotic, Keats's Endymion drinks in feeling looks much as does Wordsworth's infant:

> madly did I kiss
> The wooing arms which held me, and did give
> My eyes at once to death: but 'twas to live,

> To take in draughts of life from the gold fount
> Of kind and passionate looks.[26]

Rousseau's "effeminé" protagonist St. Preux in *La Nouvelle Héloïse* envies
Julie her greater capacity for love—her woman's soul is "plus aimante"—
but pretends to incorporate her higher empathy through a literalized
inspiration, taking in her breath: "avec ta douce haleine tu m'inspirais une
âme nouvelle"; he claims later: "mon première âme est disparue, et que je
suis animé de celle que tu m'as donnée."[27]

The Romantic emblem for the infant's internalization of maternal sympathy, nursing figures as therapeutic or redemptive both at the social and
individual levels. Rousseau advances an almost millennial view of breast-
feeding in *Émile:* "Mais que les mères daignent nourris leurs enfants, les
moeurs vont se réformer d'elles mêmes, les sentiments de la nature se
réveiller dans tous les coeurs: l'État va se repeupler: ce premier point, ce
point seul va tout réunir."[28] Wordsworth's Vaudracour seeks spiritual restoration at one of Julia's breasts while their infant sucks from the other:

> Oftener he was seen
> Propping a pale and melancholy face
> Upon the mother's bosom, resting thus
> His head upon one breast, while from the other
> The babe was drawing in its quiet food.[29]

In a common reversal, nursing can humanize the mother as well, restoring
sympathetic powers that may have lapsed. Wordsworth's "Mad Mother"
provides the most striking instance:

> Suck, little babe, oh suck again!
> It cools my blood, it cools my brain;
> Thy lips I feel them, baby! they
> Draw from my heart the pain away.
> Oh! press me with thy little hand;
> It loosens something at my chest;
> About that tight and deadly band
> I feel thy little fingers prest.

Two of Shelley's heroines, Cythna and Rosalind, are redeemed—one from
madness, the other from despondency—by nursing their infants. Peacock
maintained that the refusal of Shelley's first wife, Harriet, to breast-feed
their child Ianthe paved the way for their later separation; Shelley was so
put out that "at last, in his despair, and thinking that the passion in him
would make a miracle, he pulled his shirt away and tried himself to suckle
the child."[30] However desperate this last measure seems to us, it fits well
with the Romantic poet's feminized self-conception. In the same spirit, De
Musset, allegorizing the poet in his "Nuit de Mai," revises the image of the
pelican, conventionally associated with Christ because it was thought to
pierce its own breast with its bill in order to feed its young, into a figure for

the Romantic poet whose bleeding breast becomes a male equivalent for lactation, a "sanglante mamelle."[31]

Here we are brought up with what Barbara Gelpi has called "the politics of androgyny," a term that, as used by the Romantics, promises a utopian image of wholeness but generally delivers still another version of the male incorporation of the feminine.[32] Yet critics who discuss androgyny—whether Jean Hagstrum on Pope's "perfect" woman or Carolyn Heilbrun on Manfred's incestuous fusion with Astarte—have tended to present it as an uncomplicated ideal, and this tendency shows no sign of diminishing.[33] But when androgyny functions as another manifestation of the male poet's urge to absorb feminine characteristics, his (or his protagonist's) female counterpart stands to risk obliteration. Catherine Macaulay (whose *Letters on Education* had so decisive an influence on Wollstonecraft) exposed this problem long ago by ironically reversing the line from Pope's *Epistle to a Lady* quoted above: "Pope has elegantly said *a perfect woman's but a softer man*. And if we take in the consideration, that there can be but one rule of moral excellence for beings made of the same materials, organized after the same manner, and subjected to similar laws of Nature, we must either agree with Mr. Pope, or we must reverse the proposition, and say, that *a perfect man is a woman formed after a coarser mold*."[34] Such a threat of exclusion or even obliteration lies behind the mysterious death of Astarte in Byron's *Manfred*. For Manfred describes his sister not as a beloved object but as an idealized, feminized version of himself:

> She was like me in lineaments—her eyes,
> Her hair, her features, all, to the very tone
> Even of her voice, they said were like to mine;
> But softened all, and temper'd into beauty;
> She had the same lone thoughts and wanderings,
> The quest of hidden knowledge, and a mind
> To comprehend the universe: nor these
> Alone, but with them gentler powers than mine,
> Pity, and smiles, and tears—which I had not;
> And tenderness—but that I had for her;
> Humility—and that I never had.
> I loved her, and destroy'd her![35]

Manfred's love necessarily destroys its object, because his end is not union with Astarte but the assimilation of her. As the infant's incorporation of the mother or aspects of the mother is founded in what psychoanalysis calls "primary narcissism," the assimilation of a sister or lover (or both in one) follows a later narcissistic relation described by Freud in a passage that seems to echo Manfred's confession: "When narcissistic gratification encounters actual hindrances, the sexual ideal may be used as a substitutive gratification. In such a case a person loves (in conformity with the narcissistic type of object-choice) someone whom he was and no longer is, or also someone who possesses excellences which he never had at all."[36] In

Romantic portrayals of either narcissistic relation, the goal remains constant: appropriation of feminine, maternal characteristics and functions.

A similar strategy informs both Shelley's *Alastor* and his epic *Laon and Cythna* (later revised as *The Revolt of Islam*). The Alastor poet envisions and pursues a feminized self-projection—"Her voice was like the voice of his own soul"—who exemplifies the emotional depth he lacks:

> wild numbers then
> She raised, with voice stifled in tremulous sobs
> Subdued by its own pathos.[37]

Laon gains from his sister, who exemplifies the "female mind / Untainted," the "wider sympathy," which Wordsworth owed to Dorothy; he also reduces Cythna to a subordinate, feminized double: "As mine own shadow was this child to me, / A second self" (Cythna eventually changes her name to "Laone"). Her maternal qualities emerge most clearly in her role as midwife to Laon's visionary "conceptions":

> And this beloved child thus felt the sway
> Of my conceptions, gathering like a cloud
> The very wind on which it rolls away:
> Here too were all my thoughts, ere yet, endowed
> With music and with light, their fountains flowed
> In poesy.[38]

Again, fusion with the sister ultimately involves re-fusion with the mother, in a one-sided pursuit of "wholeness" that Irene Tayler and Gina Luria have related to Blackstone's unapologetically patriarchal definition of marriage current throughout the period: "The husband and wife are one person in law; that is, the very being or legal existence of the woman is suspended during the marriage, or at least is incorporated and consolidated into that of the husband."[39]

Blake poses, as usual, an especially complicated case. His critique of "Patriarchal pomp and cruelty" and his contention near the end of *Jerusalem* that "Sexes must vanish & cease / To be, when Albion arises from his dread repose" seem to point toward a more balanced conception of androgyny, perhaps reflected also in Coleridge's remark that "a great mind must be androgynous" (cited approvingly by Virginia Woolf in *A Room of One's Own*) or Shelley's fusion of a passive Prometheus with an active Asia in *Prometheus Unbound*.[40] If sexes vanish, if the "death-dealing binary oppositions of masculinity and femininity" are broken down, then androgyny dismantles rather than refines patriarchal domination.[41] But Blake's conception of "emanation" as feminine belies his utopian vision, for here again we see woman's sympathetic, maternal capacities subordinated to a male agenda: "Man is adjoined to man by his Emanative portion."[42] Another passage from *Jerusalem* shows both Blake's desire to escape conventional notions of gender and his inability to do so:

> When in Eternity Man converses with Man they enter
> Into each others Bosom (which are Universes of delight)
> In mutual interchange. and first their Emanations meet
> Surrounded by their Children. if they embrace & comingle
> The Human Four-fold Forms mingle also in thunders of Intellect
> But if the Emanations mingle not; with Storms & agitations
> Of earthquakes & consuming fires they roll apart in fear
> For Man cannot unite with Man but by their Emanations
> Which stand both Male & Female at the Gates of each Humanity.[43]

The emanations are here supposed androgynous ("both Male & Female"), and yet even so they are clearly maternal and valued for their feminine capacities for sympathy and empathy. It seems deeply ironic (as the passage continues) that the androgynous vision can be realized only if Enitharmon, the Queen of Heaven, submits to Los: "How then can I ever again be united as Man with Man / While thou my Emanation refusest my Fibres of dominion."

So far I have concentrated on male writers and their appropriation of the feminine, but it seems needful to at least touch on the reactions of their female contemporaries. If indeed Romantic poets and eighteenth-century men of feeling coveted conventionally "feminine" qualities to the point of striving to incorporate them, figuratively cannibalizing their nearest female relatives in the process, how did women writers of the time respond? Why didn't they simply claim these characteristics as, after all, their own and become (or create) Romantic heroines in their own right? There was in fact something of a vogue for the "woman of sensibility" in the late eighteenth and early nineteenth centuries, as witnessed by Helen Maria William's *Julia*, Mary Burton's *Self-Control*, and Jane Austen's *Mansfield Park*.[44] But the option of accepting and extending men's depictions of the feminine was problematic at best. We have noticed in passing that early feminists like Macaulay and Wollstonecraft were fundamentally (and necessarily) opposed to the very distinction between rational male and sensible female that male writers—even when it led them into such devious imaginative strategies—continued to uphold. Literary women had been relegated for too long to the realm of sentiment; they were becoming far less interested in cultivating further refinements of sensibility than in demonstrating their claims to common sense. Mary Jacobus has argued that if femininity was privileged by male writers during the Romantic period it was by the same token debased: if women were valued for natural, intuitive feeling, so were children and idiots.[45]

At least one notable woman writer of the period recognized, and parodied, the Romantic poet's urge to assimilate feminine qualities. As Sandra Gilbert and Susan Gubar have suggested, Mary Shelley's story of Victor Frankenstein tells of a man who, in creating a monstrous child, not only pretends to deific power but (literally) travesties woman's biological prerogative as well.[46] Victor draws what redeeming qualities he has from his "more than sister" Elizabeth, yet another type of maternal feeling: "Her sympathy was ours . . . She was the living spirit of love to soften and attract: I might have become sullen in my study, rough through the ardour of my nature, but she was there to subdue me to a semblance of her own gentleness."[47] But Victor ultimately takes more after Manfred than Astarte, and his adopted sister is similarly destroyed by a brother's attempt to appropriate the feminine. Frankenstein can create a kind of life; what he cannot give is precisely what the reproduction of mothering in women assures: sympathy, love, nurturing. It is a charge repeatedly brought against Frankenstein by his creature, who destroys (Elizabeth and others) only because he is not loved. In attempting to bear a child with the aid only of rationality and science, in assuming the extreme pose of a feminized Romantic creator, Shelley's Frankenstein is far more a monster than the pitiable, but fatally unpitied, creature that for us bears his name.

Feminist critiques of men's representation of woman often assume a strict duality of male writer as subject and woman (usually conflated with nature) as object. This model is a powerful one, suggesting a fundamental critique of representation itself (at least within Western culture). But too rigid a dichotomy of male subject and female object allows us to forget that, even according to men's depiction of themselves, subjectivity is initially produced through interaction with a woman. The Romantic tradition did not simply objectify women. It also subjected them, in a dual sense, portraying woman as subject in order to appropriate the feminine for male subjectivity. The implications of this Romantic program—that questions of gender and subjectivity are more likely to involve a dialectical relation than a simple dichotomy—should be kept in mind as we, men and women, continue to criticize our own subject positions.

NOTES

1. Elaine Showalter, *A Literature of Their Own: British Women Novelists from Brontë to Lessing* (Princeton: Princeton University Press, 1977); and Mary Poovey, *The Proper Lady and the Woman Writer: Ideology as Style in the Works of Mary Wollstonecraft, Mary Shelley, and Jane Austen* (Chicago: University of Chicago Press, 1984).

2. Margaret Homans, *Women Writers and Poetic Identity: Dorothy Wordsworth, Emily Brontë, and Emily Dickinson* (Princeton: Princeton University Press, 1980), p. 37.

3. E.g., Marlon Ross, "Naturalizing Gender: Woman's Place in Wordsworth's Ideological Landscape," *ELH* 53 (1986): 391–410.

4. Coppélia Kahn, "The Hand That Rocks the Cradle: Recent Gender Theories and Their Implications," in *The (M)other Tongue: Essays in Feminist Psychoanalytic Interpretations*, ed. Shirley Nelson Garner, Claire Kahane, Madelon Sprengnether (Ithaca: Cornell University Press, 1985), p. 88.

5. Nancy Chodorow, *The Reproduction of Mothering: Psychoanalysis and the Sociology of Gender* (Berkeley and Los Angeles: University of California Press, 1978), pp. 92, 167.

6. Chodorow, pp. 169, 181.

7. R. W. Chapman (ed.), *Boswell's Life of Johnson* (London: Oxford University Press, 1953), p. 327; Chesterfield quoted in Katherine Rogers, *The Troublesome*

Helpmate: A History of Misogyny in Literature (Seattle: University of Washington Press, 1966), p. 178. See also Rogers, "Anne Finch, Countess of Winchelsea: An Augustan Woman Poet" in *Shakespeare's Sisters,* ed. Sandra M. Gilbert and Susan Gubar (Bloomington: Indiana University Press, 1979).

8. See Carol Houlihan Flynn, " 'A Softer Man': Pope's, Swift's and Farquhar's Feminine Ideal," *South Atlantic Quarterly* 84 (1985): 51–62.

9. Mary Wollstonecraft, *A Vindication of the Rights of Woman,* ed. Carol H. Poston (New York: Norton, 1975), p. 52.

10. Chodorow, pp. 32, 180–90.

11. Lawrence Stone, *The Family, Sex and Marriage in England 1500–1800* (1977; abridged ed., New York: Harper, 1979).

12. See W. J. Bate, *From Classic to Romantic* (1946; reprint ed., New York: Harper, 1961), esp. chap. 5; Roy Male, Jr., "Shelley and the Doctrine of Sympathy," *Studies in English* 29 (1950): 183–203; James Engell, *The Creative Imagination* (Cambridge, Mass.: Harvard University Press, 1981), esp. chap. 11.

13. Francois-René de Chateaubriand, *Génie du Christianisme,* 2 vols. (Paris: Garnier-Flammarion, 1966) 1: 309.

14. David Lee Clark, ed., *Shelley's Prose: The Trumpet of a Prophecy* (Albuquerque: University of New Mexico Press, 1954), p. 283.

15. Chodorow, p. 73.

16. *Urizen,* plate 18, line 4 in David V. Erdman, ed., *The Complete Poetry and Prose of William Blake,* rev. ed. (Berkeley and Los Angeles: University of California Press, 1982).

17. *Tatler* 181, in Robert J. Allen, ed., *Addison and Steele: Selections from the Tatler and Spectator* (New York: Rinehart, 1970), p. 79.

18. Jean-Jacques Rousseau, *Les Confessions,* 2 vols. (Paris: Garnier-Flammarion, 1968) 1: 49. Irving Babbitt's comment on Rousseau's revaluation of the feminine (following his comparison of Jean-Jacques to "a high-strung impressionable woman") is worth quoting if only as an index of how long the thinking exemplified by Johnson and Chesterfield has persisted: "It is almost woman's prerogative to err on the side of sympathy . . . In basing conduct on feeling Rousseau may be said to have founded a new sophistry. The ancient sophist at least made man the measure of all things. By subjecting judgment to sensibility, Rousseau may be said to have made woman the measure of all things." *Rousseau and Romanticism* (1919; reprint ed., Cleveland: Meridian Books, 1955), pp. 120, 132.

19. Laurence Sterne, *A Sentimental Journey through France and Italy by Mr. Yorick,* ed. Ian Jack (London: Oxford University Press, 1968), pp. 115–16.

20. *Jerusalem* (in Erdman), plate 18, lines 5–8.

21. Stendhal, *Romans et Nouvelles,* 2 vols. (Paris: Gallimard, 1952) 1: 241.

22. From "The Sparrow's Nest"; my text for Wordsworth's poems (excluding *The Prelude*) is *William Wordsworth: The Poems,* ed. John O. Hayden, 2 vols. (Harmondsworth: Penguin, 1977).

23. *The Prelude,* 1805, 13. 213–14 in *William Wordsworth: The Prelude, 1799, 1805, 1850* (New York: Norton, 1979); references are to book and line numbers. For a discussion of Dorothy as a displacement of the mother see Richard Onorato, *The Character of the Poet: Wordsworth in The Prelude* (Princeton: Princeton University Press, 1971), p. 83.

24. *The Prelude,* 1850, 2. 234–37.

25. *Childe Harold* 4. 149 and 2. 37 in Lord Byron, *The Complete Poetical Works,* ed. Jerome J. McGann (Oxford: Clarendon Press, 1980), vol. 2; reference is to canto and stanza.

26. *Endymion* 1. 653–57 in *The Poems of John Keats,* ed. Jack Stillinger (Cambridge: Harvard University Press, 1978); reference is to book and line numbers.

27. Rousseau, *Julie ou la Nouvelle Héloïse,* ed. R. Pomeau (Paris: Garnier, 1960), pp. 189, 124, 206.

28. Rousseau, *Émile ou de l'education* (Paris: Garnier-Flammarion, 1966), pp. 47–48. The period saw a widespread return to breast-feeding on the part of upper- and middle-class mothers; see Stone, *Family*, pp. 269–73.

29. *Prelude*, 1805, 9. 811–15.

30. Newman Ivey White, *Shelley*, 2 vols. (New York: Knopf, 1940), 1: 326.

31. Alfred de Musset, *Premières Poésies, Poésies Nouvelles* (Paris: Gallimard, 1976), p. 247. One could note in this context that Karen Horney in her essay "The Flight from Womanhood" traces men's depreciation of femininity to an unacknowledged and "intense envy of motherhood"; see *Feminine Psychology*, ed. Harold Kelman (New York: Norton, 1967), pp. 60–61.

32. Barbara Charlesworth Gelpi, "The Politics of Androgyny," *Women's Studies* 2 (1974): 151–60.

33. For a recent reading of Romantic androgyny as expressing a "longing of imperfect beings for wholeness" see Cynthia M. Baer, " 'Lofty Hopes of Divine Liberty': The Myth of the Androgyne in *Alastor, Endymion*, and *Manfred*," *Romanticism Past and Present* 9 (1985): 25–49. William Veeder, in *Mary Shelley and Frankenstein: The Fate of Androgyny* (Chicago: University of Chicago Press, 1986), goes so far as to present androgyny as an idealized vision comparable to (and based upon) the traditional Christian conception of marriage, singling out such couples as Tom and Sophia in *Tom Jones* and Pamela and Squire B. in *Pamela* as exemplary nuptual androgynes (pp. 23–46).

34. Catherine Macaulay, *Letters on Education* (London: Dilly, 1790), p. 205.

35. *Manfred*, 2. 2.199–211, *The Poetical Works of Byron*, ed. Robert Gleckner (Boston: Houghton Mifflin, 1975); reference is to act, scene, and line. I borrow this and several other examples from my article "The Dangers of Sympathy: Sibling Incest in English Romantic Poetry," *SEL* 25 (1985): 737–54.

36. Sigmund Freud, "On Narcissism: An Introduction," in *General Psychological Theory: Papers on Metapsychology*, ed. Philip Rieff (New York: Collier, 1963), p. 81. Romantic incest is related to Freud's conception of narcissism by Peter L. Thorslev, Jr., in "Incest as a Romantic Symbol," *Comparative Literature Studies* 2 (1965): 41–58 and by Barbara Schapiro in *The Romantic Mother: Narcissistic Patterns in Romantic Poetry* (Baltimore: Johns Hopkins University Press, 1983), esp. pp. 1–24.

37. *Alastor*, lines 153, 163–65 in *Shelley's Poetry and Prose* ed. Donald H. Reiman and Sharon B. Powers (New York: Norton, 1977).

38. *Laon and Cythna*, 2. 24, 2. 31–32; references are to canto and stanza.

39. Sir William Blackstone, *Commentaries on the Law of England* (Oxford, 1765) quoted in Irene Tayler and Gina Luria, "Gender and Genre: Women in British Romantic Literature," *What Manner of Woman: Essays in English and American Life and Letters*, ed. Marlene Springer (New York: New York University Press, 1977), p. 98.

40. *Jerusalem*, plate 83, line 4 and plate 92, lines 14–15. Woolf slightly misquotes Coleridge ("a great mind is androgynous") in *A Room of One's Own* (New York: Harcourt Brace Janovich, 1957), p. 102. Although Woolf's conception of androgyny has been criticized as a "flight" from feminist engagement (Showalter, pp. 263–97), Toril Moi defends it as deconstructive of the oppositions upon which patriarchy relies in *Sexual/Textual Politics: Feminist Literary Theory* (London: Methuen, 1985), pp. 1–18. On Shelley's related depiction of androgyny in *Prometheus Unbound* see Ross Woodman, "The Androgyne in *Prometheus Unbound*," *Studies in Romanticism* 20 (1981): 225–47; and Nathaniel Brown, "The 'Double Soul': Virginia Woolf, Shelley, and Androgyny," *Keats-Shelley Journal* 33 (1984): 182–204.

41. Moi, p. 13.

42. *Jerusalem*, plate 39, line 38. I am indebted here to Susan Fox, "The Female as Metaphor in William Blake's Poetry," *Critical Inquiry* 3 (1977): 507–19.

43. *Jerusalem*, plate 88, lines 3–13.

44. Tayler and Luria, pp. 111–13.

45. Mary Jacobus, "The Buried Letter: Feminism and Romanticism in *Villette*" in

Women Writing and Writing about Women, ed. Jacobus (London: Croom Helm, 1979), p. 58.

46. Gilbert and Gubar, *The Madwoman in the Attic: The Woman Writer and the Nineteenth-Century Literary Imagination* (New Haven: Yale University Press, 1979), p. 232.

47. Mary W. Shelley, *Frankenstein or The Modern Prometheus,* ed. M. K. Joseph (London: Oxford University Press, 1969), p. 38. Cf. Walton's acknowledgment to his sister, Mrs. Saville, of her "gentle and feminine fosterage," which "refined the groundwork" of his character (p. 20).

ROMANTIC QUEST AND CONQUEST

TROPING MASCULINE POWER IN THE CRISIS OF POETIC IDENTITY

Marlon B. Ross

> Possessions have I that are solely mine,
> Something within, which yet is shared by
> none—
> Not even the nearest to me and most
> dear—
> Something which power and effort may
> impart.
> I would impart it; I would spread it wide,
> Immortal in the world which is to come.
>
> (*Home at Grasmere*, 686–91)

When Wordsworth, referring to his poem on the growth of a poet's mind, recognizes that his project is "a thing unprecedented in Literary history that a man should talk so much about himself,"[1] he is also bringing attention to the anxious self-consciousness that pervades all Romantic poetry, to the persistent effort of the Romantic poet to find in his own voice an aboriginal self that re-creates the world and that emblematizes the capacity for seizing meaning in the world. And of course Wordsworth is right. We cannot imagine any poet before him or his time writing a poem about the coming to being of the poetic self. Romantic poets are driven to a quest for self-creation, for self-comprehension, for self-positioning that is unprecedented in literature. Convinced that within the individual an autonomous and forceful agent makes creation possible, they struggle to control that agent and manipulate its energy; they struggle for self-possession—a state in which the individual has mastered his genealogy, his internal contradictions, his doubts about his power of mastery and the world that seems to obstruct its sway; a state in which the self has managed to see the world whole, to assimilate both time and space into a vision that is both individual and collective, to assemble all conflicting aspects of the self and put them to creative use, and by doing so to assert the power of the self to engender itself.

When Harold Bloom, identifying the cause of this quest for poetic self-possession as cultural belatedness, claims that "as poetry has become more subjective, the shadow cast by the precursors has become more dominant,"[2] he also is underscoring, like Wordsworth, the precariousness of the poet's status in relation to his world since the end of the eighteenth century. Bloom, himself a Romantic as well as a Romanticist, tends to read all poetry from the position of the Romantic self-crisis and develops a poetics of influence based on the accurate insight that "self-appropriation involves the immense anxieties of indebtedness" (*Influence,* p. 5). In other words, the self can be established only in relation to other things on which it depends for its self-definition. For Bloom, the unapologetic belated Romantic, all poetry becomes a tug-of-war between poets and their literary fathers, and only the "strong" man wins, for only he can create himself despite the father's overriding claims of insemination, authority, and paternal possession. Bloom also recognizes, however, that the son is always at a disadvantage because his quest for self-creation is doomed by its impossibility. The son wins self-possession only tentatively, if at all, in the same way that he may realize that he has made himself who he is *only* because he could not be what his father has already become. As Bloom states, "from his start as a poet he quests for an impossible object, as his precursor quested before him" (*Influence,* p. 10). The Romantic poet quests for the originating self within the self only to discover, whether he recognizes his tragedy or not, a relation or ratio, only to discover his indebtedness to the world of his forefathers in making him capable of seeming to possess himself.

In "The Internalization of Quest-Romance,"[3] the seminal essay that fathers *The Anxiety of Influence,* Bloom focuses on the paradoxical nature of Romantic self-questing, as he points out that the Romantic poet moves farther and farther within, in an attempt to find the source of the self, in an attempt to embrace all that is without. Imagination, that capacity which apotheosizes individual vision, is also a going out of self; it is simultaneously the egotistical sublime and negative capability. Imagination is the attempt to stabilize the world (or whatever one calls that external expanse that delimits selfhood) by destabilizing the self that seems to block the potential for total vision, the potential for totally embracing that outer expanse. The poet's relation to the world, much like his relation to his father, is fraught with anxiety, because the apparent externality of that world threatens the necessary myth that he fathers vision by fathering himself. Anything within the purview of that world is also a potential vehicle as well as a threat, for every external pressure, though it stresses the limits of selfhood and the impossibility of self-creation, can be exploited to move the poet and his audience toward the myth of self-possession. Solipsistically magical, the "self" can transform any external object into an aspect of itself while pretending to deny the externality of that object; it can envision and contain the infinite world by peering into the finite self, appearing to liberate the self from its own borders, appearing to capture the world for itself, appearing to father the world. The Romantic self, then, is always at strife with its progenitors and with its siblings, with generation and contextuality, which make a myth of self possible.

In their now-classic study *The Madwoman in the Attic*, Gilbert and Gubar point out the appropriateness of Bloom's gendered poetics for the patriarchal nature of the Western literary tradition. They examine the various ways in which Western writers have used the "metaphor of literary paternity" and how this patriarchal conception of writing has reduced women "to mere *properties*, to characters and images imprisoned in male texts because generated solely . . . by male expectations and designs."[4] In her excellent study *Women Writers and Poetic Identity* (which appeared a year after *Madwoman*), Margaret Homans demonstrates how three female poets (Dorothy Wordsworth, Emily Brontë, and Emily Dickinson), confronted with a hegemonic masculine tradition, attempt to write within that tradition while reshaping it for the feminine voice. Coincidentally making an argument similar to Gilbert and Gubar's, Homans points out, speaking specifically about the masculinist Romantic tradition, how "the powerful self is inextricable from the use of efficacious language, since the powerful self is so often the poet, or a poet. He constructs the strong self from his own strong language."[5] Both studies lay fertile ground for a reexamination of the historical manifestations of self-imaging in literature and of how such self-imaging has been based on the gendered socialization of poets. Building on these studies, we must flesh out the myriad ways in which the poetic vocation has been socio-historically defined as distinctively masculine and how such definition historically has affected not only women's attempts to speak within the context of an alienating tradition but also men's attempts to speak a universal and holistic language in the context of a gendered tradition that alienates them, as well, from the whole. Not only must we examine how Romantic poetry is constituted by its own distinctive masculinist postures and premises; we must also ask how the specific Romantic manifestation of the masculinist tradition interrelates with the socio-historical conditions of poets writing during the time.

As Gilbert, Gubar, and Homans point out, the metaphor of potent father informs the self-image of Western writers from the beginning. The Romantics, however, grant the poet a higher place, a more powerful influence and a more crucial mission in the world than any writers before them. Nor is it arbitrary that poets of the Romantic era are driven to self-possession as the motivating force for poetic expression. This essay examines why a poet like Wordsworth is compelled to write a self-possessing poem, one not imaginable before his time, in the context of the socio-historical conditions that inform, and are informed by, his writing. The myth of masculine self-possession results from an impending change in socioeconomic status for the poet, a change in his relationship to his audience and his society, and a change in the relation to his sources of inspiration. The myth of self-possession enables the historical resituation of the poet, allows him to adapt psychologically, philosophically, and pragmatically to historical forces that are beyond his control as a human being but that nurture the myth of self-control as the primary means for *containing* those forces (limiting their influence while accepting their inevitability). The self-questing of the Romantic poet enacts the attempt to reestablish a relation with—a hold on—the world, a relation that is predetermined by the nature of the historical changes that envelope and transform the poetic vocation itself. The Romantics resort to masculine metaphors of power not only because they are socialized and indoctrinated into a masculinist tradition but also (and tautologically) because these metaphors allow them to reassert the power of a vocation that is on the verge of losing whatever influence it had within and over that tradition.

1. Empowering the Self, Reclaiming Masculine Identity

Romanticism is not simply a historical period that includes any writer publishing work between two arbitrary dates; it is—or it has become—a complex of values and beliefs, a set of structural, thematic, and generic tendencies, an approach to the world with its own assumptions and aims, an ideology, however contentious and diverse its proponents. As critics have pointed out, Romantic poets write from a position and a perspective that would be impossible for a woman living during the time to take. This is not just because of the cultural stereotypes of gender roles during the period—though such roles are crucial determinants[6]—but also because Romanticism is historically a masculine phenomenon. Romantic poetizing is not just what women cannot do because they are not expected to; it is also what some men do in order to reconfirm their capacity to influence the world in ways socio-historically determined as masculine. The categories of gender, both in their lives and in their work, help the Romantics establish rites of passage toward poetic identity and toward masculine empowerment. Even when the women themselves are writers, they become anchors for the male poets' own pursuit for masculine self-possession.

Even though women begin to write publicly and to be known by the reading public as writers during what we have come to call the Romantic period, their influence is felt not in the "high" poetic genres for which that period has become critically acclaimed.[7] The canon of Romantics remains wholly male at a time when rediscovered women writers are finding more or less comfortable homes in many other periods and genres. Although Dorothy Wordsworth and Mary Shelley might be considered female Romantic writers, their inclusion in the Romantic canon proves extremely problematic. If one of Romanticism's definitive characteristics is the self-conscious search for poetic identity, how can Wordsworth, who tended not to conceive of herself as a poet, be considered a "Romantic"?[8] Dorothy's journal entries are rarely rewritten as poems—the way we see William rewriting his and her entries or Percy Bysshe Shelley rewriting his; her

journal insights are rarely offered to the public and are seldom transformed into the poetic conventions considered at the time to be the highest
and most honorable kind of elocution. Mary Shelley's writing, besides being
in "prose" (the "lower" form of expression), dissents with Romanticism, and
Mary's loving devotion to the editing of Bysshe's poems displays a confidence in his work that she does not seem to have in her own.[9]

The comparison of these two women is instructive. Dorothy certainly
never received the kind of encouragement from William that Mary received from Bysshe; yet in both cases the women were overshadowed (and
overshadowed themselves) by the men they saw as poetic geniuses, and in
both cases the woman intertwines admiration for the poet's genius with
devotion and love supposedly not predicated by the genius alone. It would
be impossible to disentangle the woman's literary and intellectual modesty
from the specific emotions each felt for her beloved. Both women must
have sensed the extent to which these men needed a loving other, and an
other whose interest is constituted more by a capacity to listen than a
tendency to converse, whose concern is defined more as devotion than as
friendly rivalry, as difference rather than sameness. It is no mistake that
these women are written into the men's poems as extensions of themselves
(Dorothy in "Tintern Abbey" and Mary in the Dedication to the *Revolt of
Islam,* for instance), but when these men need conversants and rivals, they
turn to their fellow (i.e., male) poets, not the women they are closest to (as
William turns to Coleridge in *The Prelude* and Bysshe turns to Byron in
Julian and Maddalo). Dorothy and Mary serve to represent William's and
Bysshe's better half, a visionary ideal, a goal to achieve, an object to desire.
Whereas the poet's female companion functions as an anchor for the self, as
a way of realizing and validating the power and autonomy of the creative
agent, the male companion is seen more as a counterpart or, more precisely, as a counteragent, a way of gauging the poet's own creative progress.
For even though the female is herself a writer, she is seen as creative in a
different sense, in a way that can be felt as less threatening to the male poet.
Because her gender "naturally" places her in a different arena, he can de-
emphasize any competitive urge between them and instead appropriate her
difference as a source of inspiration and as leverage for his will to self-
possession. The male-female relation predicated by society and nature, as
the poet understands such, is one of complementarity rather than con-
testation, so if women could be conceived of as competing at all for poetic
mastery, they would be seen as competing with other women in their own
arena, not with men.

Bloom's "strong" poet is a useful epithet because it identifies so clearly the
reigning conception of poetry during the Romantic and post-Romantic
periods and it indicates how that conception is rooted in premises of
masculine potency. Even before the Romantic period, poetry was considered a contest in which men could test their powers, but for the Romantics
this masculine contest accrues profound and intense meaning with consequences that are seen as universal and momentous. It is no longer just

one way of cleverly proving one's wit, gentility, and classical humaneness. It becomes the sole means of conquering the wilderness of personal and societal confusion, settling the borders of self potential, and civilizing the new territories of social enterprise. It becomes chivalric jousting transformed to meet the conditions of a social system in which power manifests itself no longer in physical strength but in the strength of various kinds of cognitive and metaphorical exchanges. As political power has become progressively derived not from the combined strength of individual men in combat but from a complex of mental operations (military strategy, technical inventiveness, parliamentary deliberation, propaganda, etc.), the individual or society that devises ways of establishing and sustaining cognitive hegemony becomes the strongest and rules the world. Just as economic power becomes primarily constituted by abstract transactions of capital rather than by the immediacy of agricultural and mercantile bartering, so political power becomes metonymic and abstract, the province of literacy (broadly defined) and intellect. Men rule by proxy and by mental musculature rather than by their physical presence and the allegiance owed to that presence. The American and French Revolutions had shown graphically how secular ideologies and propaganda can controvert preordained physical realities, had shown how the ideas of individual men could be stronger than the actual strength of the most powerful armies. In this sense, Romanticism is not so much a reaction against the Enlightenment spirit, but a culmination of it. More than any poets before them, the Romantics believe that power is constituted by *ideas*—whether the knowledge is scientific, historical, political, philosophical, or narrowly technological. And they believe that to govern these ideas—to wrestle them into an organic whole that seems to make sense in universal terms—is to govern the world itself. In a very real sense the Romantics, some of them unwittingly, help prepare England for its imperial destiny. They help teach the English to universalize the experience of "I," a self-conscious task for Wordsworth, whose massive philosophical poem *The Recluse* sets out to organize the universe by celebrating the universal validity of parochial English values. Blake, Wordsworth, Coleridge, Southey, Shelley, and to some extent Byron all started careers as propagandists, as men concerned with self-consciously propagating certain ideologies through their poetry in the hope of transforming political reality. And why not? If the idea is the source of power, why cannot poets, who deal in the interchange of ideas, join in the contest for power? Indeed, since poets practice the skills of inspiring allegiance to what is otherwise unreal (in being figurative and fictional) and making concrete and familiar what is otherwise abstract and alien, they have perhaps the best chance of accruing power. And since they need not rule directly, but only by proxy, they need not display the official signs of power to be strong.

With the Romantics, poetry becomes serious warfare, much more serious (in the eyes of the Romantics themselves) than the courtly skirmishes of Pope and Cibber, for the Romantics believe that on their individual visions and on the visions of all strong poets depends not just the fate of a party or nation, but the fate of humanity itself, the capacity for humanity to envision its own fate. The Romantic poet, then, bestows upon himself the mantle of the medieval romance quester not only because he writes internalized romances but also, and more importantly, because he has taken the virile role of the chivalric savior. On his exploits—now intellectualized and metonymic, based on individual vision that operates always in forms of displacement from the social whole—civilization itself depends. Like the medieval knight, the Romantic poet arms himself to compete for the collective good. He attempts to stand out as the best, as the strongest, for the sake of all who are weak and need protection; medieval peasants and ladies are replaced with the lower classes, orphans, beggars, widows, idiots, virgins, and those particular women in the poets' lives who inspire them to greater heights of self-possession. And like the knight, the Romantic poet proves the strength of his vision, his right to defend and protect, through masculine rivalry, through competition with other men who also claim to be strong enough to sustain the whole and protect the weak with single-handed might.

Conveniently, the Romantic poet is able to retain his masculine identity as romance quester, for he also identifies subliminally with two new masculine roles (even as he self-consciously counters these emergent roles) that become significant in the early nineteenth century: the scientist and the capitalist.[10] The scientist searches for laws that he takes to be natural and universal, and, as inventor, he originates powerful ways of applying these laws to transform the material conditions of society. The poet wants to claim the same powers: mastery over nature, originality, and capacity to transform the material conditions of society through his poetic inventions. The Romantic poet, however, wants to claim even greater powers of mastery over the world. Limited by the limitations of material cause and effect, the scientist can effect material change only. But the poet's power is limited only by his own capacity for self-possession. Since his materials derive from the human spirit or soul, from powerful feelings and deep thoughts, his power is more universal, higher and profounder, and it can influence not only the spiritual realm but also the actual material conditions, which owe their existence to that higher realm. To use Shelley's terms, to follow scientists instead of poets is to become enslaved to the material conditions that we want to control. Because the poet's relation to nature is of a higher kind and because he studies the relation between human nature and natural law, he supposedly can offer mastery of nature without the risk of enslavement or exploitation, for part of his mission is to balance a material use of nature and a mysterious union with nature. The scientific calling, then, becomes a crude and weak form of the poetic vocation, capable of great harm through its inherent limitations.[11]

The capitalist-industrialist competes with the scientist to become the new strong man, and his province is the new economic terrain of fierce competition, risk, power, and influence. The capitalist will create empires out of his individual vision, fighting off the threat of his competitors and claiming a larger purpose of collective good, as he individually grows in power and widens his empire. He, like the Romantic poet (or vice versa), believes that power derives from self-creation, that the stability of the whole relies on the capacity for individual self-possession. The competitive market in which he is forced to prove his power represents a risk of contamination for the poet. The poet claims that his capital is the element of pure vision, unlike the crude and corrupting alloy of money through which the capitalist seizes his empire. The market of readers, however, serves as a constant reminder to the Romantic poet that his power is actually, like the capitalist's, impure, for it is dependent on the interest of a fickle public. The Romantics have to contend, more than any writers before their time, with a market-based readership that always threatens to undermine the myth that poetic influence derives from some self-generating power that transcends all variables of time, place, and mere human assent.

As the contest moves from the court and the patronage of gentlemen to the publishing house and the market of the common reader, the poet's success becomes literally more dependent on the power of self-possession, the potency of his individual vision, his ability to captivate and rule a diverse, saturated, and fickle public, and part of his power will depend on the newness and originality of his appeal among readers. As long as his vocation is defined by its dependency on an aristocratic class, his project is more or less traditional and customary, a matter of representing the strength of his discourse by displaying its continuity with poetic tradition and displaying its allegiance to the party of his patron. To stray too far from his literary inheritance would symbolize a threat to the validity of his patron's inherited authority and would in turn threaten his own means of support. The patronized poet writes from the context of a world whose predefined stability is ritualized through his relation to the official political hierarchy. To bring too much attention to his own individuality would demean that relation and the honor bestowed upon him as an inheritor of the literary-political tradition and as a citizen with a specifiable and immediately identifiable place in the literary-political hierarchy. The aristocrat rules through the continuity of primogeniture, whose legitimacy is reflected in the continuity of the literary tradition, and the poet rules through the mediation of the patron, whose support symbolizes the poet's legitimation of both continuities. The more powerful, wealthy, and ancient the patron's claims, the more skilled and enduring the poet's work.

Unlike the patronized poet, however, who represents social stability and the collective consciousness already preordained through his identification with those who actually rule, the Romantic poet seeks to stabilize his readership through his own individual power and to become a representative of collective consciousness by gaining the allegiance of an ever-widening audience. His rule is metonymic in a different sense: it is indirect in relation to the actual structures of governance, but it is directly related to his creative power over those who must be ruled. He need not have any

relationship with those in power in order to be a celebrated poet, and in fact
lower class status and familial obscurity can be sufficient cause for his
celebrity as it stresses the myth of the great poet's unmediated condition, his
"natural" talent and originality, his virile power of self-creation and self-
possession. Although he may be a fierce ideologue, the Romantic poet
refuses to see himself as a political partisan, for that would reduce his vision
to the ephemeral politics of the faction, the party, and the nation. He claims
that his vision transcends party politics and social hierarchies, even the
literary conventions that grow out of such politics and hierarchies, but
simultaneously he does not want to give up the capacity to chart the fate of
the worldly empires he supposedly transcends.

However we assess his new role, whether in relation to his audience, to
his economic status, to his vision, to his fellow poets, to his self-image, to his
literary inheritance, or to his sociopolitical function, the Romantic poet is
thrown back upon his power of self-possession, a power that is repeatedly
willed in the poetry by both overt and subliminal appeals to the virility and
masculinity of his creative project, and a power repeatedly reconfirmed
through his specific relations with the feminine in his poetry and his life.
The poet's quest for masculine self-possession can be seen from many
different perspectives and in a variety of ways. What follows is a brief
sketch of only some of the most crucial ways, with some indication of the
kind of concrete detail that can be garnered just from a few representative
Romantic documents. We shall examine how gender-identity helps the
Romantic poet shape his creative project by focusing on the two poets who
would seem to be the most dissimilar in the Romantic canon, Wordsworth
and Byron.

2. The Poet's Manly Charge,
Reclaiming the Masculinity of Emotion

When Byron attacks his fellow poets in *English Bards and Scotch Reviewers*,
he returns again and again to a handful of interrelated complaints leveled
against each poet: their appeal among women and the lower classes; the
wild, common, and pathetic (in the nineteenth-century sense) subject matter; the softness (one of his favorite descriptive terms in the poem) of the
poet's persona; the bastardization of literary conventions; and the process
of market publishing that opens the poetic vocation to anyone self-confident enough to consider himself (or herself even) a poet. Byron, though
politically republican, is the most conservative Romantic in terms of theoretical pronouncements on the function of poetry. Unlike any of the other
Romantics, he looks backward nostalgically—even as he forges ambivalently ahead—to when the primary role of the poet was to reconfirm
cultural values and to offer pleasure and wit by exploiting conventional
forms. *English Bards* harbors a sense of frustration about the course poetry
has taken in Byron's time, and through the insistence and consistency of his

individual complaints, rather than through any systematic critique of contemporary practice, he reveals the primary source of his vexation and his
ambivalence. Most of his complaints are capsulized in the following lines,
which sketch a caricature of the popular Thomas Moore:

> Who in soft guise, surrounded by a choir
> Of virgins melting, not to Vesta's fire,
> With sparkling eyes, and cheek by passion flush'd,
> Strikes his wild lyre, whilst listening dames are hush'd?
> 'Tis Little! young Catullus of his day,
> As sweet, but as immortal, in his lay! (283–87)

As Byron castigates the "soft guise" of Moore, he is also criticizing the poet's
aim, the female audience. Repeatedly Byron reminds us that women have
become a primary audience for poetry and always he targets that audience
as representative of the detriment done to poetry in his own age. The poet
who writes primarily for women feminizes the whole poetic process. With
the feminized audience in mind, the poet must steer a difficult course
between stirring the audience to facile passion and tracing "chaste descriptions of thy page, / To please the females of our modest age" (271–72).
Byron's portrait of Bowles is even more damning. He pictures him "still
whimpering through three-score of years," the "great oracle of tender
souls." Whether Bowles writes of the "fall of empires, or a yellow leaf" his
poetry is contaminated by sympathy's "soft idea," and he, like Moore,
achieves popularity through this feminized appeal:

> All love thy strain, but children like it best.
> 'Tis thine, with gentle Little's moral song,
> To soothe the mania of the amorous throng!
> With thee our nursery damsels shed their tears,
> Ere miss as yet completes her infant years. (342–46)

Byron's "gentle" here is ironic, for he is claiming that poetry has replaced its
true gentility with a gentleness that is a sort of amorous mania. Part of
Byron's complaint is the sheer popularity of poetry—its appeal to so many
from so many classes and occupations, the female and the child serving
repeatedly to indicate how low the craft has sunk. Just as the poet and the
audience have become soft, so has the subject matter and the poetic forms.
"The simple Wordsworth, framer of a lay / As soft as evening" (237–38) and
"gentle Coleridge," "the bard who soars to elegise an ass" (262) are two of
the major culprits. This feminized process causes otherwise skillful male
poets, such as Scott, to trivialize their talents and encourages common men
to aspire to gentleness by way of the poetic vocation.

> When some brisk youth, the tenant of a stall,
> Employs a pen less pointed than his awl,
> Leaves his snug shop, forsakes his store of shoes,
> St. Crispin quits, and cobbles for the muse,

Heavens! how the vulgar stare! how crowds applaud!
How ladies read, and literati laud! (765–70)

The marketing of poetry inevitably results in the vulgarization and feminization of literature, so that the very basis of taste is eroded by crowds that
applaud and ladies who read. Byron's manly Popian satire represents not
only an attempt to vilify his "soft" fellow poets but also an attempt to
demonstrate his own patrilineal descent from the line of Dryden and Pope.

Yet the parodies Byron sketches of Moore and Bowles could well be used
against Byron himself. No poet masters the art of emotional manipulation
better than he, none exploits the combination of pathos, wildness, and
passion more successfully to gain the applause of crowds and the readership of ladies. Yet Byron self-consciously avoids becoming the kind of
effeminate poet that he is ridiculing in his caricatures. Instead, he cultivates
the image of a literary womanizer, a poet who lives for the experience of
emotion, not for the emotion of experience, a poet who can simultaneously
make the cheek flush with passion and the lips form a smirk of derision (as
he does especially well with Don Juan's various love affairs). Byron's ambivalence only deepens as he matures as a poet: although he writes for the
vulgarized and feminized market, he never forsakes the image of writing
for his own boyish enjoyment, of writing for some self-generating desire
for play and mastery. No matter how many copies of his tales are possessed
by "the females of our modest age," Byron himself cannot be possessed. He
distinguishes his voice from his fellow poets' and raises it above the din of
the common herd through self-controlling and self-probing satire and
through self-overreaching and self-torturing tragedy. Whether it is Harold,
Napoleon, Cain, the narrator of *Don Juan*, Prometheus, or Manfred who
tests the limits of selfhood, Byron always celebrates his own protean self-
possession by making himself a masquerading hero of his own tale. He
somehow manages to combine the self-involved questing of the Romantics
with the self-abnegating satire of the Augustans, and he somehow manages
to write lays of wild passion, self-pity, and amorous sentiment without
"softening" his masculine guise.

English Bards, written at the beginning of Byron's career, reflects a young
poet's anxieties about his own self-definition as much as his frustration with
contemporary poetic and social practices. It is as if he is standing up to his
older brothers (Scott, Wordsworth, Coleridge, Southey) in order to get the
attention of the fathers (Dryden, Pope), in order to prove that he has
outgrown the softness of his own early poetry (which had been criticized
for its lack of restraint by some "Scotch reviewers"), in order to prove his
manhood. Even as Byron matures and gains more self-confidence, even as
he gains critical notoriety and accrues the largest audience of his time, he is
careful to avoid "softness." As a poet and a man, he seems to identify
softness with vulnerability, vulnerability with earnest feeling, and earnest
feeling with weakness. Any display of emotional effusion in his poetry must
therefore be framed with a feminine cause or undercut with masculine

derision or both. For instance, at the beginning of *Childe Harold,* as other men aboard the ship are overcome with grief in their leavetaking, Harold remains philosophically and emotionally resolute, even as he is touched by his comrades' deep feelings. It is the softness of domesticity that melts these other men's armor; as they remember the women and children that they are leaving behind and unprotected, they, ironically embarking on manly adventure, internalize the feminine in order to take it with them. At the beginning of canto 3, the narrator himself is moved by a later leavetaking; he is compelled, however, to justify the power of his emotional outburst by placing it in the context of a father being estranged from his beloved daughter. It is Ada who becomes the focus of our emotional "excess"; it is Ada who becomes the source of vulnerability, not the narrator himself. When Don Juan is overcome by a similar leavetaking from his beloved Julia, the narrator undercuts Juan's emotional display with locker-room satire. Juan's lovesickness is exchanged for seasickness. Juan, the man capable of cuckolding a much older man, becomes an unseasoned and untraveled boy, overwhelmed by the first lurch of the sea and the first lunge of the heart. Juan's tender feeling is literally defeminized as the natural harshness of the ocean's waves displaces the "naturally" seductive softening effect of Julia's words. Julia's feminine seductiveness and Juan's potential feminization serve to empower the narrator's satirical thrust. Thus, Byron is able to exploit the powerful flow of emotion without also giving in to the vulnerability of emotion, without giving up his playfully evasive guise, his manly shield.

Wordsworth, in a very different way, is involved in the same kind of pursuit, an attempt to bring the "feminine" vulnerability of emotion into the realm of "masculine" power. Wordsworth, however, stakes his poetic identity on the capacity to reveal in its totality and nakedness the natural and active power of feeling, or at least to make his readers feel that he has made such a revelation. Byron indicates how well he senses this when he insults Wordsworth thus:

> So close on each pathetic part he dwells,
> And each adventure so sublimely tells,
> That all who view the 'idiot in his glory'
> Conceive the bard the hero of the story. (251–54)

Although Byron's stories always involve his own self-questing, he never disarms himself, never makes himself vulnerable to his public by revealing the bard as a naked hero. He always unmasks himself by self-consciously displaying the masks within himself. As Byron suggests, however, Wordsworth repeatedly unmasks his own self-questing by baring himself to his public. Wordsworth not only talks more about himself than any previous poet, he does so without acknowledging the ritual masks honored by all poets before his time. Wordsworth claims that the aboriginal self can be empowered only through honest self-inspection and sincere disrobing of the self to readers. I am not suggesting, however, that Wordsworth's project of discovering and disrobing the aboriginal self can actually be achieved. What Wordsworth does achieve is a similacrum of the disrobed self. Wordsworth's *persona* of a poet empowered by Nature and unveiled by his own quest for self-transcendence is itself a mask, but a mask that he holds onto with such consistency and earnestness that it *apparently* becomes the naked self. If Wordsworth were to strip the mask away—an unthinkable act, he would risk not only poetic disempowerment but also poetic suicide. If his persona "be but a vain belief," then his powerful flow of emotion, his strength of vision, is meaningless. It is a prospect that Wordsworth seems incapable of facing. Just as he turns away from the prospect of "vain belief" in "Tintern Abbey" and turns instead toward the prospect of the Wye and the retrospect of his mythic nascent self bounding like a doe over Nature's expanse, so in his poetic career in general he turns farther away from the prospect of a self that is either totally elusive or entirely illusive and becomes a self-fulfilling prophet, ensconced in his own version of self-revelation and his own vision of self-possession. No games need be played, for he is totally self-confident that the naked self is in fact the most virile and natural expression of creative power.

If one of Byron's favorite castigating adjectives is "soft," Wordsworth's favorite laudatory term is "power." For him poetry is constituted by a quest for poetic self-identity that is mirrored by the quest for manhood. No poet before him associates the achievement of poetic identity so closely with the passage to masculine maturity. When Wordsworth says that a poet is a man speaking to men, we should not take the gendered locution lightly. Poems as varied as *The Prelude, The Ruined Cottage, The White Doe of Rylstone,* "Tintern Abbey," the Lucy lyrics, and *The Recluse* all ally the quest for masculine self-possession with the gaining of poetic identity. Even in "Tintern Abbey," where his immediate audience is presumably Dorothy, his objective remains the same.[12] The man who realizes himself is the one who achieves a powerful inner vision that embraces all who come in contact with him, or it is the man who is capable of enforcing such a vision on others. Like the numerous young men in his poems who learn either from the immediate experience of nature or from an older man who has imbibed the power of nature, the poet transforms the seemingly passive feeling of inner life within the self into the outward action of achieved manhood.

Wordsworth's repeated claim of returning to the ordinary language of men in a state of nature must be viewed not only in terms of its duplicitous tendency to elevate the language of the common classes and to celebrate the primordial power of natural experience. It must also be viewed in terms of the image of the poet that Wordsworth is attempting to promote. He concocts a history of the poet that makes him a sort of first man, the natural man who is compelled to write from his direct experience in a life of action. In the Appendix to the 1802 Preface to *Lyrical Ballads,* he writes:

> The earliest poets of all nations generally wrote from passion excited by real events; they wrote naturally, and as men: feeling powerfully as they did,

> their language was daring, and figurative. In succeeding times, Poets, and
> Men ambitious of the fame of Poets, perceiving the influence of such
> language, and desirous of producing the same effect without being ani-
> mated by the same passion, set themselves to a mechanical adoption of these
> figures of speech, and made use of them, sometimes with propriety, but
> much more frequently applied them to feelings and thoughts with which
> they had no natural connection whatsoever. A language was thus insensibly
> produced, differing materially from the real language of men in *any situa-
> tion.*[13]

The origin of poetry in the active life of "real events" stresses the power and
influence of the poetic vocation. Ambitious men attempt to achieve the
fame of these first poets by mimicking their influential language. The
movement from "real events" to "poetic diction," a kind of "progress of
refinement" (p. 406), is as well a process of decay; Wordsworth's task is to
return the language, and by extension the feeling and thought, to its
aboriginal source in the real events, to embolden the language and re-
empower the influence of the poet. Not far beneath Wordsworth's prose
lies an ideal of the natural man of action, if not the noble savage, whose
daring conquest of the wilderness is naturally expressed in "daring" figures
of speech. This is what Wordsworth calls "the language of extraordinary
occasions" (pp. 405–06), and although he never specifies these occasions, I
think we can imagine the kinds of daring events his earliest poets would be
engaged in and record, notably the hunt, the battle, the winning of a
woman's love, the conquest.

What remains a submerged but governing paradigm of the poetic vocation in the Preface and its Appendix becomes blatant in the Essay, Supplementary to the Preface of 1815. Like Byron, Wordsworth here attempts to
identify the qualities of great poetry by categorizing and criticizing contemporary readers of poetry, an indication once again of the Romantic poet's
distress with market-based readership. He begins the essay by noting the
effect of poetry on the young of both sexes:

> With the young of both sexes, Poetry is, like love, a passion; but, for much
> the greater part of those who have been proud of its power over their minds,
> a necessity soon arises of breaking the pleasing bondage; or it relaxes of
> itself;—the thoughts being occupied in domestic cares, or the time en-
> grossed by business. (p. 409)

The adolescent interest in poetry is emotional, both in that it evokes
immediate, noncontemplative, unregulated responses (unlike the response
of those who are mature, who have "thought long and deeply") and in that
it is all-consuming and undifferentiated desire. This obsession, not dissimilar from the self-indulgent obsession of pubescent love, must, like that
love, be broken away from as the young move into responsible adulthood,
into domestic cares (for women?), and into business (for men?). As Wordsworth acknowledges the necessity (and therefore the social good) of breaking his passionate bond with poetry, he nonetheless wants to assert another

kind of passion for poetry appropriate for the adult, another kind of powerful feeling that is neither thoughtless nor undifferentiated. In order to salvage the influence of poetry during the phase of social responsibility, he must discriminate between vulnerable juvenile emotion and powerful emotion recollected and regulated by the "philosophic mind."

Byron makes a similar gesture when he bids adieu to "childish joys" in "To Romance." As Byron leaves romance's "votive train of girls and boys," however, he wants to claim that he is moving beyond the domain of emotion, beyond unregulated emotional experience, to an experience in which emotion is always subordinated to the sobering sway of reality. Byron emphasizes the disjunction between naive subjection to feeling and sophisticated awareness of the limits of feeling, an awareness that is often the source of wit. The romance votive "turns aside from real woe, / To steep in dew thy [romance's] gaudy shrine." The subjection to emotion, characteristic of romance, leads to "deceit," "affectation," and "sickly Sensibility," that is, to self-deceit (thinking that we can fully trust our feelings), as well as to a loss of sense of proportion concerning the significance of our feeling to others and to the indifferent world. As Byron acknowledges, " 'tis hard to quit the dreams / [w]hich haunt the unsuspicious soul," but in order for Byron to mature as a man and as a poet, he must break away from this adolescent self-indulgence:

> I break the fetters of my youth;
> No more I tread thy mystic round,
> But leave thy realms for those of Truth.

Unlike Wordsworth, Byron wants to distance himself from poetry derived from the power of emotion because such poetry inevitably creates a "Fond fool," who loves "a sparkling eye," rather than a hardened worldly realist (the *Don Juan* narrator). The effect of both Byron's and Wordsworth's strategy, however, is the same: poetry becomes a form of masculine empowerment rather than becoming, as it threatens to, a sign of "feminine" or boyish vulnerability, and it becomes a paradigmatic form of manly action in the world rather than an ineffectual and puerile preoccupation.

In his Supplementary essay, Wordsworth proceeds to categorize the kinds of readers that result from the breaking of this original passionate ("passion" being another of his favorite terms) bondage. Poetry, in each of these categories, becomes trivialized, its power diminished, and its "occasional" (meaning both infrequent and unserious) readers incapable of judging great poetry. Whether these readers resort to poetry as a "fashionable pleasure," as a "consolation," or as a "study" in old age, they misapprehend and abuse its function. Wordsworth is interested not only in establishing the idea that popularity is no sign of lasting power, that he has "not laboured in vain . . . that the products of [his] industry will endure" (p. 426), but also in clarifying wherein the power of the true poet (and therefore the genuine reader) lies. Like Byron, he recognizes the massive power that rests in the reading decisions of the public, but his appeal to that power is uneasy and duplicitous. With one hand he grants readers the power they must definitely hold over his poetic fate, yet with the other hand he reinvests the poet himself with full power to determine the influence and endurance of his vision. It is not the "Public," he says, but the "People" that "preserve" great poetry. The difference between the two, however, is less forthcoming. It would seem to be primarily that the people are as divinely inspired as the poet himself, "their intellect and their wisdom" being neither of "transitory" nor of "local" origin, whereas the public consists of the "clamour of that small though loud portion of the community, ever governed by factitious influence, which, under the name of the Public, passes itself, upon the unthinking, for the People" (p. 430). Wordsworth's logic is questionable. Who are the "unthinking" if not the very people who with time become the "voice that issues from this Spirit"? If we push his logic far enough, we see that the people are actually those who have a power akin to the poet's and that their decision endures, quite simply, because the "Deity" has ordained it in the same way that the Poet's power partakes of the "Vision and the Faculty divine" (p. 430).

Wordsworth must repress the actual power possessed by the public and he must suppress the relation of identity between his "Public" and his "People" because it is the readers themselves who pose perhaps the greatest threat to the myth of poetic divinity, to the myth that the poet, a little self-engendering god, transcends place and time. As he describes the poetic vocation, we see as well its basis in Wordsworth's assumptions about masculine self-possession, manhood, and male conquest:

> If there be one conclusion more forcibly pressed upon us than another by the review which has been given of the fortunes and fate of poetical Works, it is this,—that every author, as far as he is great and at the same time *original*, has had the task of *creating* the taste by which he is to be enjoyed: so has it been, so will it continue to be. . . . The predecessors of an original Genius of a high order will have smoothed the way for all that he has in common with them;—and much he will have in common; but, for what is peculiarly his own, he will be called upon to clear and often to shape his own road:—he will be in the condition of Hannibal among the Alps. (p. 426)

This is Bloom's poetics of influence and the strong poet; it is Carlyle's poet as great man in germinal form. We should note especially the metaphor that caps the passage and that then serves as the guiding figure for the rest of the essay. (And, as we shall see, the association of the great and original poet with the Alps is neither arbitrary nor singular; it is a Romantic commonplace with a masculinist rationale.) The condition of Hannibal among the Alps is the condition of the man who single-handedly conquers the world, makes a road for others to follow, but makes them lesser men in following and makes other and greater roads more difficult to create. It is the poet as man of action, as masculine quester, as ruler of visionary empires. Wordsworth begins by remembering the participation of both sexes in the reading of poetry, but he ends by repressing the feminine presence in the poetic transaction. His world of poetry quickly becomes, unconsciously but purposively, a world of aggressive desire and conquest. The association of poetry with juvenile love, with puerile emotion, has been scrapped for a more virile association that subsumes the vulnerability of emotion as an active and "profound" power. The wise reader becomes a little Hannibal, who dares to read with an originality that cooperates with the poet's own. Just as the poet aims at transmuting the raw power of passion into daring and influential language, the reader's lesser mission becomes achieving the capacity to read that daring and original language.

> Passion, it must be observed, is derived from a word which signifies *suffering;* but the connection which suffering has with effort, with exertion, and *action,* is immediate and inseparable. So strikingly is this property of human nature exhibited by the fact, that, in popular language, to be in a passion, is to be angry!—But,
>
> > "Anger in hasty *words* or *blows*
> > Itself discharges on its foes."
>
> To be moved, then, by a passion, is to be excited, often to external, and always to internal, effort; whether for the continuance and strengthening of the passion, or for its suppression. (p. 427)

Wordsworth himself stresses the relation between "words" and "blows," between seemingly passive inner feeling and external active conquest. Poetic language is no less potent than the actual physical strength of the warrior. Able to strike his blow inward as well as outward, the poet—unlike the scientist, the industrialist, or the conqueror—can wed the internal conquest of spiritual possession to the external conquest of material possessions. And, as Wordsworth so frequently points out, the poet's conquest is universal, for its realm is the "widening . . . sphere of human sensibility" (p. 428), which allows it to establish its reign over all human beings.

> Genius is the introduction of a new element into the intellectual universe: or, if that be not allowed, it is the application of powers to objects on which they had not before been exercised, or the employment of them in such a manner as to produce effects hitherto unknown. What is all this but an advance, or a conquest, made by the soul of the poet? (p. 428)

Like the scientist, the poet introduces new elements, or like the inventor, he applies powers to new objects. Like the conqueror, his "new mission" is "to extend [the] kindom" (p. 428), but not simply an external kingdom of things, of territory and people, but also the internal kingdom of ideas and feelings.

As Wordsworth re-empowers the poetic vocation and capitalizes on its capacity to cultivate the province of feeling for the manly action of conquest, he also stresses poetry's alliance with science, the discipline that seems to threaten it most. "The appropriate business of poetry," Wordsworth claims in an aside, "is as permanent as pure science" (p. 410). It is in the Preface itself, however, that we get his most lucid claims for the priority of poetry over science. Science, he suggests, is mediated, local, simply a personal acquisition and limited knowledge, whereas poetry is immediate, universal, and comprehensive knowledge.

> The knowledge both of the Poet and the Man of science is pleasure; but the knowledge of the one cleaves to us as a necessary part of our existence, our natural and unalienable inheritance; the other is a personal and individual acquisition, slow to come to us, and by no habitual and direct sympathy connecting us with our fellow-beings. The Man of science seeks truth as a remote and unknown benefactor; he cherishes and loves it in his solitude: the Poet, singing a song in which all human beings join with him, rejoices in the presence of truth as our visible friend and hourly companion. Poetry is the breath and finer spirit of all knowledge; it is the impassioned expression which is in the countenance of all Science. (p. 396)

On the verge of science's ascendency, Wordsworth (and the other Romantics) reassert poetry's more universal and potent capacity, suggesting that it is the poet who leads the way, not the scientist, that it is the poet who serves as the source of authority, not the scientist. And once again his assertion is expressed in a metaphor of masculine conquest, of empire building, that suggests a spiritual Hannibal conquering Alps both of the soul and of the physical world:

> In spite of difference of soil and climate, of language and manners, of laws and customs: in spite of things silently gone out of mind, and things violently destroyed; the Poet binds together by passion and knowledge the vast empire of human society, as it is spread over the whole earth, and over all time. The objects of the Poet's thoughts are every where; though the eyes and senses of man are, it is true, his favourite guides, yet he will follow wheresoever he can find an atmosphere of sensation in which to move his wings. Poetry is the first and last of all knowledge—it is as immortal as the heart of man. (p. 396)

Unlike the scientist, the poet can establish a kingdom without physical boundaries, alpha and omega, world without end, because the strong poet possesses a realm of internal vision that can be extended through the infinity of time and space. The poet comes before the scientist and also after. "If the labours of Men of science should ever create any material revolution, direct or indirect, in our condition, and in the impressions which we habitually receive," Wordsworth states, "the Poet will sleep then no more than at present; he will be ready to follow the steps of the Man of science, not only in those general indirect effects, but he will be at his side, carrying sensation into the midst of the objects of the science itself" (p. 396). Wordsworth is anxious to move the realm of sensation—the poet's inner expanse—into the realm of the "manifestly and palpably material." Even when poets follow—or move alongside—scientists in the revolutions of human history, they are the actual conquerors and rulers of the universe, for without their "divine spirit" the "transfiguration" cannot be achieved.

What is only implicit in Wordsworth, but what Shelley in his *Defence of Poetry,* following Wordsworth's lead, makes explicit, is the poet's function of regulating humanity's ability to master the material world. Since the "creative faculty" is "the basis of all knowledge," it "creates new materials for knowledge and power and pleasure . . . and engenders in the mind a desire to reproduce and arrange them."[14] According to Shelley, if people do not heed this creative faculty, if they blindly follow the scientist without heeding the poet, only catastrophe can result: "The cultivation of those sciences which have enlarged the limits of the empire of man over the external world has, for want of the poetical faculty, proportionally circumscribed those of the internal world; and man, having enslaved the elements, remains himself a slave" (pp. 190–91). More politically adept than Wordsworth, Shelley understands well how "a cultivation of the mechanical arts in a degree disproportioned to the presence of the creative faculty" leads to "the inequality of mankind" (p. 190), but both are concerned with establishing the reign of imagination in a time when conquest itself has become overwhelmingly the province of the scientist, the inventor, and the industrialist.

3. Conquest in the Alps, Extending Poetic Dominion

One reason Romantic poets are so obsessed with climbing mountains is that the activity perfectly emblematizes the poet's charge of self quest and world conquest. Mountain climbing and viewing is the ultimate sublime experience; testing the power and limits of self, it stresses the solitude of self-questing and pits the self against nature's power. The height of the mountain represents both the ever-spiraling ascent of imagination and the ever-present threat of falling, the loss of self-identity, the reabsorption into nature's overriding power. It is from mountains that prophets proclaim their truths; for the poet-prophet the mountain symbolizes the necessary solitude of the leaders of men and the necessary stance of truth—its transcendence, its elusiveness, and its immense might. It is another metaphor of masculine potency, which, through association, reinvests the poetic vocation with power and influence.

In the Napoleonic passage of canto 3 of *Childe Harold's Pilgrimage,* we can see clearly the relation between the poet's quest for self-possession and the conqueror's quest for world possession, each turning into the other with dizzying rapidity.

> [T]here is a fire
> And motion of the soul which will not dwell
> In its own narrow being, but aspire

> Beyond the fitting medium of desire;
> And, but once kindled, quenchless evermore,
> Preys upon high adventure, nor can tire
> Of aught but rest; a fever at the core,
> Fatal to him who bears, to all who ever bore. (42. 371–78)

This "lust to shine or rule" is a contagion shared by "Conquerors and Kings, / Founders of sects and systems, to whom add / Sophists, Bards, Statesmen" (43. 380–82). The association of the poet with the conqueror and the king has become so commonplace since the Romantic period that it is easy to forget that the association has not always been made, that it is an idea fostered by the specific socio-historical conditions of poets during the beginning of the nineteenth century. Byron's cynical irony disallows the kind of optimism that characterizes Blake's, Coleridge's, Wordsworth's, and Shelley's view of the poet as conqueror, but it does not diminish his need to identify with the conqueror. Byron reminds us that "[h]e who ascends to mountain-tops, shall find the loftiest peaks most wrapt in clouds and snow" (45. 397–98); the solitude of self-possession can be damning and the "reward" of the "summits" [e]nvied, yet how unenviable!" For Byron the quest for self-possession must inevitably become a mad and aimless masquerade, and the empires gained in conquest must become "[a] wider space, an ornamented grave" (48. 431). Wordsworth's ever-widening empire of poetic vision becomes for Byron the narrow space of an ornamented grave.

When Byron points out that power, even the power of imagination bridled by the self-possessing poet, breeds only contagion, madness, "keen contest and destruction," and ends, like all things, in death, he is subverting the very basis of poetic self-questing. By suggesting that the power of the soul's empire leads to the same outcome as the power of worldly empires, he calls into question the aim of the quest for self-possession and the wisdom of poetic conquest. Nevertheless, since poets and conquerors are driven by desire that is intensified the more it is quenched, Byron has no choice but to climb the Alps and look down, like Napoleon or Hannibal, at the folly he has conquered. "The clouds above me to the white Alps tend," he says, "And I must pierce them, and survey whate'er / May be permitted" (109. 117–19).

Byron's mask, his identity as a poet, is so tied to the quest for heroic self-possession and visionary conquest that he is unable to end the quest or take off the mask. What enables him to continue questing and conquering, despite the fact that the quest is aimless and the conquest folly, is the presence of the feminine—the prospect of feminine nature, the promise of feminine love, the need to protect feminine purity. Byron turns to "Maternal Nature," to Augusta Leigh, to Julia, to Julie, and to Ada, the only eternally pure presences in his aimless quest. Even though the Romantic poet's desire is insatiable, it moves him always toward the hope of consummation with feminine purity. In Byron this feminine presence paradoxically is both the nurturer of the desire that impels the quest and the only escape, however momentary, from "a contentious world, striving where none are strong" (49. 661):

> Is it not better, then, to be alone,
> And love Earth only for its earthly sake?
> By the blue rushing of the arrowy Rhone,
> Or the pure bosom of its nursing lake,
> Which feeds it as a mother who doth make
> A fair but froward infant her own care,
> Kissing its cries away as these awake;—
> Is it not better thus our lives to wear,
> Than join the crushing crowd, doom'd to inflict or bear? (71. 671–79)

The feminine presence in canto 3 of *Childe Harold* is Byron's only hope. It helps him clarify his identity as quester and conqueror and it serves as an ostensible reward that can be contemplated, though never grasped. The feminine consoles his "sorrow," his need to "act and suffer," and encourages him to "remount at last / [w]ith a fresh pinion" (73. 691–93).

Byron borrows the idea of maternal nature as consolation to the quest-weary from Wordsworth via Shelley. Of course, in Wordsworth nature as nurturing mother plays an even more crucial role. For him mother nature not only consoles, she is the primary force in constructing the identity of the poet and fostering the passage of the poet into active manhood.[15] She can, therefore, also be construed as a primary threat to the myth of self-possession. We must be careful not to confuse nature's capacity to bear forth and nurture with that self-justifying power that nature merely serves. Whether we locate that power in the aboriginal self within the self that the strong poet attempts to possess or in some transcendent force above and behind nature that gives meaning to natural signs, it is the alpha and omega of the poetic quest for Wordsworth; it engenders desire and it ever holds out the promise of fulfilled desire, of the fully possessed self, of unmediated and unlimited vision, of the world conquered by the might of self-engendering imagination.

The poem in which Wordsworth talks so much about himself is a quest story, a story that traces one man's search for a self, for a position from which to view the self, and for a position from which to grasp the world once the self is possessed. It is a story that must end in conquest, in a world envisioned and claimed, if the validity of the quest itself is to be ensured. The poem begins with a self-conscious contest between Wordsworth and his literary fathers, especially Milton, and between Wordsworth and his fellow poet, Coleridge, whose threat is disarmed and whose sympathy is appropriated. Making Coleridge the ears of the poem, Wordsworth cleverly borrows from his competitor's strength and diminishes his fellow poet's capacity to become, instead, the voice of the poem. With Coleridge helping establish the ever-widening borders of the poet's own identity and with the feminine presence of nature exciting his desire and urging him toward self-possession, Wordsworth, after some initial self-doubt, moves confidently toward the "honourable toil" of "manhood now mature" (1. 625–26).[16]

Predictably, a climactic moment of the quest (if not the climax itself) occurs as a conquest in the Alps. Ironically, Wordsworth's moment of conquest is constituted not by a vision of the Alps themselves, not by nature's verification of his self-possessed identity, but by a failure of such vision. Wordsworth's conquest comes not at the peak—where the mountains would offer him a view of the world he is to claim—but in the descent. The poet stresses here that the power that allows for conquest is beyond or above nature, is situated on some mysterious plane that not even nature's highest mountain can reach. The conquest is all the more miraculous in occuring in the descent, the phase of falling, rather than at Napoleonic heights.

The moment of at-lostness, which seizes Wordsworth when the actual vision of having traversed the Alps fails him, is transformed into a moment of re-vision. Through imagination he is able to fulfill the promise of conquest, and furthermore he is able to do so apparently without the troublesome mediation of maternal nature:

> Imagination—here the Power so called
> Through sad incompetence of human speech,
> That awful Power rose from the mind's abyss
> Like an unfathered vapour that enwraps,
> At once, some lonely traveller. I was lost;
> Halted without an effort to break through;
> But to my conscious soul I now can say—
> "I recognize thy glory": in such strength
> Of usurpation, when the light of sense
> Goes out, but with a flash that has revealed
> The invisible world, doth greatness make abode. (6. 592–602)

Imagination's "strength of usurpation" is greater than the "light of sense" on which any natural vision would depend. The power that moves Wordsworth toward his poetic identity, that moves him toward his masculine maturity, and that enables him to envision his own world is a power beyond even nature's ultimate control. When Wordsworth compares imagination to an "unfathered vapour," he brings attention to its source of authority, or more precisely to the lack of such authority. He does not use the word "unmothered," a word conceptually awkward (and psychologically troubling from the masculinist Romantic perspective) but linguistically feasible, because he is not so much referring here to the birth or origin as to the final cause that ordains and justifies existence itself. (Likewise, "unparented" would not work for him in the passsage because it brings to mind mere progenitorship rather than justification for existence.) Wordsworth is saying that imagination, or what he more accurately identifies as infinitude and desire, ordains itself, is its own justification, is its own source of authority. Wordsworth's allusion to Genesis (the vapour and the abyss) helps establish

the idea that desire gives birth to the human (from the male vantage point)
world of perception and value in the same way that God gives birth to the
universe and its hierarchies, not as a mother who bears her child from an
impregnated seed, but as a father who inseminates existence from
nothingness. Mothering implies for Wordsworth bearing forth and sustaining life, giving birth and giving sustenance, an activity that he places
secondarily both in terms of temporality and value. In Wordsworth's
scheme, mothering does not justify and order existence, it merely enacts
and nourishes what has already been ordained by motherless fathering. By
making imagination father itself, and by unmothering the originating act of
fathering, Wordsworth, following Judeo-Christian tradition, manages, in
this climactic moment of his quest poem, to defeminize the conquest that
has been made possible through the good auspices of feminine nature.[17]

The conquest is the quest itself, a never-ending movement toward
fulfilled vision and self-comprehension, an ever-intensifying desire for
what is desired. It is the optimistic side of Byron's aimless masquerade and
foolish conquest:

> Our destiny, our being's heart and home,
> Is with infinitude, and only there;
> With hope it is, hope that can never die,
> Effort, and expectation, and desire,
> And something evermore about to be. (6. 604–08)

As Wordsworth bares his soul to Coleridge, to us, he hopes to convince us
that what is within the deepest self, when earnestly searched out, can be
unmasked, that the kernel of self-engendering feeling at the heart of self is
not weak and undirected but the active regeneration of primal strength. Its
constitution is not the vulnerability of aimless, undifferentiated, and un-
controllable desire, but the strength of usurpation, the capacity for total
vision and unmediated truth, "[t]he types and symbols of Eternity, / [o]f
first, and last, and midst, and without end" (6. 639–40).

When we come to the end of Wordsworth's quest poem, then, we come to
its beginning, to Wordsworth's beginning as a poet and as a man. As we
come to know his vision, we are conquered by it, unless we are stronger
than he. For Wordsworth, this, of course, need not be an inimical conquest;
it takes on, rather, the qualities of a benign (and divine) reign. These are
the final lines of his poem:

> Prophets of Nature, we to them will speak
> A lasting inspiration, sanctified
> By reason, blest by faith: what we have loved,
> Others will love, and we will teach them how;
> Instruct them how the mind of man becomes
> A thousand times more beautiful than the earth
> (Which, 'mid all revolution in the hopes
> And fears of men, doth still remain unchanged)

> In beauty exalted, as it is itself
> Of quality and fabric more divine. (14. 446–55)

Wordsworth's "lasting inspiration," to use his own words from the Preface, "binds together by passion and knowledge the vast empire of human society, as it is spread over the whole earth, and over all time."

Wordsworth's earnest optimism and his uncritical self-confidence hinder him from questioning the implications of the idea that poetic identity is constituted by masculine self-questing and visionary conquest. Unlike Byron, he seems most comfortable in the role when he is most conscious of its sociopolitical implications. His vision after *The Prelude* is even more hemmed in by the complacency of masculine self-possession and even more tyrannized by an imperial, sometimes even dictatorial, voice. Unlike Byron or Shelley, he never questions how the Romantic poetic identity sustains sexual and political hierarchies, how it limits the poet's capacity for sympathy, how it limits readers' capacity for possessing themselves and sharing the visionary experience, how it discourages "the exertion of a co-operating *power* in the mind of the Reader," to use Wordsworth's own words (Essay, Supplementary). Both Byron and Shelley, however, are able to see and to offer a critique of such a vision because they are so sympathetic and prone to it and so conscious of its limitations in their literary father, Wordsworth. But not even the second generation of Romantics, who are much more attuned to the implications of these masculinist metaphors of power, are able to sever their poetic identity from those metaphors. It indicates how culturally entrenched is the feeling that influence must express itself in terms of self identity, possession, and conquest and that power must be defined through distinctions of gender. Poetry motivated and shaped by the desire for self-possession, determined by the poet's aggressive relation to his fellows and the world is not intrinsically masculine, but it is sociohistorically masculine. Quest and conquest, too, though able to be appropriated by women, are historically the means through which men have appropriated power for themselves and over women. The Romantic desire to articulate visions that can speak for the whole, in the end, is betrayed by the poet's need to adopt a masculine posture in order to fulfill that desire, a posture made to seem natural and universal by suppressing its own vital relation to the politics of gender.

NOTES

1. Letter 268, To George Beaumont, 1 May 1805, *The Letters of William and Dorothy Wordsworth*, vol. 1: *The Early Years*, 2nd ed., ed. Ernest de Selincourt and rev. Chester L. Shaver (Oxford: Oxford University Press, 1967), pp. 586–87.

2. *The Anxiety of Influence: A Theory of Poetry* (London: Oxford University Press, 1973), p. 5.

3. See *Romanticism and Consciousness: Essays in Criticism*, ed. Harold Bloom (New York: W.W. Norton, 1970), pp. 3–24.

4. Sandra M. Gilbert and Susan Gubar, *The Madwoman in the Attic: The Woman Writer and the Nineteenth-Century Literary Imagination* (New Haven: Yale University Press, 1979), p.12.

5. *Women Writers and Poetic Identity: Dorothy Wordsworth, Emily Brontë, and Emily Dickinson* (Princeton: Princeton University Press, 1980), p. 33.

6. An excellent discussion of the sociopolitical and educational status of women in the Romantic period and how this status affects their capacity to write poetry can be found in Irene Tayler and Gina Luria, "Gender and Genre: Women in British Romantic Poetry," in the volume *What Manner of Woman: Essays in English and American Life and Literature*, ed. Marlene Springer (New York: New York University Press, 1977), pp. 98–123.

7. There were female poets more popular in their own time than all the canonized Romantic poets except Byron: notably, Joanna Baillie, Letitia Elizabeth Landon, and Felicia Hemans. Yet critics—even feminist critics—have tended to overlook these first published female poets, because the very standards used to define poetry and the poet are based on masculinist assumptions promoted by the Romantic poets themselves.

8. This is exactly the kind of question that Homans asks about Dorothy Wordsworth in chapter 2 of her study and answers with precision and thoroughness. Homans also compares Dorothy's poetics with William's, explaining how their differences can be attributed to gender socialization. It is interesting to contrast Homans's discussion of the differences between Dorothy and William with the explanations of John F. Danby and William Heath. Both Danby and Heath depict William's poetic development as influenced by, but growing beyond, Dorothy's sensibility. Heath writes: "Wordsworth's subordination—if that is the word for it—to his sister's sensibility was short-lived. The act of freeing himself from this dependence, whether deliberately or unconsciously, was the composition of his finest short poem [*Resolution and Independence*], which seems to bring together all that Wordsworth had known and wanted to be since they came to Grasmere." See Heath, *Wordsworth and Coleridge: A Study of Their Literary Relations in 1801–1802* (Oxford: Oxford University Press, 1970), pp. 108–20; and Danby, *The Simple Wordsworth: Studies in the Poems 1797–1807* (New York: Barnes and Noble, 1961), p. 98.

9. In her study *The Proper Lady and the Woman Writer: Ideology as Style in the Works of Mary Wollstonecraft, Mary Shelley, and Jane Austen* (Chicago: University of Chicago Press, 1984), Mary Poovey analyzes Mary Shelley's "characteristic ambivalence with regard to female self-assertion" (p. 115) and reads her work as a critique of Romanticism (see esp. chap. 4).

10. This indicates the continuity of gender-identity through changing economic-historical phases—a sort of masculine prototype that transcends the changes themselves—as well as the pressure on men who desire power to identify with the prototype in order to feel and become empowered.

11. For a good discussion of the Romantics' conflicting attitudes toward science, see Hans Eichner, "The Rise of Modern Science and the Genesis of Romanticism," *PMLA* 97 (1982): 8–30.

12. For further discussion of Dorothy's gendered role in William's poetry (and especially in "Tintern Abbey"), see Homans, "Eliot, Wordsworth, and the Scenes of the Sisters' Instruction," *Critical Inquiry* 8 (1981): 223; and my article "Naturalizing Gender: Woman's Place in Wordsworth's Ideological Landscape," *ELH* 53 (1986): 391–410.

13. For the prefaces I am using Ernest de Selincourt's edition of *The Poetical Works of William Wordsworth*, vol. 2 (Oxford: Oxford University Press, 1944), p. 405.

14. See *Shelley: Political Writings*, ed. Roland A. Duerksen (New York: Appleton-Century-Crofts, 1970), pp. 190–91.

15. The now-standard reading of Wordsworth, and I think a valid one, is to downplay nature's *controlling* role and to stress how the aim of his development is to grow beyond nature. It is, however, still easy to overestimate Wordsworth's ready acceptance of nature's importance to him. For instance, Michael Cooke tends to do so in his study *Acts of Inclusion: Studies Bearing on an Elementary Theory of Romanticism* (New Haven: Yale University Press, 1979), where he argues in general that the Romantics incorporate and empower the feminine and dispose a change in the masculine, using the crucial role of Wordsworth's feminine nature as a primary case (see chap. 3, "The Feminine as the Crux of Value"). Although this argument seems truer for the second generation, it is extremely problematic for the first. Cooke bases his claims on the premise of the "complementary wholeness" of the sexes sought by the Romantics, but it is exactly this idea of complementariness that encourages the disempowerment of women, especially during the nineteenth century. As Kate Millett has shown in *Sexual Politics* (New York: Ballantine Books, 1969), one of the most effective ways of subverting women's demands for equality during the nineteenth century was for men to point to the way the sexes complement each other and then grant the equal value of each sex's virtues (see esp. pp. 106–11, 179–201). And as Gilbert and Gubar point out, no matter how potentially sympathetic Romantic radicalism and rebelliousness might make these poets to women, they were "after all fundamentally 'masculinist' with Milton" (p. 211).

16. I am using the Norton Critical Edition of *The Prelude*, ed. Jonathan Wordsworth, M. H. Abrams, and Stephen Gill (New York: W. W. Norton, 1979). References are to book and line numbers.

17. Gayatri Chakravorty Spivak makes a similar point in her essay "Sex and History in *The Prelude*," *Texas Studies in Language and Literature* 23 (1981): "Wordsworth projects the possibility of being son *and* lover, father *and* mother of poems, male *and* female at once" (p. 326). In "'Behold the Parent Hen': Pedagogy and *The Prelude*," Mary Jacobus explains this phenomenon in relation to Wordsworth's and Rousseau's educational systems: "*The Prelude* is not, as it represents itself, an account of Wordsworth's education at the hands of Nature. Rather, it's an educational treatise directed at the missing mother. . . . *The Prelude* repeats the self-constituting trope which makes *Émile* an account of how the child becomes father to the man without the help of his mother" (paper delivered at the English Institute, Cambridge, Mass., September 1986).

THE CULT OF DOMESTICITY

DOROTHY AND WILLIAM WORDSWORTH AT GRASMERE

Kurt Heinzelman

> Then, last wish—
> My last and favorite aspiration—then
> I yearn towards some philosophic song
> Of truth that cherishes our daily life . . .
>
> *The Prelude* (1805), 1. 228–31[1]

Although Dorothy and William Wordsworth had already set up housekeeping together in Dorset, in Somerset, and then again in Germany, it was not until they moved back to their native Lake District just before Christmas 1799 that they began to represent to themselves a new sense of the household—*their* household—as a principal site of value, a place where value could be created as well as perceived. In their household, these representations inevitably took the form of writing—journal, letter, poem. Domesticity, the Wordsworths came to see, was a result of just this mutual labor: it was not merely a function of being together or of maintaining a place of joint residence but a quality engendered through the actual work of the individual household members.

This essay analyzes William and Dorothy's different but complementary understanding of that domestic work by focusing on the ways in which the Grasmere writings of both brother and sister attempt to socialize the activity of writing and thus to place it within a larger idea of economy that included not only their own household but also the households of their neighbors and friends. The most significant social act of the early Grasmere years became the assimilation of Mary Hutchinson into the household as William's wife. Assimilation, in fact, is virtually the Wordsworthian activity par excellence during this period. The estrangement from Coleridge, the social distancing of the Wordsworths from the likes of De Quincey (who married a local girl and later moved into Dove Cottage), and the tension over ideas of domestic protocol that sometimes strained relations with the largely female household of Coleridges at Greta Hall lay in the future. My concern in this essay is the Wordsworth household before it became codified and acquired its Victorian interiors—before, that is, the radical Wordsworthian mythos, deliberately articulated by both brother and sister, became enmeshed in what historically may be called a "cult of domesticity."

By "cult of domesticity" I mean the belief that the household is the site of value not merely or even primarily because of what it produces in the economic sense but because it provides the place where the individual personality may grow and the occasion to discover in that growth a way of integrating self and society, family and polis.[2] The means by which that integration occurs and the form that it takes may differ according to the gender of the family member and the economic circumstances of the family unit. But the critical point is that the cultic valorizing of the household and of "homemaking" evolves by definition only *after* commodity production has been separated from the home. The cult of domesticity was a replacement for or sublimation of the family as a viable, self-sustaining economic entity; it thus depended upon a division of female and male labor in which commodity production came to be seen as the masculine activity while female economic activity was regarded as reproductive, whether literally in the case of childbearing or metaphorically in the form of service-based employment such as nanny, maid, governess, or indeed houseworker in general. The point is that the Wordsworths' early views of the labors of the sexes, especially as those labors cross and germinate into the idea of a household or domestic economy, resist this notion of a sexual division of labor. The problem is that this resistance, in the Grasmere years, is not immediately apparent, owing to the Wordsworths' own *later* success in institutionalizing a different domestic ideal.

At Grasmere the Wordsworths enjoyed for the first time an extended leasehold, thanks to the Calvert inheritance. The effect was that the cottage at Town End seemed more their own property than had any of their previous dwellings. Racedown in Dorset was still largely a self-sustaining country estate for the owners, a family who preferred to live in Bristol, when the Wordsworths moved in as nonlaboring, nonpaying guests. What William said about Grasmere is more strictly true of the Racedown period (1795–97): "there did [we] lie from earthly labour free."[3] Although they continued to keep young Basil Montague as a ward partly because they needed to earn some money, they had the service of a maid (the trusty Peggy, who stayed with them until they moved to Germany) and a custodial staff who maintained the grounds and garden and who provided the owners' own china, linen, and the like when the Wordsworths themselves had houseguests. Similarly, at Alfoxden in Somerset (1798) the Wordsworths were just short-term renters at a good-sized manor house that was "standing empty and fully furnished"[4] and that was fortuitously close to Coleridge's cottage at Nether Stowey. They never regarded this site as home, and they made no effort to domesticate it, although they felt possessive about certain natural features of the site, such as the huge beech tree on the lawn, the woods rising behind the house, and the waterfall in the glen below.

At Grasmere, however, the Wordsworths were on their own, and they immediately began to landscape and to "improve" their "property," first terracing the steep backyard into a garden, then filling it with plantings they gathered from the surrounding countryside on their walks, walks that also sometimes produced poems, which then needed to be transcribed, revised, read aloud, and recopied once back home. To walk abroad was thus to gather material that would fully occupy the household indoors as well, this circularity of activities mirroring (but not embodying, as I will explain in a moment) the self-sufficient, largely agricultural households of many of their neighbors. With sound georgic vision, William pruned and maintained the overgrown orchard in the back, later adding steps up to the garden and a garden seat, which partially fulfilled a fancy he had voiced in a poem of 1800;[5] Dorothy, like Eve in Milton's paradise, tended the flowers. Although not wealthy, they were well enough off that they could contemplate possessing the material happiness they had often imagined. W. W. Douglas shrewdly remarked many years ago that "Wordsworth's interest in money was one of the determining factors in his life," but it is more precise to say that the Wordsworths always reckoned their blessings in terms of actual property.[6] The place of their childhood became the place where they chose to establish their permanent dwelling even as it was becoming the place of choice for increasing numbers of "tourists," as both William and Dorothy disparagingly call these presences who, by definition, live elsewhere. Disparagement aside, though, the Wordsworths' celebration of their "Power of choice" (*The Prelude* [1850], 1. 166) in becoming "The Master of a little lot of ground" (*Home at Grasmere,* line 473) was constantly being reinforced by social and economic indications that Lakeland itself was a chosen place indeed.

Grasmere was a fortuitous spot as well in that industrial development had not yet revalorized the households of the Lake District (as had occurred in other parts of England), redefining the kinds of value that the self-sufficient family unit *could* produce. The Wordsworths were not literally self-sufficient like some of their neighbors, such as the Ashburners or, even more meagerly, the Greens of Blentarn Gill. They were more like the Clarksons of Pooley Bridge, people who had the means to purchase sufficiency, if sufficiency was circumspectly defined.[7] It took William and Dorothy some practice and some experience at living alone together to be able to understand how the blessings of domesticity could be—indeed, had to be—created as well as fortuitously bestowed. It took William's getting married, in fact, to make the Wordsworths see both the full importance of work to maintaining their household as a household and the necessity of expanding their idea of work to include that of others. His marriage was the catalyst that forced them to redefine the value of their household. The three-year period between their arrival at Grasmere in late 1799 and the establishment of the marital household in late 1802, which Dorothy's Grasmere *Journal* covers almost exactly, is sacralized by her *Journal* as the time of "our pilgrimage together" (p. 160). But brother and sister did not know what the shrine at the end of that pilgrimage was until *after* William's marriage. Or, rather, bridegroom and sister-in-law confronted the disruption of the marriage primarily by reaffirming Grasmere as the shrine, geographically speaking, and their domestic life as the shrine, psychologically speaking.

The two Wordsworths read this "shrining" differently. William affirms again and again in his Grasmere writings that a sense of "ancient homeliness" (*Prelude* [1805], 9. 219) guided his character development and shaped his poetic identity, and he locates this ancient homeliness in the traditional domesticity found among Lake District families. Certain qualities—manners, simplicity, candor, comfort—follow from this domestic nurture and make domesticity a public, rather than a private, virtue. William speaks of "household laws" in a sonnet composed during the emotionally critical summer of 1802 when his own household was disrupted first by his revisiting Annette Vallon in France and then by his marriage to Mary. While these household laws apply to domestic conduct, they are philosophically central to a masculine tradition of political discourse in public themes; psychologically, they emphasize individual work and the cultural value of vocation. The end goal of the work of writing may be to cherish "our daily life," as William says in the *Prelude* (1. 231), but the daily work of household management should aspire to the condition of textual production. This is William's daydream: a labor-intensive, task-specific view of domestic activity as an infrastructure of support for creativity.

Dorothy had her own idea of household laws and a pragmatically different sense of what creativity and support should look like. Her Grasmere *Journal* is, I shall argue, a kind of account book of that difference, as well as a work of intrinsic interest. Many critics have judged Dorothy the woman as they have judged her texts—that is, as adjuncts to William's labor of poetry writing—a procedure dramatically reversed by Margaret Homans, who sees the writings as a negative record of what Dorothy did not or could not or would not do to become a poet.[8] One can draw "Wordsworth Circles" that center or decenter, make tangential or ellipsoidal, particular figures at particular times, but the geometry of Dorothy's life and work must at least take into account the Wordsworths' unique way in the Grasmere years of using their various writings as heuristic models for one another—William borrowing from Dorothy's writings even as Dorothy's *Journal* conditions her ideas of writing from the sight of William writing, which she cites and sites in her own daily entries. Although arriving at different judgments of worth, both Homans and many prefeminist critics want to assess Dorothy's writing as an end in itself, as task-specific. But this is to throw too strong a light on the idea of task or vocation as such, an idea that Nancy Chodorow and others have argued is a culturally learned and male way of viewing responsibility.

Dorothy's vision of domesticity begins, like William's, in a daydream; but whereas William's is a daydream of owning his labor as a poet, Dorothy's is a more architectonic, spatially precise daydream of owning a piece of property "where, if we could erect a little cottage and call it *our own* we should be the happiest of human beings."[9] That is, the pure struggle to acquire a poetic identity through the work of writing is not an issue for her. But the arrangement of the domestic household is. It is Dorothy's Grasmere *Journal,* I argue, that articulates and sustains the idea that the equating of creativity and work is necessary to the success of the household unit. Her dream is a totalizing vision of the household as the material means of life. In this dream the coefficient of happiness is the coherent management of all the labors of a household, including the production of texts. Dorothy uses her *Journal* to place her brother's work of writing within a calendar of fluid domestic labors—reading, sewing, baking, giving alms, mending, walking, conversing, eating—her own keeping of the *Journal* being the bonding force between them but not the only or the principal locus of household attention.

In short, one of the Wordsworths' critical tasks during the Grasmere "experiment," as both liked to call it, was not just to record their domestic blessings or even to explain why they felt they *were* blessed but to articulate for the first time a sense of home economics. They strove to write their household into being, even as they were engaged in the material process of shaping a rather unpromising, smoky, dank, and overgrown cottage into a home. What emerges from their accounts of domesticity is a recognizable "Wordsworthian" mythos, but a mythos emphasized distinctively by brother and sister as they drew on different discursive traditions.

These different discursive traditions have not been comparatively analyzed. As I will show in some detail, William's concept of domesticity was rooted in political and philosophical discourse. Dorothy, who was probably not as well read as William in contemporary social and economic theory, was at least as informed about the poetic analogue to such theory, which we may generally call the georgic tradition. To explain the curious eclipse of the pastoral tradition by the georgic in the eighteenth century, John Barrell has surmised that "It was not until a language had been developed by which society could be described in economic, rather than in philosophic or political theoretical terms, that Georgic could describe, without mock heroic apology, the various tasks of industry in some detail."[10] Barrell's suggestion that the rise of the georgic as a poetic genre coincides necessarily with the rise of economics as a distinct form of discourse has never been systematically explored. I will argue that Dorothy provided the economic analysis to explain the industry of their household "in some detail." In effect, her Grasmere *Journal* is a piece of georgic writing that sometimes expostulates, sometimes expropriates William's own analysis of "household laws."

To reconstruct this process we need to be mindful of how the Wordsworths evolved in later years a sentimentalized and ritualized understanding of domesticity that restored it to a kind of pastoral (as well as apologetically heroic) status. For the Wordsworths, this later view is grounded in the much different kind of household that existed after 1813 at Rydal Mount, that manor house on the hill whose many-acred grounds William himself laid out and landscaped into a private garden. From the height of the Mount, William identified the household nostalgically with those patriots "who revere, / And would preserve as things above all price, / The old domestic morals of the land, / Her simple manners, and the stable worth / That dignified and cheered a low estate."[11] These lines from the *Excursion* of 1814 (8. 234–38) suffuse an eighteenth-century republicanism within a language of pastoral elegy, their celebrative tone being derived from the genre of the country-house poem, like Ben Jonson's "To Penshurst." Although the Wordsworths read Jonson's poem with particular enthusiasm at Grasmere,[12] their idea of domesticity at Grasmere was less programmatic and hardly nostalgic at all because it was dependent upon that *labor improbus* or hard labor which, from Virgil onwards, was one specific way of distinguishing a georgic from a pastoral or idyllic modality.[13] Moreover, by placing the value of domesticity "above all price" and by rooting it in what he benignly calls "the land," William evades in 1814 the very issue that so occupied him and Dorothy at Grasmere— namely, how to put a specific value on their own household and on the work they did there. Property, not "land," is what they wanted—a house of their own. Pricing was metaphorically just what the Wordsworths' Grasmere writings sought to accomplish, although in 1800 they could not have imagined publishing such writing at the extraordinary price, even by the inflationary late-war standards of 1814, that the *Excursion* brought: two guineas. Grasmere is to Rydal Mount as the genre of georgic is to the specialized pastoral of the country-house poem.[14]

When William asserts in the 1805 *Prelude* that "patriotic and domestic Love" are "analogous" to the "feeling" one has for nature and for natural phenomena (2. 195–96), he is positioning himself squarely in the Virgilian georgic tradition; when he refers to the "fair seed-time" of his soul (1. 305) and of being "transplanted" (1. 309) to his birthplace, he is positing the *work* of self-making within the frame of georgic seriality; and when he declares his "last and favorite aspiration" to be a song "that cherishes our daily life" (1. 229, 231), he is making his song subject to the georgic's concern with everydayness.[15] That, at least, is the literary background to this analogy. The philosophical tradition behind the analogous linking of patriotic and domestic love goes back to Plato's *Statesman*[16] and is plangently affirmed in Edmund Burke's notion that the vital connection between political and domestic households is not only salutary but quintessentially English. The English, Burke says, "have given to our frame of polity the image of a relation in blood: binding up the Constitution of our country with our dearest domestic ties; adopting our fundamental laws into the bosom of our family affections."[17] The economic theorists, whom Wordsworth in *The*

Prelude calls "modern statists" of "the wealth of nations" (12. 78, 80), tended
to model economic production on a household that attains self-sufficiency
primarily by means of agricultural labor, whether supplied by the members
of the household themselves or by their operatives. At the same time, these
theorists tended to model economic behavior—that is, modes of consumption—upon the notion of individualistic decision-making within a society of
duly constituted individuals acting in generally similar, self-interested
ways.[18] This latter model became the heuristic device called "economic
man," first identified as such in 1827 by one of Wordsworth's most important early readers, John Stuart Mill.[19] The result of using a model of
production based upon the household simultaneously with a model of
consumption based upon the isolated individual called "economic man"
meant that eighteenth-century economic theory did not and could not
account for the value of any labor other than male labor, the work of men.
Or, to put it another way, "economic man" is essentially a male-conquest
myth. Marx jested that such a myth was "Adamic," thus satirically linking
the Scotsman's economics to an idealistic, paradisal household, and he liked
to call theories based on this myth "Robinsonades"—theories that, like the
adventure story *Robinson Crusoe*, were grounded in male-specific concepts
of individual production and self-sustaining consumption.

Classical economic theory presumes that no productive relationship ap-
pertains between the work of men and the work of women. It presumes,
that is, a sexual division of labor. In the case of Thomas Paine this division is
expressed in what would seem to be a nonprejudicial way: "It is wrong to
say God made *rich* and *poor;* He made only *male* and *female;* and He gave
them the earth for their inheritance."[20] But men and women inherit the
earth differently, not only because inheritance laws favor the sexes differently but also because their work is judged to have different economic
status. Unmaliciously, perhaps, Paine's biblical language reminds us that
this difference has a long and firm theological grounding, just as his syntax
pairs rich with male and poor with female.

The most notorious statement in Wordsworth's time of the sexual division of labor was, of course, Reverend Malthus's *Essay on the Principle of
Population,* first published in the same year as the *Lyrical Ballads,* 1798.
Bluntly put, Malthus imagines that male and female labor are always at
odds and will inevitably cancel each other out. By male labor he means
essentially agricultural labor or the work of producing primary foodstuffs,
and by female labor he means essentially childbearing. For Malthus, the
economy of the family household is directly opposed to the political economy of the state. Malthusian "economic man" is one who will rationally
choose to improve his economic situation but will then irrationally tend to
interpret any partial improvement as proof that unlimited progress is
possible; and he will try to confirm this interpretation by means of increased sexual activity. Economic production, male labor, will promote an
optimism that results in greater sexual reproduction, essentially female
labor. Reproduction will outpace production exponentially just as money

outruns commodities. The sexual division of labor, pitting production against reproduction, is an antinomian conflict in which mankind confronts the evil inherent in human industry as such.

The critical question, which none of Malthus's contemporary critics addressed, is why female labor should be so singularly identified as childbearing. One answer is that Malthus's thesis of mankind's rapacious growth was perched, not at the height but deliberately at the foot of that great argument of *Paradise Lost:*

> Want pinched the less fortunate members of the society, and, at length, the impossibility of supporting such a number together became too evident to be resisted. Young scions were then pushed out from the parent-stock and instructed to explore fresh regions and to gain happier seats for themselves by their swords. "The world was all before them where to chuse."[21]

Malthus's ironic quotation from the end of *Paradise Lost* as Adam and Eve leave paradise for the fallen world exemplifies how allusion, in the absence of statistics, provides Malthus with persuasive evidence—the logic of metaphor. The point is that the Fall is recapitulated in each generation as a new set of children is expelled out of the household and into the world, the choices open to those children being geometrically reduced with each expulsion. The household thus generates its own destruction, or, as Marx bitterly lamented, Malthusian theory strips labor of even the power to reproduce itself, for such theory takes the sexual division of labor as a given and necessary dichotomy, following Milton and orthodox Christianity.

Wordsworth interpreted literature—Milton, especially—in a different way, partly because he had experienced a different kind of sexual division of labor both in the household of his Lake District neighbors and to some extent in his own household. Like Adam Smith, Wordsworth understood the small proprietary farm to be the crux of a just economy, but for Wordsworth this economy of estatesmen or "statesmen" was not yet a wholly nostalgic model in the early Grasmere years. One of the salient characteristics of the statesman's household was that it used two equally important modes of production: "first, the produce of [the man's] lands and flocks; and, secondly, the profit drawn from the employment of the women and children, as manufacturers; spinning their own wool in their own houses . . . and carrying it to market for sale."[22] In Wordsworth's *Guide to the Lakes* of 1810, from which this passage is taken, Wordsworth laments the coopting of this latter manufacturing by the new textile mills, a mode of production that took the women and children out of the home and literally gave the word "manufacturing" a new significance, no longer associated with the etymological idea of hand-fashioning. Writing in 1809, Coleridge excoriated "the vast Machines of Lancashire" for having "overwhelmed and rendered helpless the domestic Industry of the Females in the Cottages and small Farm-houses of Westmorland [sic] and Cumberland."[23] Historians tell us that by 1837 there was virtually no domestic or cottage industry in the Lakes, where once it had been so integral.[24]

Despite its twofold method of production, the traditional statesman economy did not depend upon a sexual division of labor in the same way that Malthusian theory or industrial manufacturing does. In the Lake District household, men tended to do the field work and women tended to do the final knitting that resulted in homespun, but those labors were not divided categorically. Female labor could extend to the fields, male labor to the nursery and kitchen. Thus, a contemporary observer of mid-eighteenth-century life in the Lake District noted that "husband, wife, sons and daughters all turn out to work in the fields"; and another, writing near the end of the century, describes "daughters and female servants" who "assist in carting, harrowing and weeding, as also in hay-making and harvesting; and even sometimes, they stay in the barn with the threshers, and wrap the straw into small bundles."[25] (Dorothy, traveling through Kent on the trip to France in July, 1802, was sufficiently struck by the differences between the agricultural economies of northwestern and southeastern England to comment in her *Journal*.[26]) This fluidity of employment in the Lake District meant that William's remark that "extreme penury is here unknown" (*Home at Grasmere*, 444) was largely accurate.

The Wordsworths themselves give several pictures of men doing so-called female labor and vice versa. There is Michael, for instance, in William's poem of that name, who performs for his baby son

> female service, not alone
> For dalliance and delight, as is the use
> Of Fathers, but with patient mind enforced
> To acts of tenderness. . . . (164–67)

There is also the story of the Ashburners, a family of five daughters, related in Dorothy's *Journal*. Peggy Ashburner, second wife of Thomas, told Dorothy of the "pains and industry [with which the family] had made up their taxes, interest, etc. etc., how they all got up at 5 o'clock in the morning to spin and Thomas carded, and . . . they had paid off a hundred pounds of the interest" (*Journal*, p. 61). This story is akin to—some have said it is the model for—the story of the old, blind widower with six daughters described in an early manuscript of *Home at Grasmere* (c. 1801) and subsequently transposed to *The Excursion* in 1814. One of the daughters, "a hardy Girl," performs for her father "the service of a Boy." She accompanies him, Antigone-like, on "his pastoral course," and she does the landscaping and gardening around the family cottage (*Home at Grasmere*, 547 ff.). Another daughter, the eldest, directs domestic business, but she has learned this "female" labor "from her Father's honored hands, herself / While She was yet a Little-one" (603–04).

This family apprenticeship, in which members of the sisterhood learn about household work from their blind father, alludes, I would suggest, to the domestic situation of Milton and his daughters in their collective role as amanuenses. Milton figures in Wordsworth's thinking throughout the period when he was composing *Home at Grasmere,* a poem with the avowed purpose of establishing the Grasmere household as a substitute for and a redemption of the "Home extinct" from which the Wordsworth children had been orphaned. If Grasmere was to become paradise regained, however, a new (home) economics would be needed to replace the lost Edenic one, which had become reified into the fallen economic law of Malthus.

The Fall comes about in book 9 of *Paradise Lost* because Eve insists upon a division of labor for sexual reasons. But what Eve means by a sexual division of labor is not what the term came to mean when applied to late eighteenth-century economic life. Eve asserts that the "wanton growth" of the garden is not manageable "till more hands / Aid us," (207–08), and so she reasons that she and Adam should separate for greater efficiency.[27] "Let us divide our labours" (9. 214), she says. But Eve does not mean by this commandment what the second Adam, Adam Smith, would mean. She is not suggesting that she and Adam should specialize their labors, each performing a small and discrete facet of a larger manufacturing process. Indeed, she imagines that while she and Adam are apart they will do exactly the same work: namely, the only labor that has to be done in Paradise, pruning and trimming (or, to use Eve's unfallen word, "redressing" [219]) the luxurious growth. Eve's argument for working apart is that, when she and Adam work together, "Looks intervene and smiles, or object new / Casual discourse draw on, which intermits / Our days work brought to little . . ." (222–24). Undivided labor leads to sexual dalliance, which undermines the efficiency of production.

Contrary to the point of view of someone who had read Adam Smith, Eve's argument for dividing labor is really just a plea for a little solitude. And to his credit, Adam (or Eve's "husband" as he is called immediately before [204] the poem's extended discourse on the nature of Edenic husbandry) understands her tacit plea. His way of heeding it, however, creates a new set of problems. To start with, he answers her essentially non-economic argument by using a language saturated with economic terms. Spouses should "lend" aid, he avers (260); the malicious foe will "work us" evil, he warns (255); Eve has "imployd" her thoughts well, he concedes (229). Even when Adam is speaking of things far removed from the question of labor, his language is economically intensive. Thus, he talks of their "joint hands" (244), of "yield[ing]" (248) her for a while to a solitude from which he expects her "sweet returne" (250).

Adam does not, that is, hear any "fallenness" in his own discourse. Nor perhaps did Milton.[28] In explaining to Eve the "fallacy" in her reasoning, Adam praises her for being mindful of the management of the household. In seeking to show Eve why their labor should not be divided, however, Adam proceeds to divide it along sexual lines. "[N]othing lovelier can be found / In Woman," he opines, "than to study household good, / And good works in her Husband to promote" (232–34). In dividing household good from good works, women from husbands, and domesticity from husbandry, Adam is, unconsciously perhaps, preparing Eve to understand the life of household economy to which sexual reproduction will consign her whether they avoid temptation or not. His entire economist-like response to her noneconomic suggestion is to instruct her in seeing how production ought to lead to reproduction. The Lord, Adam says, has not "impos'd Labour" so as to "debarr" what Adam exquisitely calls "this sweet inter-course" (235–38). Mixing images of "food" and thought, of nutrition and cognition, of mental and material labor, Adam lets the gentle equivocation of "intercourse" lead him on to his equivocal conclusion that "Love [is] not the lowest end of human life" (241). Thus, if Eve sounds to fallen ears like Adam Smith, Adam answers her with a kind of Ur-version of Malthus.

At times in the early Grasmere years the relationship between good works and household good was more ecstatically transparent than either Milton's Adam or Eve could say, as in this effusion from William's *Home at Grasmere* where female labor is appropriated into the service of textual husbandry:

> Possessions have I wholly, solely, mine,
> Something within, which yet is shared by none,
> Not even the dearest to me and most dear,
> Something which power and effort may impart.
> I would impart it; I would spread it wide,
> Immortal in the world which is to come. (897–902)

This extraordinary assertion of vocation identifies the poet's power not only in terms of possessive individualism but also in terms of sexual prowess. And yet the precise gender of the sexual metaphor is difficult to determine here. Is this a male dream of dissemination based loosely on the scattering or broadcasting of seed in a field? ("I would spread it wide.") Or is it a female dream (one dreamed by a man, to be sure) of parturition? ("Posses-sions have I. . . ." "Something within, which yet is shared by none. . . ." "I would impart it. . . .") The point is that each labor-process is a vehicle for the other: it is a double dream of production as reproduction and repro-duction as production.

By 1802, however, the relationship between love and household good, between fame and domesticity, was not susceptible to the same kind of bravado, and one of the reasons for this was the imminent change in the Wordsworths' domestic situation. William had decided by the end of 1801 to marry Mary Hutchinson, but the Peace of Amiens made possible for the first time in many years a visit to France, and Annette wanted to see him. Thus, the marriage to Mary was scheduled for October so that William, accompanied by Dorothy, could revisit Annette and their child, whom William had never seen. They met in Calais, on the coast, during August. This trip into William's domestic past, on the eve of a restructuring of his domestic future, produced a generous handful of sonnets, none of them directly concerned with Wordsworth's domestic life, most of them focused on the mismanagement of political households, both French and English.

The Calais sonnets tend to measure contemporary events in postrevolutionary France against Wordsworth's own recollections of French politics from his earlier visits, one of which produced Caroline (although the sonnets do not explicitly include that particular memory). The London sonnets, written in September, after Wordsworth's return, tend to indict England for its deteriorating moral resolve and to measure the English polis of 1802 against its own seventeenth-century, revolutionary history.

How did William come to write sonnets at all, and why did they hold such appeal for him during the tumultuous summer and autumn of 1802? In the narrow rooms of Dove Cottage, warmed as William wrote "By my half-kitchen my half-parlour fire" ("I am not One," 12), Dorothy had read her brother Milton's sonnets in May 1802 (*Journal*, p. 127), and he immediately tried out the form. In William's 1802 sonnets, Milton figures explicitly as a political thinker (as in "Milton! Thou should'st be living at this hour"), as well, of course, as the paterfamilias of the poetic form itself. I would suggest, however, that Wordsworth may also have been remembering not just the public poet who was secretary to the Commonwealth but the domestic Milton, the failed husband of whom Dr. Johnson wrote: "marriage afforded not much of his happiness. The first wife left him in disgust, and was brought back only by terror; the second, indeed, seems to have been more a favourite, but her life was short. The third . . . oppressed his children in his life-time, and cheated them at his death."[29] Certainly the sonnet form suggested the domestic space to William, a space soon to be altered by the taking of a new wife who would become the third important woman to him along with Dorothy and Annette. Recalling perhaps that the single stanza structure of the sonnet acts out the Italian sense of *stanza* as a room or chamber, William in a letter of November 1802 praised the "manly and dignified" Miltonic sonnet for "crowding into narrow room more of the combined effect of rhyme and blank verse than can be done by any other kind of verse I know of" (*E.Y.*, p. 379). Using the very language that describes the Grasmere property, another sonnet from late 1802 speaks of "the Sonnet's scanty plot of ground" ("Nuns fret not," 11). The sonnet, in short, epitomizes the domestic space that William celebrated at Grasmere and bestows upon that space an aesthetic analogue.

The following sonnet explicitly combines patriotic and domestic love in the manner of Milton and problemizes that combination in the manner of Wordsworth:

> O Friend! I know not which way I must look
> For comfort, being, as I am, opprest,
> To think that now our Life is only drest
> For shew; mean handywork of craftsman, cook,
> Or groom!—We must run glittering like a Brook
> In the open sunshine, or we are unblest:
> The wealthiest man among us is the best:
> No grandeur now in nature or in book
> Delights us. Rapine, avarice, expence,

> This is idolatry; and these we adore:
> Plain living and high thinking are no more:
> The homely beauty of the good old cause
> Is gone; our peace, our fearful innocence,
> And pure religion breathing household laws.

The "household laws" exhaled by pure religion are what Enlightenment social theorists took to be *moeurs*—that is, unwritten customs affecting the disposition of the individual personality in an understood matrix of communal behavior and social deportment. At the time he wrote this poem (in London, September 1802), Wordsworth was geographically as well as metaphorically in the middle of an isosceles triangle of households whose *loci* were Grasmere, Calais, and Gallow Hill in Yorkshire where Mary Hutchinson kept house for her tenant-farming brother Tom. In other words, the subject of the poem has the potential to become personal but its voice remains a public voice. The thrust of the poem is to bring all households together de jure under the single Miltonic codification of a public sonnet on a political theme, addressed to a friend. In Milton, that friend would doubtless be male. But in Wordsworth's poem, the friend is uncharacteristically abstract—in effect, a figure of speech, a personification enabling the poem's public stance.

Or, rather, the friend is less like either Coleridge or Dorothy than like the "others who called Milton Friend," whom Wordsworth identifies in another sonnet ("Great Men have been among us," 4), probably written about the same time, as Algernon Sidney, Andrew Marvell, James Harrington, and Sir Henry Vane the younger. These political theorists and polemicists would have understood the "good old cause" to be what scholars now call the ideology of civic humanism, in which "virtue and the faculties within" (to quote yet another Wordsworth sonnet from this same general period ("These times strike monied worldlings," 12) stand in antithesis to commerce and its corrupting influence on both public policy-making and the construction of the private personality. Like Wordsworth, these civic humanists held an idea of patriotism that was anticommercial but pro–private property.[30]

The point of these generalizations is simply that Wordsworth is speaking within the conventions governing the humanist lament about the private household's privative place in policy debates, a lament made more poignant by Malthus's allegation of the household's *de*privative place. Once one recognizes the conventions, one can then see that behind the criticism of "shew" in the poem's opening lines is not merely opposition to what was loosely thematized as "luxury" but, rather, a dissatisfaction with the idea of the specialization of labor, as J.G.A. Pocock explains:

> Specialization . . . was a prime cause of corruption; only the citizen as amateur, propertied, independent, and willing to perform in his own person all functions essential to the polis, could be said to practice virtue or live

in a city where justice was truly distributed. There was no *arte* that he must not be willing to make his own. (p. 499)

"Shew" in Wordsworth's poem depends upon and is supported by specializations such as that of artisanal labor ("mean handywork of craftsman") and that of domestic service, the latter identified in its gender-specific forms as female (cook) and male (groom) service. "Shew" "look[s] for comfort" as merely cosmetic and gourmandizing successes. What constitutes "idolatry" here is that this "shew" betokens a lost totality of being. "Shew" is a fragmentation of being as specialization is a fragmentation of labor, the division being representable in either economic or sexual terms. Conversely, the integration of personality into a self capable of performing all works for himself is what "plain living and high thinking" make possible—or so Wordsworth likes to think, poised as he is in the city of injustice (London) between households vanishing and about to be (re)born.

The one striking rhetorical figure in the sonnet above is the phrase "fearful innocence." What is gone, the sonnet laments, is an innocence "fearful" in the archaic sense of the word, an innocence capable of producing reverence and awe in others, an innocence that is paradoxically well-armed against corruptions from outside the household. What has taken its place is an innocence that is fearful in the more usual sense of the word—full of fears at what might be. This latter sense carries overtones of emasculation, as in Wordsworth's later sonnet where he exhorts England to "wean / Thy heart from its emasculating food" ("England! the time is come," 1–2). The breakdown of the analogous relationship between patriotic and domestic love was fearful, then, because of its potential to unman. Virtue crossed by such fear leaves the speaker not in awe but in an impotent state of perplexity: "I know not which way I must look." In 1802, Wordsworth's perplexities were as much familial as sociopolitical, although it is the latter sort of husbandry—as the management of the polis understood in the abstract terms of civic humanism—that provides Wordsworth in sonnet after sonnet from the long summer of 1802 with a language to express the anxieties of the former.

Contemporary economic theory belied the kind of households that the Wordsworths could observe around them in the Lake District, and the experience of these actual households also helped them reread the sexual division of labor in Milton and heal that division in their own household. It was Dorothy, as I shall show in a moment, who put that rereading into effect. To this point we have looked at William only, who, at the critical moment in the transformation of his own domestic economy, conducted an extended meditation in Miltonic sonnets on the analogy between patriotic and domestic love, between public "shew" and private "comfort," and the consequences of the analogy for the growth or decline of the individual personality. Of the role of the female in particular, Wordsworth remained

conveniently equivocal, but he could voice that equivocation unconven-
tionally. Near the end of the 1805 *Prelude,* William dramatically treats the
feminizing influence of domesticity not as emasculation but as a kind of
metaphorical husbandry that *improves* the (male) personality. Household
laws inspire a softening or humanizing of the speaker's severe and im-
passive form. Here, Dorothy is cast explicitly as the improving agent, and
William is bodily metamorphosed into a piece of landscape, cultivated and
refined by Dorothy's art of gardening into a *locus amoenus:*

> I too exclusively esteemed that love,
> And sought that beauty, which as Milton sings
> Hath terror in it. Thou didst soften down
> This over-sternness; but for thee, sweet friend,
> My soul, too reckless of mild grace, had been
> Far longer what by Nature it was framed—
> Longer retained its countenance severe—
> A rock with torrents roaring, with the clouds
> Familiar, and a favorite of the stars;
> But thou didst plant its crevices with flowers,
> Hang it with shrubs that twinkle in the breeze,
> And teach the little birds to build their nests
> And warble in its chambers. (13. 224–36)

To seek that beauty which has terror in it one must turn to that very
passage in *Paradise Lost* discussed above, where Adam and Eve divide their
labors for sexual reasons, allowing Satan to approach the now vulnerable
Eve while she tends her flower garden alone (9. 490–91). Dorothy, in the
Wordsworth household, had charge of the economically marginal produce
of the garden, the flowers, whereas William tended the nutritionally more
significant fruit and nut trees:

> This plot of Orchard-ground is ours;
> My trees they are, my Sister's flowers.
> > ("I've watched you now a full half hour," 10–11)

Although not economically important, the work of the female has the social
function of bringing refinement to what would otherwise be crudely natural (i.e., geological) process, here imaged as "a rock with torrents roaring."
Dorothy's intervening feminine touch augurs that "Of female softness shall
his life be full, / Of little loves and delicate desires . . ." (13. 208–09), but her
intervention here has an immediate poetic effect as well. The above passage
alludes to and significantly rewrites a poem of 1800, "There is a Eminence."
The "eminence" is the actual mountaintop of Stone Arthur, although
William later admitted that the peak could not be seen from the orchard
seat at Grasmere as the poem claims.[31] In the poem, Dorothy, because of
whom "no place on earth / Can ever be a solitude to me" (1506), gives "this
lonesome Peak" (17) William's name. Thus, in the earlier poem William is
turned *into* a remote and rocky mountaintop, whereas in the passage from

the *Prelude* his physiology or outward aspect becomes metaphorically transformed into an interiorized space—a chasm, a chamber, an enclosure like the Grasmere orchard.

What is significant here is William's figurative equating of both self and mountain peak with the domestic household at Grasmere. In fact, William always regarded the cottage itself as a kind of mountaintop. In a letter written shortly after the move to the cottage he referred to the grounds as "our little domestic slip of mountain" (*E.Y.* p. 274). In his curious marriage poem, written in May 1802 and addressed not to the bride-to-be but to the cottage where the bride would reside, he refers to the cottage as a "little Nook of mountain ground."[32] The household economy, then, which Dorothy represents, domesticates the mountain-like self of the poet just as the physical shape of the cottage and its garden embowers a mountaintop, transfiguring it into what the marriage poem calls a "happy Garden" (57), which like Milton's Paradise sits atop a mount. William's recurring fantasy is that, thanks to Dorothy, he falls from the grand yet severe solitude of the angelic (in which he is familiar with the clouds and a favorite of the stars) into the cultivated and 'improved' state of the Edenic (in which no place is a solitude *to him*). This rather breathlessly personalized reading of Miltonic metamorphosis leaves no room for the spirit of metamorphosis itself—that is, for the satanic. The marriage poem, for instance, leaves no opportunity to wonder whether the bride, who has been living in the Yorkshire dales, will find this nook of mountain ground to her liking. Indeed, any notion of misgiving is sublimated by the marriage poem into the single anxiety that the cottage garden, cultivated with such care since the Wordsworths' arrival, will become overgrown while they are away on their domestic mission.[33] This is as close as William comes to pondering the fragility of their art of improvement.

Missing from the *Prelude*'s lines that celebrate domesticity in the image of warbling birds, and missing from William's writing about the domestic in general, is an understanding of how the world of domestic arrangements has its own terrors. In the Wordsworth household such terrors are expressed predominantly by Dorothy. In the *Prelude*, William attributes to Dorothy the power to "teach the little birds to build their nests," and in June 1802 Dorothy had been watching a pair of swallows to see if they would nest in the cottage eaves. Significantly, they choose to build at Dorothy's own bedroom window, Dorothy having recently exchanged bedrooms with William (see *Journal*, pp. 128, 137). For her, these nesting little birds become emblematic of the personality integrated into a serene and responsive home site. The image of warbling birds, which the *Prelude* associates with Dorothy's moral gardening, is in fact her image, expropriated from the *Journal*'s loving descriptions of these swallows:

> When they first came about the window they used to hang against the panes, with their white Bellies and their forked tails looking like fish, but then they

fluttered and sang their own little twittering song. . . . I watched them one
morning, when William was at Eusemere, for more than an hour. Every now
and then there was a feeling motion in their wings, a sort of tremulousness
and they sang a low song to one another. (p. 142)

A fortnight before the Wordsworths' departure for the Continent to
meet Annette and ultimately to gather Mary into the bosom of the family,
these birds lose their nest. "Poor little creatures," Dorothy writes, "they
could not themselves be more distressed than I was" (p. 142). For about ten
days she had been associating this pair of swallows with her own domestic
activity: "I had watched them early in the morning, in the day many and
many a time and in the evenings when it was almost dark I had seen them
sitting together side by side in their unfinished nest both morning and
night" (p. 142). Now, the rebuilding of this nest becomes the metaphorical
ground upon which Dorothy stages her anxieties about the coming changes
in the Wordsworths' domestic arrangements. She does not transfer these
anxieties, as William did, through the elevated language of political theory
to the sublimated world of statecraft and economics, but she does effect a
dramatization, the *Journal* serving as the theater in which Dorothy writes
the new household laws into being. Her last entry before their departure
has the air of dramatic soliloquy:

> O beautiful place! Dear Mary William. The horse is come Friday morning, so
> I must give over. William is eating his Broth. I must prepare to go. The
> Swallows I must leave them the well the garden the Roses, all. Dear crea-
> tures!! they sang last night after I was in bed—seemed to be singing to one
> another, just before they settled to rest for the night. Well, I must go.
> Farewell————(p. 146)

In William's sonnet of two months later, he will refer to the domestic labors
of cook and groom, and here their tasks have been accomplished: William
has his porridge; the horse has been brought to the door. As the Wordsworths prepare to leave their beautiful household for a world of more
public "shew," however, the beauty of this passage belies a terror that the
"settled" tone of the redomesticated birds cannot entirely mitigate. The
terror is that William will be paired with Mary ("Dear Mary William," in
Dorothy's unpunctuated valediction), while Dorothy will be paired only
with the mean handiwork of her own arts and crafts: with swallows,
garden, roses, well—in fact, with "all" the rest.

This crisis of the empty nest is central to the *Journal*'s sense of bonding.
William asserted in a poem from the germinal month of May 1802 celebrating his friendship with Coleridge, "Verse was what he had been wedded to"
("Within our happy Castle," 33). But Dorothy viewed the bonding both of
the self to its own labor and of the self to others somewhat differently. In
Dorothy's view of the household as a totality, textual production must be
grounded in the material means of life, the business of keeping "all" of the

household coherently managed. The sacrament of matrimony is not the only kind of wedding that would need to occur.

The *Journal's* complex way of explaining that other bonding to William and to herself is anticipated in Dorothy's earlier correspondance with her childhood friend Jane Pollard. In letters prior to Jane's marriage in 1795, Dorothy replays again and again a shared female memory of the household as a determined space managed and structured by women. "You remember," she tells Jane, "the Enthusiasm with which we used to be fired when in the Back-Kitchen, the croft, or in any other of our favorite Haunts we built our little Tower of Joy" (*E.Y.*, p. 93). Love, she reminds Jane, "fired our little hearts when we built our airy castles leaning upon each others arms in some corner where we have stolen from our play-fellows, and where we did not fear to hazard observations which others would have laughed at or despised as foolish and unmeaning" (*E.Y.*, p. 101). This architectural fantasy Dorothy calls "the language of the heart," thus inventing in 1793 the phrase that is the cornerstone of William's great architectural fantasy about ecclesiastical ruins and the mansion of the mind: *Tintern Abbey.*

In Dorothy's correspondence, the dream of a household finds an unexpected center in the actual figure of Dorothy's "aunt," depicted by Dorothy after childbirth: "I am now in my aunt's Room, she is in Bed beside me, and is really so well as to make me think lying-in not half so tremendous a Business as it is generally thought; she manages matters so well . . ." (*E.Y.*, p. 95). It is this understanding of female competence in a domestic setting that Dorothy's letters share with Jane and that they project into a future household managed by Dorothy, who will be, of course, living with William, but where there will be room for others as well—specifically, for another woman, for Jane. In "my little Parsonage," Dorothy muses to Jane, "I hope you will spend at least a year with me." And then she dreams up a domestic decor and indoor tasks in the georgic spirit of Thomson and Cowper:

> I have laid the particular scheme of happiness for each Season. When I think of Winter I hasten to furnish our little Parlour, I close the Shutters, set out the Tea-table, brighten the Fire. When our Refreshment is ended I produce our Work, and William brings his book to our Table and contributes at once to our Instruction and amusement, and at Intervals we lay aside the Book and each hazard our observations upon what has been read without fear of Ridicule or Censure. (*E.Y.*, p. 88)

The antecedent of "our" in "our Work" seems at first to be Jane and Dorothy exclusively, their work being some female activity like sewing or mending the linen, two actual and time-consuming winter chores in the Grasmere household. But by the end of the passage, that "our" embraces what William is doing and expands to include mutual observation, discussion, and reading.

In another letter to Jane, Dorothy precisely explains the bonding behind this "our": "I am very sure that Love will never bind me closer to any human Being than Friendship binds me to you my earliest female Friend, and to William my earliest and my dearest Male friend" (*E.Y.*, p. 96). This early affirmation of concurrent male and female bonding is particularly significant because the greatest challenge to the Grasmere *Journal's* idea of domestic order comes in the person of Mary Hutchinson—or rather, in the need to reimagine the postmarital household as continuous with the premarital one. But Mary is in Dorothy's *Journal* from the beginning—or, rather, she is the absence behind the *Journal's* origin. And Dorothy's way of resolving her anxiety about William's marriage is also inherent in the original purposefulness of the *Journal* itself.

The *Journal* was begun when Dorothy's brothers went to Yorkshire to visit Mary, and Dorothy "resolved to write a journal of the time until [they] return" (p. 15). Her resolution to write, begun in being suddenly independent of her brothers, has as one of its important ends to "give Wm Pleasure by it when he comes home again" (pp. 15–16). By the time William returns home, however, Dorothy is concerned not only that he take pleasure in her writing but principally that he see how the cottage and grounds have changed in his three-week absence. In fact, brother and sister stay up until 4 A.M. the night of his return so that William may have the "opportunity of seeing our improvements" (p. 25).

By "improvements" Dorothy undoubtedly means the aesthetic alterations caused by her assiduous planting, weeding, and watering; and by "our" she must mean the work done by her on behalf of their mutual interest. Her journal records that in William's absence she spent a lot of time culling plantings from both the countryside and from her neighbors and replanting them in her garden. But the word "improvements" casts a long socioeconomic shadow, for the word was coming to mean not merely cultivation or an increase in agricultural efficiency but also an ideology based upon the turning of a profit.[34] Significantly, the period of William's absence from their six-month-old "property" elicits from Dorothy her most concentrated series of meditations on actual socioeconomic issues affecting her Lake District neighbors. A visit by a beggar woman, for instance, leads Dorothy to think how "burying" has become "very dear." She records John Fisher's conversation with her about "the alteration in the times" that will result in a society divided into "the very rich and the very poor, for those who have small estates says he are forced to sell, and all the land goes into one hand" (p. 19). Or, one morning while sitting on the grass near a neighbor's farmhouse, she fantasizes "[i]f I had three hundred pounds and could afford to have a bad interest for my money I would buy that estate, and we would build a cottage there to end our days in" (p. 21). Meanwhile she actually does find a house for the Coleridges to let at Greta Hall, Keswick, thus reciprocating Coleridge's kindness in finding accommodations for the Wordsworths several years earlier at Alfoxden.[35]

Dorothy's daydream money becomes, in the accounting of her *Journal*, the actual labor that she puts into improving the Grasmere property in

William's absence. One assummes William was pleased at how the place looked. Dorothy certainly was. Two days after William's return she tells how a "cornotted Landau went by when we were sitting upon the sodded wall. The ladies (evidently Tourists) turned an eye of interest upon our little garden and cottage" (p. 25). Like the "wealthy son of Commerce" who casts an interested glance at the Coleridges' pretty cot,[36] these tourists as Dorothy calls them (using the word in something like its modern sense) are not looking merely for beauties unborrowed from the eye but can see that the value of property is a reflection of labor bestowed and invested in its improvement—improvement that, in Dorothy's eyes, coincides exactly with her keeping of the *Journal*. If the "interest" Dorothy elicits from the tourists is interest in the capitalist sense, then the reflexivity that Dorothy, the domestic improver and manager, attempts to elicit from William involves a more abundant recompense—his approbation of her work both on the property and in her journal.

Mary is also behind the next critical example of Wordsworthian household laws at work, as represented by Dorothy. The date of this entry is 23 March 1802, the day after William and Dorothy have decided that they should "see Annette" and then, also in Dorothy's words, "that Wm should go to Mary":

> A mild morning. William worked at the Cuckow poem. I sewed beside him. After dinner he slept I read German, and at the closing of day went to sit in the orchard. He came to me, and walked backwards and forwards. We talked about C. Wm repeated the poem to me. I left him there and in 20 minutes he came in, rather tired with attempting to write. He is now reading Ben Jonson I am going to read German it is about 10 o'clock, a quiet night. The fire flutters and watch ticks I hear nothing else save the Breathing of my Beloved and he now and then pushes his book forward and turns over a leaf. (pp. 105–106)

There is nothing unusual about this depiction of the interchangeability of activities in the premarital household except that here those activities come to seem *representative* of the household because of the way they have been aesthetically shaped and stylistically compressed. The key to that artfulness is the modulation of the journal entry into the present tense, "He is *now* reading Ben Jonson," a device that Dorothy uses rarely and always with dramatic effect (as in the earlier letter about her aunt). It is a device that makes experience seem to occur at the instant it is being written, as if experience *is* textual. Here the coincidence of domestic peace and aesthetic calm, the harmony of affect and effect, seems to reproduce the Wordsworths' mutual resolve of the night before to put William's family life (or lives) in order.

It is William who is reading at the end while Dorothy is "going to read German" but goes on writing instead, taking William as the object of her loving scrutiny. But it is Dorothy, as if reading her own text back to herself, who judges the significance of this evening's events when, in her entry for the next day (24 March), she says, "I made a vow that we would not leave this country for G[allow] Hill" (p. 106). The effect of this vow, spoken by Dorothy ("*I* made a vow") on behalf of them both ("that *we* would not leave"), means that any new household including Mary Hutchinson of Gallow Hill would have to be reconstituted in this space, on this particular Grasmere site. And it is Dorothy's own text that has movingly sacralized this space as well as recorded the vow.

Lacking a cohesive narrative structure, the *Journal* cannot be said to have a climax; but Dorothy's vow is a liminal moment, ironically comparable to Jane Eyre's "Reader, I married him." The vow henceforth distributes values into a "before" and an "after." From this point on, Dorothy is committed to reimagining life at Grasmere as a permanently expanded household in which the interchange of activities as described above would have to be less exclusively a *double* labor. We know from letters that Dorothy also had to deal with Coleridge's insistent invitation that the Wordsworths—all three of them—move to Greta Hall after the marriage, but the decision has already been made on 24 March not to let the marriage interfere with the Grasmere household.[37] That is the decision Dorothy is wedded to.

The vow to stay in the Grasmere cottage replicates, therefore, the conditions under which the *Journal* was begun. It reminds the Wordsworths why they came to Grasmere in the first place—namely to affirm their own household as a site of intrinsic value. But the original pilgrimage of the two must now be expanded or at least realigned. We do not see—or at least I do not see—in the *Journal* how Dorothy works out whatever inner struggle that vow might have exacted. We do see, however, the *effects* of a struggle—as, for instance, on William's wedding day when she presents her brother with the ring she has worn all night, or when she throws herself on the bed in a near-swoon while waiting for the news that the marriage, which she did not attend, had taken place. And we see the *results* of a struggle; we see that there *is* a resolution, which I shall now try to describe.

On his wedding night William wrote yet another sonnet, "Composed after a Journey across the Hammilton [sic] Hills, Yorkshire," the journey being the one back to Grasmere after the wedding. Dorothy's equivalent of this sonnet is the extended passage in the *Journal* where she lovingly describes the landmarks passed by the Wordsworths on their return, landmarks that recall the earlier return to the Vale in 1799 when she and William "were left to ourselves and had turned our whole hearts to Grasmere as a home in which we were to rest" (p. 158). For Dorothy, the culmination of the whole summer's voyage was not the wedding but the return to Grasmere, to the place of her choice. It is at the moment of reentering the cottage itself when we see Dorothy undergoing the psychic work of assimilating Mary, of pairing the other woman with herself, herself with the other.

The three of them arrive at the cottage at six in the evening. William and Dorothy have been away for three months. As Dorothy says, "for my part I cannot describe what I felt, and our dear Mary's feelings would I dare say not be easy to speak of" (p. 161). Out of this unspoken moment of reflection signifying adjustment and readjustment by the two women in particular, Dorothy resumes, "We went by candle light into the garden, and were astounded at the growth of the Brooms, Portugal Laurels, etc. etc. etc." William's marriage poem in May had predicted this wild growth. Because the creation of this garden had been one of the most important premarital labors in the household, the "we" here must refer primarily to William and Dorothy, for Mary could not be astounded by the growth of *their* garden. Dorothy continues without interruption: "The next day, Thursday, we unpacked the Boxes. On Friday 8th we baked Bread, and Mary and I walked, first upon the Hill side, and then in John's Grove, and then in view of Rydale, the first walk that I had taken with my Sister" (p. 161). Slowly, inexorably, the "we" of Dorothy's discourse opens up to include Mary and then, in an oddly touching way, to include *only* herself and Mary. At last they go walking together, into the widening Wordsworthian circle of familiarity.

The sequence of unpacking/baking/walking silently defines a female rhythm and suggests that a kind of bonding occurs between the two women upon the return to Grasmere that reproduces the woman's role in the household.[38] It reproduces, that is, the affection Dorothy has felt for William as a new, or newly affirmed, affection for Mary—her "Sister," as Dorothy chooses to call Mary, giving her sister-in-law her brother's name for herself. And it reproduces the pre-Grasmere daydream household of William, Dorothy, and Jane Pollard; for, long before William's marriage, Dorothy had dreamed a place in her household for two women. For Dorothy, such pairings tend to go on reproducing themselves as new pairings or as triplings or as any other mathematical combination and permutation that is necessary to keep the household as a unit of work-engendering value intact. This way of thinking may be graphically present in the almost doodlelike entry written on blotting paper and dated 16 May 1802 that arranges the names William, Dorothy, John, Coleridge, and Mary and Sara Hutchinson in columns that can be read both vertically and horizontally (see *Journal,* p. 126). These different pairings, different threesomes, emblematically expand the household into a polis of many simultaneously possible households.

The penultimate entry of the *Journal,* however, arranges these possible households into the actual one of January, 1803:

A very cold day. Wm promised me he would rise as soon as I had carried him his Breakfast but he lay in bed till between 12 and one. We talked of walking, but the blackness of the Cold made us slow to put forward and we did not walk at all. Mary read the Prologue to Chaucer's tales to me, in the morning William was working at his poem to C. Letter from Keswick and from Taylor on Wm's marriage. C. poorly, in bad spirits. Canaries. Before tea I sate 2 hours in the parlour. Read part of The Knight's Tale with exquisite delight. Since Tea Mary has been down stairs copying out Italian poems for Stuart. Wm has been working beside me, and here ends this imperfect summary. I will take a nice Calais Book and *will* for the future write regularly and, if I can legibly so much for this my resolution on Tuesday night, January 11th 1803. Now I am going to take Tapioca for my supper; and Mary an Egg. William some cold mutton—his poor chest is tired. (pp. 165–66)

Dorothy's description of this one day exhibits a structural unity that draws upon her premarital way of describing household activity. The day begins with William's broken vow and ends with Dorothy's vow to go on writing in a new notebook, a vow that she was not able to keep. That is, William breaks his vow for the same reason that Dorothy makes hers—for the sake of writing. The entry begins with breakfast taken by William from Dorothy's hands, and it ends with the three family members each choosing a different supper. The day is, in one important sense, a failure, for they have not been able to walk. Or, in other words, William's condition, referred to at both the beginning and the end of the entry, determines the quotidian events of the household. Nevertheless, within the context of his discomfort, the household is relentlessly active, and that activity is conducted, at least in the selectivity of Dorothy's recollection, according to certain palpable rhythms.

There is first the double pairing in which Mary reads to Dorothy while William writes his poem to Coleridge. Then, after the day's letters are read, there is a kind of soliloquy in which Dorothy is alone reading to herself "with exquisite delight." Finally, there is a reversal of the earlier pairings. Now Mary is downstairs copying out some poems for Stuart while Dorothy and William are working together. The work here is specifically writing, with Dorothy making a belated New Year's resolution to go on keeping the journal even as her notebook runs out of pages. This resolution to go on writing recalls, of course, the *Journal's* own beginning in Dorothy's desire to keep a record during William's absence. Now William is present, but what is "imperfect" about Dorothy's summary is its gesture toward returning the relationship between William and Dorothy to a time before the occasion of the *Journal.* For just a moment here they seem to be alone together *again,* but this time the swerve into the authorial present tense has a different resolution. "Wm has been working beside me," records Dorothy the chronicler of daily household activities; "and here ends this imperfect summary," concludes Dorothy the authorial manager of those activities.

This return to the present, with its subsequent daydream of writing in the future, leaves the entry shaped but unfinished—"imperfect," if you will. Dorothy makes one interesting gesture toward perfecting that summary. If there is to be a future journal, she says, it could be written in "a nice Calais book," for that would be a gesture embracing the French household of Annette and Caroline as well and pairing it symbolically with the present one. Returning to the present entry, however, we may see that the agent which has harmonized the household's apparently random series of events and associations and concerns is the shaping spirit of imagination that is the

Journal itself. Or, in other words, the writing has "improved" the day's activities by the various household members insofar as they have all been made to connect in *this* "imperfect summary," which is the household law that keeps William and Dorothy "working"—to use her word—beside each other even as the work of the *Journal* comes to an end.

But Dorothy's *Journal* does not conclude with its overt little gesture toward closure like a public utterance, like a poem. It concludes much less solemnly with a kind of Shandean cock-and-bull story about gingerbread, a story that centers upon a three-person household like the Wordsworths' and that ends by turning upside down the standard economists' view of production and consumption as predicated on a sexual division of labor. On an "intensely cold" Sunday in January,

> Wm had a fancy for some ginger bread I put on Molly's Cloak and my Spenser, and we walked towards Matthew Newton's. I went into the house. The blind Man and his Wife and Sister were sitting by the fire, all dressed very clean in their Sunday's Clothes, the sister reading. They took their little stock of gingerbread out of the cubboard [sic] and I bought 6 pennyworth. They were so grateful when I paid them for it that I could not find it in my heart to tell them we were going to make Gingerbread ourselves. I had asked them if they had no thick "No" answered Matthew "there was none on Friday but we'll *endeavour* to get some." The next Day the woman came just when we were baking and we bought 2 pennyworth. (p. 166)

This blind baker is surrounded not by daughters, like the Miltonic father-figure in *Home at Grasmere*, but by a wife and sister, like Wordsworth himself. On this intensely cold day, the Miltonic poet Wordsworth is in Milton's own words a "blind mouth"—a consumer waited on by the female presence of Dorothy in Molly's cloak. On her quest to satisfy William, Dorothy discovers a household that produces gingerbread, which William fancies, but not the thick sort, which he relishes. The point of this wry little jest, which has the savor of romance and the tone of fable, is mock-Malthusian: women cannot manage the household efficiently as long as (male) desire outruns the cost-benefit ratio. Here the man's seemingly capricious longing for gingerbread results in Dorothy's expenditure of more money than she would have liked to spend. For, if you want gingerbread, you will pay sixpence even if it's not the thick kind you prefer. But if the gingerbread man (or woman) shows up with the thick kind the next day, then you are obliged to buy some, even if you can now make it for yourself. Thus Dorothy buys twopence more from the Newton woman, which is bad home economics but right neighborly action.

There is more than a little Cumbrian caginess in this compressed georgic of private wishes, *labor improbus,* and civic action. The woman manages the Wordsworth household so as to satisfy the willfulness of the man's (i.e., William's) delicate desire, but at the cost of virtually owing the Newtons a purchase of some kind for their "endeavour," as the other man, Matthew

Newton, delicately emphasizes. Nevertheless, in this good-natured anecdote, which finally does conclude the *Journal* and so terminates the resolve to go on keeping a journal, Dorothy cheerfully gives her twopence to an enterprising family, which had the good sense to leave a special place for "the sister" to read to them beside the fire.[39]

NOTES

1. *The Prelude: 1799, 1805, 1850,* ed. Jonathan Wordsworth, M. H. Abrams, and Stephen Gill (New York: W. W. Norton, 1979). All subsequent references are to this edition, according to book and line numbers.

2. The term is taken from Julie A. Matthaei, *An Economic History of Women in America: Women's Work, the Sexual Division of Labor, and the Development of Capitalism* (New York: Schocken, 1982), esp. pp. 101–86, although Matthaei might wish to apply the term differently in a study of British households. A germinal economic assessment of the household as a value-producing entity is Margaret G. Reid, *Economics of Household Production* (New York: John Wiley, 1934).

3. "Within our happy Castle there dwelt one," line 68, in *William Wordsworth,* ed. Stephen Gill (New York: Oxford University Press, 1984), p. 267. All subsequent references to William's poetry, excluding *The Prelude* and *The Excursion,* will be to this edition.

4. Mary Moorman, *William Wordsworth: The Early Years 1770–1803* (1957; reprint edn., New York: Oxford University Press, 1968), p. 324. I am indebted throughout this discussion to Moorman's depictions of pre-Grasmere life at Racedown (chap. 9, pp. 279–320) and at Alfoxden (chap. 10, pp. 321–58).

5. For the building of the garden seat, see *Journals of Dorothy Wordsworth,* ed. Mary Moorman (New York: Oxford University Press, 1971), p. 121. All subsequent references, cited parenthetically as *Journal* with page number, are to this edition. William's poem of 1800, "There is an Eminence," is discussed later in the present essay.

6. W. W. Douglas, "Wordsworth as Business Man," *PMLA* 63 (1948): 641. William's, and indeed the Wordsworths', fantasy of ownership is pervasive but is particularly central in "Home at Grasmere" ("The unappropriated bliss hath found / An owner, and that owner I am he" [85–6]) and is prefigured as a trope in "Tintern Abbey," as more and more readers are discovering. (See Mark Foster, for instance, in "'Tintern Abbey' and Wordsworth's Scene of Writing," *Studies in Romanticism,* 25 [1986]: 80, where he speculates about Wordsworth's "desire . . . to invest his intuitions with some of the substance of real property.") Interestingly, the only piece of real estate actually purchased by Wordsworth was bought in order to threaten the owner of Rydal Mount with development on a nearby field if she did not allow him and his family to stay on as renters. The story is told in Mary Moorman, *William Wordsworth: The Later Years 1803–1850* (1965; reprinted, Oxford and New York: Oxford University Press, 1968), p. 421. The field, Dora's Field, remains undeveloped.

7. See Moorman, *The Early Years,* p. 475. Michael H. Friedman calls the Wordsworths rentiers in "Wordsworth's Grasmere: A Rentier's Vision," *Polit: A Journal of Literature and Politics* 1, no. 1 (1977): 35–60.

8. Margaret Homans, *Women Writers and Poetic Identity: Dorothy Wordsworth, Emily Brontë, and Emily Dickinson* (Princeton: Princeton University Press, 1980), pp. 41–103.

9. *The Letters of William and Dorothy Wordsworth: The Early Years 1787–1805,* rev.

ed. Chester L. Shaver (Oxford: Clarendon Press, 1967), p. 97. Hereafter cited parenthetically in the text as *E. Y.*

10 John Barrell, *English Literature in History 1730–80: An Equal, Wide Survey* (London: Hutchinson, 1983), p. 91.

11. Wordsworth, *Poetical Works,* ed. Thomas Hutchinson; rev. ed. Ernest de Selincourt (London: Oxford University Press, 1969). All references to *The Excursion* are to this edition.

12. See *Journal,* pp. 88, 90.

13. Most scholars would not make a distinction between Romantic pastoral and Romantic georgic vision. See, for instance, Roger Sales, *English Literature in History 1780–1830: Pastoral and Politics* (London: Hutchinson, 1983). Although Virgil Nemoianu in *Micro-Harmony: The Growth and Uses of the Idyllic Model in Literature* (Bern: Peter Lang, 1977) does not use the term georgic and is mainly concerned with continental literature, he makes a supple distinction between pastoral as a *genre* and idyll as a *model* (pp. 15 ff.). Using Schiller's terminology, Lore Metzger's *One Foot in Eden: Modes of Pastoralism in Romantic Poetry* (Chapel Hill: University of North Carolina Press, 1986) attempts to expand the definition of pastoral beyond generic distinctions. But the georgic, I would argue, is, in the *English* tradition, a mode that counters the pastoral and that was appropriated by the English Romantics as an antithetical genre. In this regard, the Virgilian georgic, with its ethic of hard labor, is opposed to the Horatian celebration of rural retirement, the more traditional way of accounting for the *sermo humilis* of Wordsworthian (and Coleridgean) conversation poems. On the distinctions between Horatian and Virgilian ideas of work and leisure, I have been instructed by Michael O'Loughlin, *The Garlands of Repose: The Literary Celebration of Civic and Retired Leisure* (Chicago: University of Chicago Press, 1978).

14. That is, the country-house poem is the exact opposite of georgic when it acts, as Raymond Williams claims "To Penshurst" does, to expurgate both the idea of labor and the very presence of laborers (*The Country and The City* [New York: Oxford University Press, 1973], p. 32).

15. The student of the georgic tradition in English literature is indebted to John Chalker, *The English Georgic* (Baltimore: Johns Hopkins University Press, 1969) and to Anthony Low, *The Georgic Revolution* (Princeton: Princeton University Press, 1985). There have been few readings of the Wordsworthian georgic, but see Annabel Patterson, "Wordsworth's Georgic: Genre and Structure in *The Excursion,*" *Wordsworth Circle* 9 (1978): 145–54; and Kurt Heinzelman, *The Economics of the Imagination* (Amherst: University of Massachusetts Press, 1980), pp. 196–233.

16. See the chapter "The Public and The Private Realm," in Hannah Arendt, *The Human Condition* (Chicago: University of Chicago Press, 1958), pp. 22–78.

17. *Reflections on the Revolution in France,* in *The Works of the Right Honorable Edmund Burke,* rev. ed., 12 vols. (Boston: Little, Brown, 1865–67), 3:275. On the general importance of Burke to Wordsworth see James K. Chandler, *Wordsworth's Second Nature: A Study of the Poetry and Politics* (Chicago: University of Chicago Press, 1984).

18. See Louis Dumont, *From Mendeville to Marx: The Genesis and Triumph of Economic Ideology* (Chicago: University of Chicago Press, 1977); and Milton L. Myers, *The Soul of Modern Economic Man: Ideas of Self-Interest, Thomas Hobbes to Adam Smith* (Chicago: University of Chicago Press, 1983).

19. "On the Definition of Political Economy and on the Method of Investigation Proper to It," in *J. S. Mill's Philosophy of Scientific Method,* ed. Ernest Nagel (New York: Hafner, 1958), pp. 407–40.

20. Thomas Paine, "Agrarian Justice," in *Complete Writings,* ed. Philip S. Foner, 2 vols. (New York, 1945), 1:609.

21. *An Essay on the Principle of Population,* ed. Philip Appleman (1906; New York: W. W. Norton, 1976), p. 29.

22. *Guide to the Lakes*, ed. Ernest de Selincourt (1906; reprint edn., London: Oxford University Press, 1977), p. 90.

23. November 9, 1809, in *The Friend*, ed. Barbara E. Rooke, 2 vols., Bollingen Series, no. 75 (Princeton: Princeton University Press, 1969), 2:1.160.

24. C. M. L. Bouch and G. P. Jones, *A Short Economic and Social History of the Lake Counties 1500–1830* (Manchester: Manchester University Press, 1961), p. 236. Bouch and Jones's contemporary source is the economist J. R. McCullough. See also Michael H. Friedman, *The Making of a Tory Humanist: Wordsworth and the Idea of Community* (New York: Columbia University Press, 1979), p. 211.

25. Cited in Bouch and Jones, p. 229.

26. On the journey past Canterbury, Dorothy and William fantasize about inhabiting the "neat gentlemen's houses" that they see there. There is one in particular, a "white house almost hid with green which we longed for." Amidst the daydream of property ownership, Dorothy is stopped by the sight of the hops grounds and by the remark of a fellow traveler (who is a woman) that "It is a sad thing for the poor people for the hop-gathering is the women's harvest . . ." (*Journal*, p. 151).

27. John Milton, *Complete Poems and Major Prose*, ed. Merritt Y. Hughes (New York: Odyssey, 1957). All references are to this edition; book (when not indicated in text) and line numbers are given in parentheses.

28. At least not the owner of "some thirty spots" (p. 97) described in J. Milton French, "Milton's Homes and Investments," *Philological Quarterly* 28 (1949): 77–97.

29. *Lives of the English Poets* (London: Oxford University Press, 1955), 1:92.

30. See J. G. A. Pocock's description of "the ideal of personality-sustaining property" (p. 463) in *The Machiavellian Moment* (Princeton: Princeton University Press, 1975), esp. pp. 462–505.

31. See *Wordsworth*, ed. Gill, pp. 697–98.

32. "Farewell thou little Nook of mountain ground," (1). William was apprehensive because he found that "neither D.[orothy] nor C.[oleridge] understand," the tone of this poem. Later he explained certain word choices in the poem to Mary by calling the work "a Spenserian poem" (*E.Y.*, p. 365). Dorothy and William had read Spenser's *Prothalamion* in April 1802 (*Journal*, p. 116).

33. "Thou easy-hearted thing! with thy wild race
Of weeds and flowers till we return be slow
And travel with the year at a slow pace . . ." (46-48).
The lines echo both Spenser's "Sweets *Themmes* runne softly, till I end my Song" and Milton's description of the Edenic diaspora: "with wandering steps and slow."

34. See Raymond Williams, "The Morality of Improvement" in *The Country and the City*, pp. 60–67; and "Improve" in Raymond Williams, *Keywords: A Vocabulary of Culture and Society* (London: Fontana, 1976), pp. 132–33.

35. See Moorman, *Early Years*, p. 477.

36. "Reflections on having left a Place of Retirement," (l. 11) in Coleridge, *Poetical Works*, ed. E. H. Coleridge (1912; reprint edn., London: Oxford University Press, 1969), p. 106.

37. See Moorman, *Early Years*, p. 557.

38. On the family as a "relational institution" in which the interrelatedness of women is reproduced, see Nancy Chodorow, *The Reproduction of Mothering: Psychoanalysis and the Sociology of Gender* (Berkeley and Los Angeles: University of California Press, 1978), p. 178 et passim.

39. I wish to thank Andrew Cooper, Susan Sage Heinzelman, Theresa M. Kelley, and Bradford K. Mudge for timely comments that helped me shape this essay—and especially Susan J. Wolfson for affording me more opportunities to develop this argument than one ought to have needed.

III.
Writing the Female

HARASSING THE MUSE

Karen Swann

> Now, between philosophers and poets, the
> latter, paradoxically, are perhaps the least
> naive. For if today's philosophers think they
> know that they don't know, the poets, for
> their part, know that they do know, but
> don't know what.
>
> —Shoshana Felman

John Keats's "La Belle Dame Sans Merci" appears to dramatize a scene of
instruction. Confronted with certain puzzling signs and desirous of an
explanation, an interlocutor questions a knight-at-arms he encounters in a
deathly landscape: "Oh what can ail thee, knight at arms, / Alone and palely
loitering?" The knight seems willing to assist the interlocutor in getting to
the bottom of his mysterious circumstances. Yet readers of the poem often
feel that the story he tells—of his romantic dalliance with a fairy lady and
her subsequent disappearance—finally begs more questions than it answers. The knight cannot tell who the Romantic woman was, or where she
went, or why; rather, he simply recounts a series of events, which he invites
us to assume but does not claim are related. Finally he gathers all "this" into
the last stanza, which, in the form of an answer, merely seizes on and
hollowly repeats the terms of the interlocutor's original question:

> And this is why I sojourn here,
>   Alone and palely loitering,
> Though the sedge is wither'd from the lake,
>   And no birds sing.[1]

Like many framed Romantic narratives, then, Keats's poem stages a scene
of instruction only to frustrate a desire to know. The knight would seem to
grasp neither the lady nor his own story, while his story in turn perplexes
rather than enlightens his audience. In the passage that serves as the
epigraph to this essay, Shoshana Felman invites us to read this very re-
calcitrance as the sign of poetic knowledge: poet that he is, the knight
knows that he knows, but doesn't know what.[2] But one could also account
for the poem's reserve more tendentiously—saying, for instance, that the
poem hints it could reveal more, but then refuses to give up the goods. This

crasser formulation, in a manner that no longer shocks, draws attention to the way a value we can call "knowingness" comes into play in discussions of what poets know. For it implies that, at the very least, Keats knows to deploy poetic reserve strategically—in order to entice, to seduce, to enthrall. At the same time, it flaunts the critic's presumption, not to know in some absolute sense, but simply to know more. The literary critic "knows" that the philosopher's naiveté consists in his settling on an answer, even if he only comes to see his own ignorance; in contrast, the critic knows that no story is the whole story.

Recasting Felman in more flagrantly knowing language serves to divert; the epistemological question—what do poets know?—gives way before a fascination with how that question is staged. In the pages that follow I will be arguing that the Romantic woman, like flagrantly seductive style, functions similarly to divert: she secures poetry's enticing reserve and the knowingness of poets and critics by allowing interpretive dramas to be seen as fascinating romantic encounters. The first section of this analysis wanders farthest from the landscape of "La Belle Dame Sans Merci," to the terrain of recent critical discussions of the poem and, more broadly, of the Romantic woman. Whatever else divides them in these discussions, critics agree on the value of knowingness—or, in the terms of the poem, on the undesirability of falling into the role of the knight, the innocent and chivalrous victim of a romance plot. But from the impossible point of view of the woman who may not even exist, the difference between naive and knowing efforts at mastery may be less decisive than it is for the critics. This feminist perspective uncovers a certain complicity between the knight who naively presumes to win the lady and the master who knows not to get too involved; from this vantage point both seem equally implicated in an old story whose victim is the woman.

I

The lady of "La Belle Dame Sans Merci" cannot be grasped, but one can try to get somewhere with her. Indeed, until quite recently critics of the poem have focused almost exclusively on the question of her identity, which has seemed inextricably bound up with the meaning of the poem itself. As David Perkins's headnote to the poem in his popular teaching anthology puts it: "The essence of Keats's ballad is the mystery of 'la belle dame.'"[3] The student reader is warned, however, that this is not a mystery to be resolved. One can only eliminate possibilities, learn what the lady is not: "She is not quite mortal, though she is loved by a mortal. She is not sinister, though the love of her has led the knight to his present woeful state (a state that might be attributed to the hopelessness of his love for something superhuman rather than to 'la belle dame' herself)." Alternatively, one can learn that the lady is much more than one thing. This is the lesson of another student text, the Longman edition of Keats, which in its headnote to "La Belle Dame" quotes Robert Graves's assertion that "the Belle Dame represent[s] Love, Death by Consumption . . . and Poetry all at once."[4] Both of these scenes of instruction suggest that the lady secures the power of literature by making reading more romantic. Not quite mortal, neither ideal lover nor fatal seductress but something of both, and representing love, death, and poetry all at once, the Romantic woman figures and contains the significance of the irreducibly ambiguous, richly and painfully enigmatic Romantic poem. Her enchanting character lends its mystique to the poem's interpretive puzzles; while it affords the critic who knows not to push her too far a certain *je ne sais quoi,* against which the naive student reader appears, at best, fatally misguided, at worst, clumsy and naive.

These representative and previously uncontroversial accounts of the poem themselves now seem a bit innocent. We've become more knowing about the plangent oppositional vocabulary that would set the ideal against the real, the transcendent or escapist against the mortal, art or at least certain romances against life; we've become more suspicious of the gesture that would establish the woman as the privileged representative of poetry's truth. We are also quicker to recognize our implication in interpretive drama: where Graves and Perkins presume to know the naiveté of the knight (and, by implication, of the young John Keats, hopelessly in love with truth, beauty, and romance), we are apt to feel that such confidence on the part of the reader is naive. A fine recent analysis of "La Belle Dame Sans Merci" by Susan Wolfson, for example, sees this poem as less "about" woman or love or poetry or even consumption as about a problematic of interpretation.[5] Focusing on the complex framing of the narrative, Wolfson rightly points out that the "action" of the poem, such as it is, consists not in the knight's encounter with the lady but with the interlocutor, whose "irresolution" can be linked to the reader's. The knight is as mysterious to his readers as the lady is to the knight; the woman is thus not the privileged repository of the poem's significance (and insofar as we are led to think so she functions as a lure) but one among numerous mysteries merely "accentuat[ing] the gap between the strangeness of signs and their proposed translations," eluding interpretive certainty.[6]

Wolfson's analysis by no means empties the poem by turning into philosophy as Felman defines it; rather, she charts how the poem invites our questions but preserves its mysteries, refusing even to yield up the "answer" that we do not know. But her reading—which sees the poem cannily undoing its own gestures toward meaning—does suggest the difficulty of keeping the Romantic woman in view in the present critical climate. If Graves now seems to have cast himself into the role of the knight who couldn't take his eyes off the mysterious lady, today's Romanticists, who feel that the lady has had previous readers of the poem too much in thrall, may threaten to effect her magical disappearance from the landscape of debate. For how does one take up the question of the Romantic woman when

Keats's knowing deployment of the plot in which she figures—his complex framing of it so as to de-center the lady—suggests that her only function is to be a lure, not simply for the knight, but for the reader?

Merely posing the question in these terms reveals its disingenuousness, since the woman who functions as a lure is a central figure in the psychoanalytic theory of Jacques Lacan. Lacan's Woman is close cousin of Keats's—she is complement and absolute Other, faithful lover and transcendent value, truth, poetry, and unconscious all at once. In his seminar *Encore*, Lacan considers the Woman as fantasm and lure, as she who functions only to divert attention from a gap opened up by the signifier within and between subjects. "There is no sexual relation," "there is no relation," because the subject in language is self-divided, structured in relation not to an other but to the phallus—the subject is subject, that is, to castration. Man's dream, the Woman serves to deny castration and the absence of relation, on the one hand by functioning as that onto which he projects his lack, and on the other—*as* Other—by representing an imaginary oneness that allows him to deny lack altogether. Thus, "the Woman does not exist" except as a fantasy in which man would find his own completion.[7] That it is possible to take up the question of this woman is apparent, not just from Lacan's work, but also from the charged discussion it has provoked. Here I want briefly to consider one such discussion, orchestrated by Jane Gallop in her book *The Daughter's Seduction* and involving Lacan, Stephen Heath, and Gallop herself, because of the tantalizing way the question of the woman and issues of critical knowingness get played out in a drama Gallop chooses to cast as romantic—involving a gallant knight, a "woman [who] does not [properly] exist," and a cavalier master who knows the dame has us too much in thrall. Acknowledging that the woman functions as lure, we might best reintroduce her to the critical debate by looking at this drama played out on the poem's margins.

Gallop's chapter "Encore *Encore*" focuses on Heath's essay "Difference," an extended critique of Lacan's seminar *Encore,* for its complicity with an ideology of representation that, by privileging the visible and apparently "natural," shores up the very order psychoanalysis presumes to critique.[8] Gallop's reading of Heath, however, attends surprisingly little to this argument, concentrating instead on a limited number of his rhetorical moves: she points out a moment when Heath seems to translate Lacan so as to make him more obviously answerable to charges that his claims to know (what Heath calls his "confidence of knowledge") are dependent on the presumed immediacy of the visual; she dwells on a long footnote on "authority" and what "authorizes" psychoanalytic theory, which he appends to the first page of the text, and on a passage at the end of the essay where, speculating about the potentially imperialistic gesture of his speaking for the feminist position, Heath refers to himself as "not a woman."[9] For Gallop, these gestures are symptomatic of Heath's ambivalence about legitimacy and authority; he wants to champion "unauthorized" feminist practice, but continually falls back into the "confidence of knowledge" he is exposing in Lacan.

That Gallop virtually overlooks the argument of Heath's long, dense analysis might strike one as cavalier. Charging her with infidelity to the text becomes problematic, however, because of the way her essay celebrates infidelity over legitimacy, and gesture or style over systematic analysis. Here is Gallop setting up Heath against Lacan, knight against rake, Anglo fidelity against French *je ne sais quoi*:

> The choice is between Heath's gallant chivalry (he effacingly refers to himself as "me not a woman"—p. 111; one of "those not woman"—p. 99; he wrote this article to *honour a commitment* to some feminists—p. 111) and Lacan's cavalier approach ("Woman does not exist," "[women] don't know what they're saying, that's all the difference between them and me"—p. 68): chivalry or cavalier approach? The choice seems obvious, but is it? (p. 44)

What does woman want? Although one might expect Heath's "devotion" to look better than Lacan's fast and loose play (what Gallop later calls his "macho aggression" [p. 44]), Gallop, anyway, prefers the mode of the latter. At issue, I want to suggest, is knowingness: who unknowingly repeats the same old romantic story? who knowingly exposes its strategems? For Heath, Lacan and feminists who adopt Lacanian theory threaten to become complicitous with a phallocentric identification of the woman with lack, unconscious, disorder, God. But for Gallop, it is Heath who risks complicity with a phallic order that would subject everything to the measure of a rigorously sustained single standard: his Marxian and feminist analysis of psychoanalytic theory merely sets up once more the Name of the Father ("a feminist system, one constant, faithful to the tenets and dogmas of feminism, would be but another Name of the Father, feminism as a position and possession" [p. 48]).

Somewhat cavalierly Gallop calls such a system "chivalrous"—faithful to "the woman"—and subjects it to Lacan's critique of courtly love:

> Lacan says that "for the man, whose lady was entirely, in the most servile sense, his subject, [courtly love was] the only elegant way to pull out of the absence of any sexual relation" . . . "Courtly love," according to Lacan, "is a totally refined way of supplementing the absence of sexual relations, by pretending that it is we who put the obstacle there." . . .
>
> Chivalry then, devotion to the lady, is a way of supplementing, making up for, getting away from, masking the glaring absence . . . of sexual relations. (p. 44)

Trying to critique an old romantic story, Heath, the gallant knight, repeats the misrecognition that is that story's support: naively, he takes up the standard of the woman "who does not exist." In contrast, Lacan, the cavalier, knowingly enters into the old story, playing his role with such style—and such stunning bad faith—that its plot is unmasked as construction. Gallop aligns Lacan with a feminist practice of infidelity, a resistance to the law that hollows it out from within: "Infidelity is not outside the system of marriage, the symbolic, patriarchy, but hollows it out, ruins it, from within" (p. 48). The woman who plays fast and loose—as Gallop does here with her cavalier, "unfaithful" reading of Heath—resists appropriation to the Name of the Father, which operates to produce the relation of the sexes as natural and complementary: "Any suspicion of the mother's infidelity betrays the Name-of-the-Father as the arbitrary imposition it is" (p. 48). In a similar manner, Lacan overplays his role, the role of the master presumed to know, and thus exposes the extravagance of phallic privilege and the excessiveness of paternal desire; like the unfaithful woman, then, whose desire flamboyantly exceeds the economy that would reduce it to exchange value and regulate it, the performative master Lacan reveals the symbolic as inequitable and unnatural. In an earlier chapter, Gallop equates this unfaithful practice, which exposes both the desire of the woman and of the father, with "seduction." The cavalier ladies' man is finally complicitous with the seductive woman in undoing the hold of the law: "Feminists have been hard on the ladies' man, presuming that his intentions are strictly dishonourable. They're right. But should not feminism be working to undo the reign of honor, and all those virile virtues?" (p. 35).

Granted, however, that undoing virile virtue is in the lady's best interest, does it follow that her best hope is collusion with the artful master? Gallop's own argument suggests that, at least at times, the daughter who would practice infidelity only finds herself more firmly under the rule of the law. In the chapter following "Encore *Encore*," commenting on the work of the feminist psychoanalyst Luce Irigaray, Gallop describes such a "vicious circle":

> Irigaray would really like to respond to Freud, provoke him into a real dialogue. But the only way to seduce the father, to avoid scaring him away, is to please him, and to please him one must submit to his law which proscribes any sexual relation. (p. 71)

The woman who enters into an economy of desire in the hope of acting as its point of resistance may find herself repeating the same old story. Using "seduction" to describe the dynamics of the daughter's encounter with the father, Gallop suggests the daughter gives up her resistance because she desires an encounter with the law. Possibly, however, Gallop, a seductive daughter herself and thus potentially already complicitous with the law's notoriously unsubtle perspective, cannot pick up the fine distinctions. And indeed, how *does* one discriminate between the daughter who, intending resistance, is unwittingly seduced into complicity and the one whose pretended, artfully exaggerated complicity amounts to true resistant practice; or even, between the daughter who submits because she wants to please the father and the daughter who has been forced into submission? To make these distinctions one must know what the daughter had in mind. The law, however, has only one category for the woman who practices infidelity, no matter how skilled and knowing her performance—to the law she is "la belle dame sans merci."

For Gallop, Lacan's knowingness aligns him with "art" over against the philosophers ("Not simply a philosopher, but, artfully, a performer, he is no mere father-figure out to purvey the truth of his authority" [p. 36]). Lacan's artfulness—his poetic mastery—puts him on the lady's side. This celebration of the poet's knowingness may be naive, however. Imagining that "infidelity" hollows out the categories active/passive, master/devotee— categories that keep the woman in her place—and presuming that "infidelity" works to undo equally the places of the woman and the master, Gallop does not take into account the way "seduction" is already accommodated by the old chivalric tale that always returns power to the father. Playing his role as though he does not believe in it, the father becomes more charismatic, more than father, "no mere father-figure"; while provoked by his insouciance, the woman who tries to seduce him is brought back under the control of the law. Ultimately, then, it may not matter so much whether one encounters the woman naively, in the manner of the knight, or knowingly, like the poet/master who knows she is only a lure. In either case, she lends her allure to a romantic plot whose victim is not so much the knight or the hapless reader as it is the woman.

Picking up on these hints of collusion among naive knight, poetic master, and the law, the knowing feminist reader might resolve to be less charmed by beknighted innocence *or* cavalier knowingness, less seduced by romance. Instead, she might attempt to collude with the Romantic woman—who may not exist, but in whose resistance she could provisionally believe. In the rest of this essay I would like to take my cue from another feminist practice, aimed not at seducing the law but at challenging the way the law reads seduction. By redefining seduction as "harassment," this feminist legal practice would make encounters between subjects who are situated differently with respect to power look less romantic, and it would draw our attention to a certain complicity between apparently chivalrous and apparently cavalier approaches to the lady. Possibly the knight of "La Belle Dame Sans Merci" is more knowing than he seems, and only pretends innocence. Perhaps he enters into his relationship with the lady in the meads in bad faith, knowing full well he hasn't got a chance with her; perhaps he, but also the artful poet who exploits without endorsing the plot of seduction, is harassing the Romantic muse, using her to defend literature against other, less thrilling constraints.

II

The pleasures of "romance" are often characterized as excessive and escapist, yet the form is paradoxically bound up in a thematics of containment. This is certainly true of the love plot Keats's knight seems to want to realize—a plot we might classify as "domestic" romance. According to the story he tells the poem's interlocutor, when he first meets the fairy lady she's free, even wild: "Her hair was long, her foot was light / And her eyes were wild." Although he seems to find this self-abandonment smiting, his first impulse is still to control her, to bind her, even if with lovely chains: he makes a "garland for her head," "bracelets," and a "fragrant zone." To all appearances this program of domestication is successful: to quote Keats, accounting for another lady's capitulation to the "tyranny" of her suitor Lycius (or what Gallop might call "macho aggression"), "women love to be forced to do a thing."[10] The lady makes the knight supper ("She found me roots of relish sweet / And honey wild, and manna dew"), takes him home with her, and sings him to sleep. Moreover, she seems to love it: the knight tells us, "she look'd at me as she did love, / And made sweet moan"; "And sure in language strange she said— / I love thee true."

As the knight describes it, his courtship realizes a familiar plot whose main character is the Ideal Woman and whose dynamics are a happily asymmetrical reciprocity: his active capture of the fairy lady brings about her passive, reflective response of "love" together with its domestic signs— meals, sexual favors, lullabies. The reader, however, sees and hears more: the regular alternations of active agents in the knight's story—"I made," "she looked," "I set"—and, finally, a suggestion of the lady's ascendency over the knight in stanzas 7 and 8, which list an unbroken series of her actions—"she found," "she took," "she wept." Gazing on the lady's face the knight "nothing else saw all day long"—captivated by the mirror he constructs, he fails to realize it may simply reflect back his own enchantment.

That we can read these signs of the knight's enthrallment does not necessarily indicate our greater critical acumen. We have the advantage of position: of the knight's position as narrator who knows how the tale ends and thus might be giving us these clues; of our position as reader, which seems to afford us the possibility of one-upmanship—we read the knight's reading of his experiences. We also have the advantage of our position as experienced readers of romance. For like the knight, we too are tempted to interpret this encounter through a familiar romance plot—recognizing, not the domestic angel but a false florimel, a Duessa, a Morgan le Fay, or a belle dame sans merci, not the ideal but the fatally ambiguous woman. Indeed, critics have traditionally supported their sense of the lady's character with source studies: Robert Graves, for example, knows that the lady represents "Love, Death by Consumption, . . . and Poetry all at once" from "a study of the romances from which Keats developed the poem." Like Robert Graves we know from books that it's a mistake for knights to allow themselves to be diverted from knightly tasks, particularly for the sake of ladies they find wandering in the woods—or, shifting to the terms of a popular romantic account of the poet's career, we know it's a mistake when aspirants to poetic fame dally too long with the poetry of wish-fulfilling fantasy and sensuous delight. The "pale kings and princes" whose warning interrupts the knight's romantic interlude are figures of us. Crying

"La belle dame sans merci / Hath thee in thrall," they simply declare what we already know to be true—that the knight has become caught up in a form whose pleasures, though great, are fatally circumscribed.

The naive reader of the lady, the knight, is caught up in idealizing fantasy; the knowing reader knows that such captivation is fatal—every ideal woman is also a deathly woman. Both of these readings attempt to contain the lady's significance with the assistance of a familiar romance plot; both limit certain ideal and/or fatal effects to the spliced term woman/ poetry. Taken together, of course, these two readers present us with a woman we have already encountered, the woman of chivalry—both complement and absolute other, both she who delusively promises to overcome, and she who takes the blame for, the absence of relations. It remains for the feminist critic, less enchanted with romance, to defend the lady. One should try not to do this in a chivalrous fashion—it may not be in the lady's or the critic's best interests to assume she exists unproblematically, in a form one wants to champion. Yet a feminist critic listening to the knight's tale picks up threads of another story: the hint of physical compulsion ("I made a garland"), the suggestion of interpretive violence ("And sure in language strange she said— / I love thee true"); this critic might wonder if certain signs—moans, sighs, tears—don't indicate resistance more than love or duplicity. She might conclude that "romance" is at least as fatal to the lady as the knight. Not only does its logic work toward her disappearance from the scene, romance blinds most readers to the woman's point of view—a point of view from which the exchange between lady and knight looks less like a domestic idyll or a fatal encounter and more like a scene of harassment.

Earlier I proposed that "harassment" is potentially a helpful term for the feminist Romanticist because of the way it invites one to see apparently different romantic enounters as aspects of a more general problem. It invites us, for example, to look for evidence of collusion between the knight who uses force because he thinks the lady loves it and the reader whose advantageous position and experience encourage him simply to disregard the woman's perspective. Recent criticism of the poem has of course been concerned to point out aspects of that collusion. So far, I've been implying that one can at least differentiate between naive and knowing readings of the lady: deluded by romance, the knight is blind to evidence of his own enchantment; enlightened by romance, the knowing reader recognizes these signs. This account, however, overlooks the way the poem's character as a framed dream narrative unsettles the boundary between interpreters and their objects of interpretation. As Susan Wolfson points out, the reader in the poem, the questioner, is only uneasily separate from the knight he interrogates: he wanders in the same barren landscape, and his speech is not set off from the knight's by quotation marks—indeed there's some question about who speaks what lines in the poem's first stanzas. We're invited to make analogies between the situations of the two characters: could the pale knight be to the questioner what the "pale kings and princes" are to the knight? Could the questioner be engaged with the knight in the way the knight is involved with the lady? These indeterminacies of course finally work to make us question the relative positions of the "knowing" reader and the "naive" knight: perhaps like the reader the knight "knows" the *entire* trajectory of the fatal plot—he dreams up the lady *and* her disappearance and his enthrallment; or on the other hand, like the knight, the reader perhaps naively seeks to command the significance of a problematic encounter by means of a familiar romance plot.

It's a temptation for a modern critical discourse which pursues connections like these to stay close to a Romantic vocabulary, to suggest there's something fatal and enthralling about the process of interpretation itself: in our efforts to determine and limit meaning we are all like the knight, tragically subject to the redounding effects of those efforts. But the connections cut both ways. For if, on the one hand, the evidence of a radical entanglement between the reader and knight-at-arms suggests that the reader who presumes to know may in fact be as fatally blind as the knight, on the other, the thoroughgoing *collusion* of reader and knight might suggest that the latter is fully as knowing as the knowing reader. We tend to assume that the knight sincerely wants to capture the lady—that the interrupting warning voices bring home a truth he couldn't have foreseen. Focusing on his loss, we fail to notice what he gains at the end of the poem—accession to an all-male community. Could this community, and not the ideal or even the fatal woman, be the true object of his quest? Is it possible that the knight is using the lady—harrassing her—in order to conjure up the warning voices, in order to be interrupted, in order, finally, to become one of the gang, one of the pale kings and princes in whose world "woman" exists only as a delusive fantasy, a memory of a dream?

As I've just described it, this "world" resembles not the "real world" of just a short time ago, when critics found something tragically incompatible between the poet/knight's love for a life of imagination and real, mortal existence, but the new criticism's equivalent, the symbolic order—the order of language, in which subject knights must bow to a deathly law, and where, according to Jacques Lacan, "the Woman does not exist" except as a fantasmatic construct, which, insofar as it occupies the place of the unattainable Other, figures the imaginary unity of identity "itself." In the most romantic modern portrayals of this order, the subject is a ghost, an effect, of plots and meanings that predate and determine it—much like Keats's knight, who turns pale and becomes a haunt of the text when it's brought home to him that he's been caught by "La Belle Dame Sans Merci," the poem he's in, the poem by Alain Chartier from which Keats's poem took its title, and, more generically, the romance plot that declares escapades like his fatal.

The knight of "La Belle Dame Sans Merci" is Everysubject; no subject can escape his doom. This discussion, like the knight's story, might thus seem to end at its starting point: the poem knowingly reveals that it is not "about" woman at all but, rather, about the unmasterability of language and the gender-neutral subject's enthrallment in the symbolic order. Focusing on the woman, though—however briefly she enters the picture—allows us to see how the knight's romantic tale, knowingly deployed by the artful poet, encodes this doom in a way that distributes its effects unequally, with all benefits accruing to the masculine subject.

To determine how the plot works, we might loiter for a moment with a sonnet, an experiment in sonnet form, which appears in the letter from John to George and Georgianna Keats that also includes "La Belle Dame Sans Merci." Like "La Belle Dame," the sonnet is about binding the muse:

> If by dull rhymes our English must be chain'd,
>   And, like Andromeda, the sonnet sweet
>   Fetter'd, in spite of pained loveliness;
> Let us find out, if we must be constrain'd,
>   Sandals more interwoven and complete
> To fit the naked foot of Poesy;
>   Let us inspect the lyre, and weight the stress
> Of every chord, and see what may be gain'd
>   By ear industrious, and attention meet;
>   Misers of sound and syllable, no less
> Than Midas of his coinage, let us be
>   Jealous of dead leaves in the bay wreath crown;
> So, if we may not let the muse be free,
>   She will be bound with garlands of her own.

The identification of woman and romance we saw operating in "La Belle Dame Sans Merci" is only a special case of a traditional identification of poetry with woman. Keats's sonnet suggests the shiftiness and contagiousness of that identification, and a corresponding mobility of the object which is or must be bound: "our English," "the sonnet sweet," "Andromeda," "the naked foot of Poesy," even "we"—practitioners of sonnetry—"must be constrained." Indeed, the sonnet as a whole suggests there's no escaping constraint. None of its characters are originally free—even the "naked foot of Poesy" is already a "foot," a measured unit; nor can the origin of "constraint" be determined—English "must" be chained, Andromeda, sonnets, and we "must" be fettered and constrained, we "may not let" the muse be free. But within the condition of unoriginated, inescapable limits, desire—mobilized by the gendering of form—allows "constraint" to be translated into happy capitulation. The muse but also "we" are seduced into constraining ourselves; like women, and through the enthralling power of feminized forms, poets come to love force.

The knight who experiences an enchanting encounter, is interrupted by a masculine prohibition, and then spends the rest of his days wandering in a landscape of signs that resist translation simply enacts a currently popular account of every subject's history. But Keats's poem, at once mysterious and urbane, "knows" that what is fatal to the artful master's endeavors is not ambiguity or even indeterminacy but flatness or excessive determination.

An old tale of chivalry, "La Belle Dame Sans Merci" transforms what could
be a banal, neutral observation—that identity is imaginary, that subjects are
effects of the symbolic—into a thrilling Romantic game of risk and capture.
In this play, the ideal lady may only seem to be the stakes. For the exemplary power of this plot, which inspires this and a host of other knights to
go after the lady again and again, to pester her in scores of romantic
encounters even when no one has ever been known to hold onto her,
invites the suspicion of the feminist critic. Knowing in her turn, she notices
that the lady gets "nothing" from this encounter—it works to her disappearance—while the knight who encounters her, and the poet who knowingly exploits without endorsing the plot in which she figures, are enabled
to experience a certain inevitable "fatality," not simply as submission to the
law of the father, but as accession to a community of poetic masters, "pale
kings and princes" who are already translated into text. These are perhaps
the "shapes of epic greatness" that haunted the young aspirant John Keats's
dreams and tempted him into harassing the muse.[11]

NOTES

1. Quotations from Keats's poetry follow *John Keats: Complete Poems*, ed. Jack
Stillinger (Cambridge, Mass.: Harvard University Press, 1982).

2. Shoshana Felman, *Writing and Madness: Literature/Philosophy/Psychoanalysis*,
trans. Martha Noel Evans (Ithaca: Cornell University Press, 1985), p. 136.

3. David Perkins, ed., *English Romantic Writers* (New York: Harcourt Brace
Jovanovich, 1967), p. 1181.

4. Miriam Allott, ed., *The Poems of John Keats* (London: Longman, 1970),
pp. 500–01.

5. Susan Wolfson, "The Language of Interpretation in Romantic Poetry: 'A
Strong Working of the Mind,'" in *Romanticism and Language*, ed. Arden Reed
(Ithaca: Cornell University Press, 1984), pp. 22–49.

6. Ibid., p. 37.

7. Two chapters of Lacan's seminar *Encore* have been translated into English and
included in *Feminine Sexuality: Jacques Lacan and the École freudienne*, ed. Juliet
Mitchell and Jacqueline Rose, trans. Jacqueline Rose (New York: Norton, 1982),
pp. 137–62.

8. Stephen Heath, "Difference," *Screen* 19, no. 3 (Autumn 1978): 51–113.

9. Jane Gallop, *The Daughter's Seduction: Feminism and Psychoanalysis* (Ithaca:
Cornell University Press, 1982), pp. 50–51; 46, 48, 50; 44, 51. Subsequent page
references to *The Daughter's Seduction* will appear in the text.

10. Hyder Edward Rollins, ed., *The Letters of John Keats* (Cambridge, Mass.:
Harvard University Press, 1972)2:164.

11. Ibid., 1:403.

THE WRITER'S RAVISHMENT

WOMEN AND THE ROMANTIC AUTHOR —THE EXAMPLE OF BYRON

Sonia Hofkosh

> Who really spoke? Is it really he and not
> someone else? With what authenticity or
> originality? And what part of his deepest
> self did he express in his discourse?

In a famous letter to the woman who had rejected him the previous autumn, Byron defines poetry as "the lava of the imagination whose eruption prevents an earth-quake." Claiming to value "the talents of *action*" over his own (not inactive) volcanic literary talents, the most popular poet of his time nonetheless articulates what has been taken to be one of the central formulations of Romantic poetics.[1] While not "high in the scale of intellect," the force of literary production is immediate and personal, originating within the poet, from his "deepest self." The poetic text is the expression and preservation of that self's integrity, composed in an impulse so fundamental as to be a matter of biological necessity. Words explode from the writer, subject only to the laws and limits of his own physiology. Invoking the bodily function of writing, the ejaculatory imperative in Byron's image of writing as erupting lava suggests that even when he does not actively or consciously will his work into being, that work confirms the poets' identity, an identity already strong, significant, full to overflowing.

But in its context, Byron's definition of poetry also complicates such a formulation. The statement that valorizes his own literary prowess and productivity while claiming to dismiss them is addressed to Annabella Milbanke, the woman whose stories about him will prove at least as compelling as Byron's own self-representations. The reputation Byron achieves overnight for his thinly veiled self-portrayal in the first two cantos of *Childe Harold's Pilgrimage* (1812) is contravened as suddenly four years later by the tales about his personal life that Lady Byron tells so well. The poet may pretend to devalue his own achievement, but the poet's estranged wife effectively preempts the claims to personal power that Byron won as a popular poet. The efficacy of Lady Byron's revelations about her husband's "deepest self" underscores some of the implications of the questions posed in my epigraph from Foucault's "What Is an Author?"—questions about the poet's privilege to generate and govern his authorship, his own name and fame.[2] The logic that would lead the women who had adored Byron as the author of the Eastern tales to cut him in Lady Jersey's drawing room suggests that the model of literary production, which assumes the priority and prestige of the individual self out of which literature is born, may not adequately account for the Romantic practice of authorship.

Byron offers his explanation of literary production, with its erotic resonance, to the woman he will woo again, win, and lose. His literary career is also the chronicle of a love affair. Figuring the dynamics of literary relations—the author's association with publishers, reviewers, readers—the love affair belies the Romantic fantasy of unmediated subjectivity underlying Byron's definition of poetry, a fantasy of self-creation and self-government. The woman in the romance enacts the marketplace forces that contest the writer's exclusive claim to his work. Byron's career exemplifies this contest in the poet's efforts to design his own image in response to a culture evolving new risks and rewards for the professional writer. When in the separation proceedings Lady Byron publicizes an account of *Childe Harold*'s author in competition with his accounts of himself, the effect aligns her power with the forces of production and evaluation in literary culture. Ineluctably separate, the woman demonstrates the way authorship, neither self-fashioned nor belatedly begotten in oedipal struggle, is always being engendered and empowered by others.

In what follows I want to explore a few moments in which various feminine figures seem to bear the burden of a male writer's anxiety of authorship. I adopt Gilbert and Gubar's term for the special struggle of the woman writer in order to suggest that the male writer also dreads, as he desires, being read by others—a reading that rewrites him and thus compromises his powers of self-creation.[3] I want to focus here not only on the masculine deployment of woman as an image, but also on the way women and images of them function to describe a model of writing that the male author represses. Such an exploration is based on a fundamental interplay between private and public realms, between the individual personality and the culture of literary production and consumption. The evolution of his personal relationship with Annabella Milbanke elucidates the pattern of Byron's literary career as well, while the play of power operative in the courtship is always a public issue, an issue of commerce.[4] This means that in my discussion the writer is also a lover—in his concern with self-presentation, response, fulfillment, mastery—a lover both of actual women and of a culture conceived increasingly in feminine terms. At the juncture of the writer's and the lover's discourse, the feminine figure variously reflects and reiterates the culture's challenge to the fantasy of autonomous creativity.[5]

I. The Author and the Gypsy

Renounced by his admiring coterie in England and in love with another woman, Byron initiates the musings of his Ravenna journal in the winter of 1821 with an incident that considers authorship at once in an economic and a sexual register.

> I was out of spirits—read the papers—thought what *fame* was, on reading, in a case of murder, that "Mr. Wych, grocer, at Tunbridge, sold some bacon, flour, cheese, and it is believed, some plums, to some gypsy woman accused. He had on his counter (I quote faithfully) a *book,* the Life of *Pamela,* which he was *tearing* for *waste* paper, &c., &c. In the cheese was found, &c., and a *leaf* of *Pamela wrapt round the bacon.*" . . . What would he [Richardson] have said? What can anybody say, save what Solomon said long before us? After all, it is but passing from one counter to another, from the bookseller's to the other tradesman's—grocer or pastry-cook. For my part, I have met with most poetry upon trunks; so that I am apt to consider the trunk-maker as the sexton of authorship. (4 Jan. 1821)

Pamela in the grocery store provides a scenario for Byron's meditation on the literary fame that ideally assures the integrity and continuity of the self in and with the work. Torn up for wrapping bacon, Richardson's text undergoes a radical commercialization that violates the author's fame with the violation of the work's integrity. The fate of the book turns the author into the kind of Grub Street hack Byron deplored, whose work is subject to the designs and demands of tradesmen, be they publishers, printers, grocers, or pastry-cooks. Mr. Wych's appropriation of the book as so much waste paper alienates the author from the distinct and stable personality— the properties of the self—that he seeks to express and confirm in his writing. As Byron acknowledges, however, the trade perpetuated by the grocer merely replicates the text's circulation in the literary marketplace. The tearing of *Pamela* only literalizes the alienation built into the concept of the work as the author's personal property: the self becomes the author when the work that is his own belongs to others, when it is published, bought, read, and reviewed.

But that Richardson's text should offer a focus for Byron's anxiety about the vagaries of fame is particularly telling. In his dual role of author and publisher, Richardson enacted for the eighteenth century what many already perceived as the alarming debasement of literature into commerce. A victim of the marketplace in Byron's journal entry, Richardson nonetheless participates in what Byron understands as the violation of authorial privilege and propriety. For Byron, who is engaged during that same winter of 1821 in championing Alexander Pope's reputation against the criticism of the editor Bowles, Richardson also represents the displacement of the poet as the ascendant voice in literary culture. The publication of *Pamela* occa-

sioned the recognition of new voices in the literary marketplace—the voice
of prose, of a literate middle class, and of women as both consumers and
producers of literature.[6] The epistolary novel also elides standards of
difference by turning the personal letter into a vehicle for public narrative
as it records the words of a serving girl turned lady of the house. Similarly,
the transformation of Richardson's literary text into wrapping paper in Mr.
Wych's grocery store obscures the very distinctions—of genre, class, or
gender—upon which Byron, manly poet and Baron of Rochdale, grounds
his reputation and his claims for immortality.

While the grocer's appropriation of *Pamela* dramatizes the violation of
authorial privilege inherent in an age of commercial reproduction, the
other violence implicit in this episode is committed by the "gypsy woman,"
who is linked to the crime circumstantially by Richardson's text. This
"gipsy-murderess" in fact signifies the threats to his own literary integrity
that Byron tries to dismiss with characteristic aplomb when he considers
"the trunk-maker as the sexton of authorship." While the trunk-maker, as
sexton, takes care of the author's remains, the gypsy woman animates the
writer's worst fears concerning his own authorial status because the murder
she commits confirms the author as nothing but remains. Her crime is
murder; but the pages of *Pamela* wrapped around her groceries tell the tale
of other crimes as well. One may be the crime of the romance reader who
buys her literature in supermarkets, supporting the industry that capitalizes on the interchangeable and reproduceable form of the writer's
identity. Even more, she, like Richardson, undergoes the very com-
modification in which she is complicitous when she buys her groceries. In
the language of the newspaper she is serialized rhetorically with "some
bacon" and "some plums"—she is merely "some gypsy woman," objectified
into an anonymous type, her distinct name and fame unrecorded and
unremembered. While the pages of the novel bear testimony to the violation she commits, the newspaper's pages condemn her to the namelessness
that the author fears may be his own fate. As a victim of her own profitable
devices, the gypsy woman embodies the simultaneous making and unmak-
ing of the writer's reputation by grocers (like Mr. Wych), editors (like Mr.
Bowles), and other tradesmen.

For the poet who by 1821 had already gained and lost so much by the
vagaries of reputation, both social and literary, ultimate fame is as fortuitous, as circumstantial, as the evidence by which the "gipsy-murderess" is
identified. But of course he was not alone. In his experience first as a
literary lion and then as a social outcast, Byron epitomizes the writer's
vulnerability to the fluctuations of reputation and to the contingent nature
of the personal authority reputation confers. He might purport in the
Preface to *Hours of Idleness* (1807)—his first volume of verse "for the Public
at large"—to "resign, without repining, the hope of immortality," but the
alternative of "ranking amongst 'the mob of gentlemen who write'" and
having his name recorded only on a "posthumous page in 'The Catalogue
of Royal and Noble Authors'" is clearly insufficient for the young writer

whose ambition is to author his own name and fame, to single himself out in and by means of the pages he writes. To be some gentleman who writes seems too much like being merely one of an anonymous mob of gypsies.

Lacking even the consolation of such a gentlemanly genealogy as Byron could always invoke, Keats renders in poetic form the anxieties at issue in Byron's meditation on the tearing up of Richardson's novel. In two sonnets on fame included in a long letter from 1819 (4 Feb.–3 May), Keats depicts his version of Byron's "gipsy-murderess" as the personification of fame's vicissitudes. The kind of promiscuous circulation whereby literature passes from one tradesman's counter to another is explicitly symbolized in Keats's "Fame, like a wayward girl" by the desirable and inconstant gypsy.

> She is a gipsey, will not speak to those
>   Who have not learnt to be content without her;
>
> . . . .
>
> A very gipsey is she, Nilus born,
>   Sister-in-law to jealous Potiphar.

By definition a wanderer, the gypsy remains resistant, elusive, the woman who cannot be possessed. Carmen-like, she may even, as suggested by the murder in Byron's anecdote, turn the violence of the lover's passion against himself. In fact, the "love-sick bard" of this sonnet is made insane by the resistant gypsy ("Ye artists lovelorn, madmen that ye are!"), and in Keats's second sonnet he becomes the "fever'd" man who, by desiring fame,

> . . . vexes all the leaves in his life's book,
>   And robs his fair name of its maidenhood;
> It is as if the rose should pluck herself,
>   Or the ripe plum finger its misty bloom. . . .

The man becomes the woman whom he seeks to violate; here, that violation is his own. Wandering in Keats's sonnet, the gypsy woman betrays the writer's own promiscuous desire for the recognition that both constitutes and subverts his authorship, both empowers him to write and undermines the singularity of his writing.

When he "vexes all the leaves in his life's book," the writer resembles Mr. Wych, who, tearing pages of *Pamela* to sell groceries, profits from the alienation of the self from the work. But the writer, thus profiting from his own alienation, also resembles the vagrant gypsy woman, whose power derives from her status as alien, as other. Keats's sonnets specifically explicate this play of power in sexual terms: they define feminine desire—promiscuous, adulterous, or narcissistic—as that which overcomes masculine self-control. Among the plums that Byron's gypsy woman buys from Mr. Wych may be the "ripe plum" that in Keats's poem figures the writer's self-contained fantasy; by appropriating that plum, the gypsy woman interrupts the author's self-sufficiency and satisfaction. Her purchase contradicts the desire of the "love-sick bard," the "fever'd man," for the fame that

would assure his integrity, the continuity of his mastery. Keats's sonnet
eroticizes the commercial threat in Byron's journal entry, turning the issue
of the work's dissemination and reception into an issue of gender relations.
The threat to male authority implicit in a woman's misdirected affection
evokes an alternative model of literary production counter to the one
valorized in Byron's imagination of self-generating eruptions. Rather than
expressing and preserving the self as it is, writing calls the identity of self
(with itself) into question. From Byron's journal entry and Keats's sonnets
on fame emerges an image of authorship as simultaneously promoted and
appropriated by others, by others epitomized in the otherness of the
feminine. When she buys groceries wrapped in *Pamela,* the woman as gypsy
obfuscates the difference between the work and waste paper, personality
and commodity; when like jealous Potiphar's wife she desires an alien in her
husband's house, (mis)taking one man for another, she blurs the line
between identity and difference by which male authorship and authority
postulates its power. That the "gipsy-murderess" in Byron's narrative and
the desire of Potiphar's wife are each in their "wayward" way criminal only
marks the association of femininity and authorship as a more pernicious
conjunction for the male writer.

Recently, Mary Poovey has shown how, especially in its early years, "the
literary market was a man's domain" and how, in order to survive in it,
rebellious women had to resort to difficult and often debilitating strategies
of indirection and accommodation.[7] But as Poovey and others have noted,
the end of the eighteenth century saw a significant expansion in the role of
women as consumers and producers of literature;[8] the metaphoric conjunction of femininity and authorship gathers force in a culture increasingly dominated by what might be called a circulating library
sensibility,[9] a culture that facilitates and capitalizes on promiscuous circulation while theoretically upholding the category of the masterly imagination,
of pure, organic creativity. The men in this "man's domain" also experienced ambivalence about pursuing a literary career. "When women en-
tered the career of authorship" in the nineteenth century, Catherine
Gallagher has argued, "they did not enter an inappropriately male territory, but a degradingly female one. They did not need to find a female
metaphor for authorship; they needed to avoid or transform the one that
was already there."[10] But as Keats's sonnets on fame suggest, this territory
was a "degradingly female one," even a "frighteningly sinister female one"
to male authors as well as to female authors, precisely because the metaphor
of the writer as whore, which Gallagher so astutely elaborates, manifests a
double pressure on the privileges of masculine discourse.[11] The alteration
of the male writer's gender—a mark of his powerlessness in his culture—
may be frightening to him; what is sinister in the metaphor is that it evokes
at once feminine powerlessness and power. The prostitute is powerless in
her dependence on masculine desire for her livelihood, but, like Keats's
promiscuous gypsy, this wandering woman is also empowered in the male

imagination by the elusive and undiscriminating nature of her own desire. She favors no individual man, eluding possession by any one man in order to sell herself repeatedly, only temporarily, to a great many, even a mob of men.

In his earliest satire, Byron attacks the "mental prostitution" of English bards and Scotch reviewers, associating the professionalization of literary practice with the degradation of the "prostituted muse."[12]

> . . . when the sons of song descend to trade,
> Their bays are sear, their former laurels fade. (175–76)

Commerce perverts "the poet's sacred name" (177) because it distorts the personal and familial bond between the self and the work. But Byron's disdain for his commercial culture finally has to do with the problematics of sorting through "the mob of gentlemen who write" in order to distinguish the true poet, that is, himself, whose work ought to be "the single wonder of a thousand years" (194). His difficulty is elaborated in the image of the "prostituted muse." Selling herself, she represents the writer who depersonalizes his self-expression by marketing it; even more, her promiscuity, her failure to distinguish among men, endangers the very foundation of self-expression—the logic of personality and propriety by which men determine who they are and what they own. As another "wayward girl," the prostitute represents the violation intrinsic to the idea of personal property. Her self-alienation advertises and reproduces the impropriety that men deplore, but that they make their own when they pay her to fulfill their desire.

II. Byron and Scott:
The Erotics of Literary Relations

An emblem of the writer and his disinheritance, the image of woman as gypsy and prostitute offers a view of the author's love affair with his culture as one fraught with what Walter Scott called, in a letter to Byron's publisher, the "pigs-kitchen brash of literary envy & petty rivalry."[13] In *English Bards and Scotch Reviewers*, the "prostituted muse" is, specifically, Walter Scott's, whose poetry Byron nonetheless uses as a model for his own early tales and who later takes up prose partly as a result of Byron's more stunning poetic success. By 1822, in a letter thanking Scott for accepting the dedication of *Cain*, Byron's feminine figure for the other writer has changed, but the new figure still bespeaks the "tremulous anxiety" provoked by the challenge to the writer's authority over his own (self) representations.

The letter addresses the poet's literary affairs generally and his relation with the other most acclaimed author of his age in particular. Explaining why it took him so long to write back, Byron begins his letter by feminizing Scott.

> I can only account for it [his delay in writing] on the same principle of
> tremulous anxiety with which one sometimes makes love to a beautiful
> woman of our own degree with whom one is enamoured in good earnest;—
> whereas we attack a fresh-colored housemaid without (I speak of course of
> earlier times) any sentimental remorse or mitigation of our virtuous pur-
> pose. (12 Jan. 1822)

The "tremulous anxiety" that the "beautiful woman of our own degree"
inspires in this earnest lover reflects an anxiety about authorship. Recount-
ing the scene in which he declared his love to Lady Frances Webster by
passing her a billet-doux during a billiard game, Byron elaborates the
anxieties of seduction in terms of the risks of writing:

> . . . here were risks certainly—first how to convey—then how it would be
> received . . . —when who should enter the room but the person who ought
> at that moment to have been in the Red Sea . . . —It was a risk—& all had
> been lost by failure. . . . (8 Oct. 1813)

The dynamics of the letter's dissemination and reception—who reads it and
what response it generates—conjoin with what Byron calls "this business"
(23 Oct. 1813) of making love: both involve a not unwilling submission of
the self to the exigencies of a speculative economy beyond authorial control.
The woman, at the scene of the writer's self-declaration, seems to hold his
fate and fulfillment, with his love note, in her hand.

The erotic metaphor Byron adopts to explain why it was so difficult to
write to Scott is in this way not unprecedented in Byronic rhetoric. It is, in
fact, a line he has used a number of times before. Byron employs the same
logic of the analogy between love and writing when he responds to the
complaint of another lover, Teresa Guiccioli, whom he had wooed "in good
earnest" a few years earlier: "Perhaps if I loved you less it would not cost me
so much to express my thoughts" (22 April 1819). The expensiveness of
expression bears witness to the intensity and depth of desire. Metaphoriz-
ing Scott into a Lady Frances Webster or a Countess Guiccioli, Byron
articulates that the other writer is important to him, that as a reader and a
reviewer he wields a certain power over him. But, like his avowal to the
countess, his admiration for Scott is couched in terms that are at once
completely sincere and in the service of a disguised tension. The metaphor
that acknowledges Scott's social equality ("of our own degree"), and thus his
power, also feminizes him ("a beautiful woman"), while the poet keeps his
own character, asserting the self-identity his trope denies the other writer.
Byron feminizes Scott in a strategic disavowal that there is anything of that
"pigs-kitchen brash of literary envy and petty rivalry" in their relationship.
But his effort to recuperate the cost of expression by characterizing his
relation to Scott as an erotic one succeeds rather in implicating his female
figures in the challenge to his literary mastery that he tries to repress. The
"beautiful woman of our own degree" in fact signals the "literary envy and
petty rivalry" from which she seems to be excluded.

The letter to Scott is a love letter, employing in a discussion of his literary relations the "earnest" language of feeling characteristic of Byron's sexual relations.

> I owe to you far more than the usual obligation for the courtesies of literature and common friendship—for [that] you went out of your way in 1817—to do me a service . . . at such a time—when 'all the World and his Wife' (or rather *mine*) . . . were trying to trample upon me was something still higher to my Self esteem. I allude to the Quarterly rev[iew] of the 3d. Canto of C[hild]e H[arol]d . . . you see you have been heaping 'coals of fire &c.' in the true Gospel manner—and I can assure you that they have burnt down to my very heart.—

The emphasis on obligation and gratitude here recalls the formal rhetoric of eighteenth-century epistolary romance.[14] Indeed, Scott's is an *uncom-mon* friendship that "[burns] down to [Byron's] very heart." Taking the place of Lady Byron and the poet's other disaffected admirers, Scott in his review of *Childe Harold* takes the poet for better and for worse. In return Byron treasures every bit of the novelist's writing, admitting that he "never move[s] without" the "Scotch novels"—they are "the only books that I [keep] by me—although I already [know] them by heart."

A marriage of minds, if not of bodies, this is an ambivalent love affair at best because the terms Byron chooses to emphasize his profound obligation to Scott as the generous reviewer of his poem link his language of desire and the heart to his concerns about the writer's relations with English bards and Scotch reviewers. Byron's denigration of Scott is suppressed with the satire, but his allusion to the proverbial "coals of fire" again suggests that these relations are not unvexed—the enemy lurks in the generous friend.[15] Moreover, it is in the figure of the desired women that this intersection of romance and writing is accomplished; she rehearses the vexations sup-pressed, with the satire, in the paradigm of writing formulated by both Byron and his critics in images of irrepressible eruption. The sexual anal-ogy gives a shape to Byron's anxieties about his literary project ("first how to convey—then how it would be received") that the letter to Scott cannot otherwise openly express; as it thus takes shape, however, the literary and masculine dynamic such an erotic form tries to veil exposes the tension disguised in the lover's discourse itself. In its entangled articulation of attraction and repulsion, Byron's letter to Scott records the erosion of his pretension to a privileged authority founded in his unique self, in his difference from others.

The poet's initial dedication of *Cain* to Scott, which is the motivating subject of the letter, already contains a fundamental duplicity. By inscribing his representation of fratricide to a reviewer of his work and the only other author to rival his prominence in what has been characterized as "the brotherhood of letters,"[16] Byron bestows with one word what his drama violently revokes with another. That is to say, the poem that appears to be a recognition of his indebtedness to a brother author/reviewer is at the same time a gesture of defensive appropriation; contradicting its dedication, the poem thematizes the fantasy of autonomy in Cain's resentment that he is subject to any creative power other than his own, even to God, who, "Sit[s] on his vast and solitary throne, / Creating worlds" (1. I. 148–49).[17]

This double posture of fraternal gratitude and violence, however, is transfigured in the letter into sexual desire and anxiety. Byron displaces his real feelings of love and rivalry onto the dual analogy of heterosexual encounter: making love "to a beautiful woman of our own degree" and attacking housemaids. Such a displacement conforms to the triangular structure by which a number of current readers recognize the gender arrangement that organizes literary practice and theory. The triangular configuration locates woman "only as an occasion of mediation, transaction, transition, transference, between man and his fellow man, indeed between man and himself."[18] The male relation, like the masculine subject, is the primary and prior one; the feminine, empty or derivative. "This triangle characteristically invokes its third (female) term only in the interests of the original rivalry and works finally to get rid of the woman."[19] In Byron's use of the sexual metaphor, the "woman of our own degree," like the house-maid, is reduced to and seduced into serving male desire—both as the object of that desire and the scene of its displacement.

But what I would argue is that Byron's erotic calculus,[20] which dimin-ishes the "beautiful woman of our own degree," also dismisses the "fresh-colored housemaid" altogether and that such absolute dismissal in fact suggests the potential threat that Byron's notion of authorship is formu-lated to preclude. Scott is explicitly not like the housemaid, whose seduction doesn't involve any of "the tremulous anxiety" inspired by her social supe-rior. But "the servant-girl is the repressed of the boss's wife,"[21] and the triangular configuration implicit in Byron's troping of Scott as "a woman of our own degree" is therefore subsumed by another geometry. Just as his dedication of his poem to a brother writer is qualified by the fratricide in *Cain* itself, the love language that turns Scott into Byron's latest passion may mask another "tremulous anxiety" suggested by the repressed figure in his analogy, the "fresh-colored housemaid." By introducing the class distinc-tion, the sexual metaphor underscores the issues of power and property at stake in Byron's sexualized literary politics; it also registers the tenuousness of this aristocratic writer's authority over his own possessions, of his self-possession, or, as he would call it, his "Self esteem." When Byron dis-tinguishes the woman as housemaid from the "woman of our own degree," he emphasizes the powerlessness of her dependence and reinforces it by assigning her a place outside of or beneath the realm of his heartfelt or "earnest" desires. Because she is below stairs,[22] the housemaid need not be courted with expressions that "cost [him] so much"; she need not be won by any very great expenditure of a poet's talents or a lover's gifts. Byron's analogy announces that it is in the inherited order of things that the housemaid's seduction can and should be a ravishment.

But if he had never known Susan Vaughan, the Newstead Abbey servant "whose infidelity had given him a bitter shock" in 1812,[23] Byron would have read Richardson, and so would have known at least one account of the way the housemaid can function to reform the order of things that he here assumes as the basis of a common, masculine experience. Indeed, Byron's cavalier parenthetical disclaimer—"I speak of course of earlier times"—can be taken to refer both to his personal past and to the historical past of Richardson's novel.[24] He would have read in *Pamela* that Mr. B. finds the seduction of his housemaid perhaps more costly to his "Self esteem," if not to his pocketbook, than the winning of any woman of his own degree might have been. Pamela finally eludes the attacks to which Byron's housemaids have been subject. It is Mr. B who has to compromise his "pride of condition, and the world's censure" (274), which would countenance the housemaid's violation before it conceded to her elevating marriage.[25]

For Byron, then, both Pamela's effective resistance to her master's attacks and her speedy rise in social position could dangerously qualify the hierarchical arrangement that seems to guarantee Byron's social and literary authority. The danger is suggested in the language of attack that describes his encounter with the housemaid and that reinvokes the fraternal strife Byron represses in his otherwise panegyrical letter to Scott. Falling upon her "like a thunderbolt,"[26] Byron does have something, perhaps "*all*," at stake in the housemaid's ravishment. Although she does not elicit the "sentimental remorse" that Pamela finally inspires in Mr. B., the housemaid, like the "woman of our own degree," nonetheless could signify a threat to the poet-lover's conception of his own status and power. Echoing the fraternal strife of the Cain story, the violence done to the housemaid marks her as a descendent of Abel, attacked by the brother who resented being created (instead of creating). As a feminine transfiguration of the biblical brother, the housemaid has in an important way already posed that threat.

The literary rivalry disguised in Byron's letter to Scott resurfaces in the character of the housemaid; although Byron claims to like lower-class women precisely because they cannot write,[27] perhaps, like her prototype Pamela, "this girl is always scribbling" (*Pam*, 15). The role of housemaid is in fact implicitly filled in the letter by another writer and reviewer of Byron's work. Repeating the juxtaposition between his "earnest" love for the "woman of our own degree" and his unsentimental attacks upon the housemaid, Byron situates his admiration for Scott in contrast to his longstanding and public animosity toward Robert Southey. The opposition reveals the motivating force both of that animosity and of the effusive praise articulated in the letter.

> I'll work the Laureate before I have done with him . . . —I like a row—& always did from a boy—in the course of which propensity I must needs say that I have found it the most easy of all to be gratified—personally and poetically.—You disclaim 'Jealousies' but I would ask as Boswell did of Johnson 'Of *whom could* you be jealous'—of none of the living certainly—and (taking all and all into consider- ation)—of which of the dead?

But does the Lord protest too much? As Boswell to Scott's Johnson, Byron denies the literary priority that his repeated abuse of Southey, from *English Bards and Scotch Reviewers* to *The Vision of Judgement* (1822), seeks to demonstrate and enforce. When he openly attacks the laureate, treating him, as he says, "like a pickpocket," Byron also jealously asserts his own superior authorial status in contemporary literary culture. Without inspiring the "sentimental remorse" of Byron's intercourse with Scott, Southey offers the housemaid's challenge to the poet's gentlemanly literary prerogative. As a successful author and influential reviewer, in effect risen from the ranks of Grub Street as Pamela rose to become Mrs. B., Southey manifests for Byron the dissolution of his literary aristocracy—a dissolution that can be traced in Byron's career from his self-conscious appeal to his nobility in the Preface to *Hours of Idleness* to his treatment of writing as a commercially profitable venture by 1816.[28] Pamela's prophetic critique of Lady Davers's endogamous argument ("ours is no upstart family," 270) could be Byron's imagination of the threat a professional writer like Southey poses to the distinction of the gentlemanly poets: "a time is coming, when they shall be obliged to submit to be on a level with us . . ." (271). Southey's participation in and influence over the literary scene, and, even more, his capacity to earn a respectable living solely by his pen, represents the leveling of literature that imperils Byron's account of writing as a uniquely personal pursuit.[29] Anybody—even "pickpockets" and "housemaids"—can do it.

III. Women Who Read and Write

In the letter that purports to reject the competition of literary culture, Byron explicitly and implicitly feminizes rival writers. He thereby tries to displace them from the literary scene and from his consciousness that they could exercise power equal to his own. Simultaneously, he discloses the structure of courtship, with its complicity of love and rivalry, in which all authors are implicated—as writers, readers, and reviewers of their own and one another's work. The force of the sexual analogy is that it both reveals Byron's "tremulous anxiety" about the power of others over his authorship and identifies woman, of whatever degree, as the sign of that power. Rather than alleviating Byron's anxiety about his literary career, about how his work is constituted and criticized, the sexual analogy exposes woman as the literary rival par excellence. In early nineteenth-century literary culture, where "women began to play an important role in literature as writers and readers,"[30] they are construed as the other factor that must but cannot (by virtue of their very otherness) be accommodated by the masculine model of autonomous creativity.

Byron's affair with Lady Caroline Lamb in the early days of his fame exemplifies the courtship of a woman that is also itself a kind of literary rivalry; in the case of Lamb, woman is indeed the literary rival par excellence precisely because she seems to have power over the writer's personal life, his "deepest self." Here, the "woman of our own degree" exacts the price of expression. In *Glenarvon* (1816), her roman à clef, Lady Caroline details the exploits of a transparently Byronic hero/villain. She also reproduces in the novel at least one of Byron's letters to her, making him repay her, as it were, for having shown her letters to Lady Melbourne in 1813. The culminating betrayal of Calantha in *Glenarvon* is Byron's betrayal of Caroline Lamb, but, by including his letters in her fiction, Lamb betrays Byron as well: " 'Twas the letters written in confidence which he shewed!"[31]

For the poet who repeatedly evaded admitting the autobiographical resonances of his own work, such a rendering of his personal language in another's text calls the very definition of his authorship *as* personal language into question. *Glenarvon* shows that the author's private life and work are always another's imaginative property.[32] As lover turned novelist, Lady Caroline authors her affair with the famous poet in other terms. Her novel points to Byron's difficulty in mastering his affairs, his failure to dictate the text of his own and others' desires. Caroline Lamb's appropriation of Byron's private text for her own purposes enacts the dispossession attendant on literary production. In a letter to Murray, Byron objects to such dispossession in the form of the publisher's omission of *Manfred*'s last line: "You have destroyed the whole effect & moral of the poem . . . why this was done I know not.—Why you persist in saying nothing of the thing itself I am equally at a loss to conjecture" (12 Aug. 1817). A week later another letter, this one to his attorney, demands explanation for the "hints & innuendoes" he has been receiving about how the sale of his estates is being handled. The two complaints take much the same form: "I never can get any person to be explicit about anything—or anybody—& my whole life is past in conjectures of what people mean—you all talk in the style of Caroline Lamb's novels" (21 Aug. 1817). The witty jab at Lamb's literary talent, her authorship, just barely disguises the "tremulous anxiety" Byron feels about the conjectural nature of his authority over his personal property, real and literary.

The most popular of major Romantic writers, and the most promiscuous, Byron's relation to his culture is fittingly described as a love affair. His career may be the conspicuous example of the way the writer's power to manage his self-representation is undermined at the moment it is constituted in love and literature. But if this is Byron's problem, Keats's sonnets on fame suggest that the Lord shares it with at least one other Romantic writer. With the reviews of "Endymion" still festering, Keats writes to his publisher in the summer of 1819 to borrow more money on his future literary composition:

> I feel every confidence that if I choose I may be a popular writer; that I will
> never be; but for all that I will get a livelihood—I equally dislike the favour
> of the public with the love of a woman—they are both a cloying treacle to the
> wings of independence.[33]

The issue for Keats is writing independent of others and of other, worldly concerns, being free to create himself, privately. But what Keats aspires to do this summer by writing "Otho the Great" is "upset the drawling of the bluestocking literary world" (14 Aug. 1819)—such drawling "batters too much the wings of [his] self-will" (27 July 1819). The pressure that the "literary world" exerts on the author's "self-will," or, in Byron, his "Self esteem," is brought to bear in the female form of the "drawling bluestocking" because the female form circumscribes the writer's independence, his fantasy of his creative autonomy.

Thus it is in the bluestockings' feminized literary world, to which Keats scorns to be but always is indebted, that critical reaction to the writer's poetic production ("the favour of the public") and the "love of a woman" converge most explicitly. The bluestockings helped precipitate the "feminisation of literature in the second half of the eighteenth century."[34] They are Dr. Johnson's "Amazons of the pen," whose defiance of masculine exclusivity in literature Richardson's friend saw as indicative of the lamentable "universal itch of writing."[35] Hazlitt later expressed popular opinion more tersely when he wrote, "I have an utter aversion to blue-stockings. I do not care a fig for any woman who knows what *an author* means."[36] Women should neither know what it means to be an author, nor what other authors, that is, male authors, mean. Any woman who reads or writes is a potential threat to the masculine conception of authorship. By reading Virgil and writing tracts on political economy, the women in William Scargill's 1827 novel, *Bluestocking Hall,* are thought to "relinquish a legitimate and undisputed empire, to engage in the silly project of conquest over regions which will never submit to their arms."[37]

In "The Blues: A Literary Eclogue" (1821), written shortly before *Cain* was completed, Byron satirizes these learned ladies in the voice of Sir Richard complaining about Lady Bluebottle, whose "heart's in the inkstand" and whose "hand [is] on the pen." "I'll be cursed if I know / Myself from my wife," is this husband's complaint—the mark of Sir Richard's masculine creativity is effectually erased as scribbling women invade the domain of literature. When they read and write, women upset domestic and literary hierarchies. The bluestockings in Byron's poem appropriate the very tool of authorial prowess, contesting the exclusive claims of male authorship and authority in public and private realms.

But as the example of Byron suggests, an author is precisely he who gives up his exclusive claims to his work—his "deepest self" and his "independence"—to those others who will read and write it for him. And as Keats's sonnets on fame suggest, the younger poet also experiences the amorous lord's desire for and dread of such dispossession. In fact, whereas in Byron's letter to Scott the feminine operates figuratively to articulate other powers the poet would conceal, in Keats's correspondence with *his* beloved, Fanny Brawne realizes that power. Byron's letter to Scott elaborates the erotic complexity of writing and of literary rivalry, while Keats's love letters demonstrate that "the love of a woman" involves competition over who writes the story of the poet's desire. The association between an erotic and a literary economy postulated both in Byron's metaphor and in Keats's letter to his publisher is borne out in Keats's relationship with his fiancée. Not just an image, the woman in this correspondence enacts the problem that others pose to the fantasy of self-representation. Without the claims to an authorial status that name and fame seem to give Byron, Keats worries all the more to legislate his love affair and his career.[38]

The "love of a woman" at stake in Keats's letter to his publisher is Fanny Brawne's love. Throughout that summer, he contends that, in order to write, he must resist the "cloying" distraction of his relationship with his fiancée. A week before his letter to the publisher, he writes to her:

> a few more moments thought of you would uncrystallize and dissolve me. I must not give way to it—but turn to my writing again—if I fail I shall die hard. O my love, your lips are growing sweet again to my fancy—I must forget them—" (16 Aug. 1819)

The passionate and even threatening extremity of Keats's involvement with the "love of [this] woman" is well known.[39] Crucial here is the direct yoking of his effort to master at once that passion in his private life—"I must not give way to it"—and the productions of his fancy in the public sphere of the literary marketplace. His desire for Fanny Brawne very nearly supplants his desire to write; dissolved by Brawne, Keats would fail to assert his "self-will" in and by writing.

But Keats cannot finally recuperate his threatened self-mastery in the realm of writing. Without being a Lady Bluebottle, or even a Caroline Lamb, Fanny Brawne nonetheless reads and writes in competition with Keats's own imaginative production. As the reader of his love letters and a writer of her own, her power for and over Keats derives from her capacity to imagine and inscribe the story of passion in other words. Such a capacity impels a situation in which Keats, unable to supervise her creativity, remains in doubt that he can govern his own creative power. His courtship of Fanny Brawne reveals the logic of his stake in his literary character, his reputation, his name and fame.

> Man must die, as Shallow says; but before that is my fate I feign would try what more pleasures than you have given so sweet a creature as you can give. Let me have another oportunity [sic] of years before me and I will not die without being remember'd. (March 1820)

The pleasures and fulfillment of the lover and the writer function isomorphically. Desiring Fanny's affection is coupled in the language of Keats's letters with desiring the satisfaction of posthumous fame. But so does the "throng of jealousies" (16 Aug. 1819) that describes the insecurity of his love affair also describe the "mire" in which his literary equanimity founders, in which his "name with the literary fashionables is vulgar—[he is] a weaver boy to them" (17–27 Sept. 1819). Conceiving that Brawne's narrative about their affair can similarly upset his own descriptions, he attempts to suppress her writing: "Do not write to me if you have done anything this month which it would have pained me to have seen" (? May 1820). The bluestockings' "silly project of conquest over regions which will never submit to their arms" is effected in Brawne's sexual conquest of Keats. While he is attacked as a "weaver-boy" by literary fashionables, Keats's love language suggests that he feels himself attacked, as if he were one of Byron's housemaids, by his beloved as well—"You have ravish'd me away by a Power I cannot resist" (13 Oct. 1819). The erotic "Power" Fanny Brawne wields is also the power of others to declare Keats either a poet or a "weaver-boy."

The words Fanny Brawne has the power to write to and of him are in fact not always the ones the poet himself would have dictated. While he is neither willing nor able to censor her writing entirely, he would try at least to edit it.

> I enclose a passage from one of your Letters which I want you to alter a little—I want (if you will have it so) the matter express'd less coldly to me. If my health would bear it, I could write a Poem which I have in my head, which would be a consolation for people in such a situation as mine. (? Aug. 1820)

His poem would be, Keats seems to claim, a rendering of his own situation far more consoling to him than Brawne's unedited version of it. But this particular poem remains in his head, unwritten. Unable to write himself because of his declining health, Keats betrays how much he relies on his lover's reproduction of him (his "situation") in her writing.

It would seem that in Keats's life the Romantic ideal of independent writing is disputed in the person of the woman who contests the writer's authority over his own imagination, his authorship of his own poems. She has an imagination too. She reads and she writes. Such a contest provides the terms for Byron's oblique discourse about authorship in the letter to Scott and reveals in Keats's exchange with Fanny Brawne that it is in the other's writing and rewriting that such authorship becomes powerful. While being "an object intensely desireable" (? May 1820) to the writer, the woman is also a subject scripting her own desires. What Keats fears in Fanny Brawne, as in the culture of bluestockings that names him "vulgar" or "weaver-boy" instead of poet, is the efficacy of the alternative accounts of him that she can engender. But if these alternative accounts inspire "tremulous anxiety," they are also, as Keats admits, "intensely desireable." As in the erotic economy the lover seeks his fulfillment in the beloved, the writer in literary culture writes precisely so that he will be read, reviewed, rewritten. The risks Byron takes in the billiard room when he expresses his love in "prose periods" are compelling both for their promise and their unpredictability: "*all* had been lost by failure—but then recollect—how much more I had to gain by the reception . . . & how much one always hazards to gain anything worth having" (8 Oct. 1813). The Romantic imagination of the feminine is equivocal, as is the writer's conception of the culture within which his authorship must come into being; the other who threatens the creative self does so by participating in that self's creation.

IV. The Writer's Ravishment

"Let no man fall in love," Hazlitt warned in 1821, "for from that moment he is 'the baby of a girl.' "[40] "Every lover who falls in love at first sight has something of a Sabine Woman" in him, Roland Barthes observes a century and a half later. "The lover—the one who has been ravished—is always implicitly feminized."[41] Referring to yet another story being circulated about him carrying off a girl from a convent, Byron remarks, perhaps only half facetiously,

> I should like to know *who* has been carried off—except poor dear *me*—I have been more ravished myself than anybody since the Trojan war—but as to the arrest and it's causes—one is as true as the other—and I can account for the invention of neither. (29 Oct. 1819)

With typical Byronic braggadocio, the poet calls attention to his sexual appeal and prowess; but his love affairs also ravish him, putting him in the woman's place. Crucial here is that such feminizing ravishment is linked to the unauthorized tales that undermine his own title to invention, to authorship. Moreover, although Byron can perhaps "brush away" these stories better than Keats can when his love life is, as he describes it, "the Theme . . . of idle Gossips" (? June 1820), other unauthorized tales put Byron "in a damned passion": "the imposters have published—*two* new *third* Cantos of *Don Juan*—the devil take the impudence of some blackguard bookseller or other." Byron literally finds others authoring his poem, though without the desperation of Keats's situation, his ravishment, like Keats's, consists in the usurpation of the authorial propriety that defines his personal model of creativity. Walter Scott heaps "coals of fire" on Byron when he treats the author of *British Bards and Scotch Reviewers* generously in his review of *Childe Harold's Pilgrimage III*. The reviewer also usurps the poet's authority by formulating the work in his own words. In Italy at the end of 1820, Keats finds his imaginative power subject to similar usurpation:

> My imagination is horribly vivid about her . . . I am afraid to write to her—to receive a letter from her—to see her hand writing would break my heart—even to hear of her any how, to see her name written would be more than I can bear . . . I have coals of fire in my breast. (1 Nov. 1820)

Brawne fuels the "coals of fire" that mark the writer's subjection to other imaginations. Feeling himself mastered, here by illness and his approaching death, Keats imagines, and *can* imagine, nothing other than Fanny Brawne's writing.

In his essay "Reading," Maurice Blanchot characterizes the silent appeal that a literary work makes to a reader,

> an appeal the reader hears only as he responds to it, that deflects the reader from his habitual relations and turns him towards the space near which reading bides and becomes an approach, a delighted reception of the generosity of the work, a reception that raises the book to the work that it is, through the same rapture that raises the work to being and turns the reception into a ravishment, the ravishment in which the work is articulated.[42]

One could argue about who is ravishing what or what is ravishing whom here. But as even Byron's comic complaint that he "has been more ravished [himself] than anybody since the Trojan war" suggests, such an argument would itself reveal that the literary erotics operating in the Romantic imagination obscure the difference between the creative work of the self and the creative work of the other. As that other to the male writer's conception of his own authorship, the woman persists in posing the question: "Who really spoke? Is it really he and not someone else?"

NOTES

1. All references to Byron's letters and journals are from Leslie Marchand, ed., *Byron's Letters and Journals,* 12 vols. (Cambridge, Mass.: Belknap Press of Harvard University Press, 1973–81). The letter to Annabella Milbanke is in vol. 3, p. 179 (29 Nov. 1813). Future references to Byron's letters and journals will be by date in the body of the text. Matthew Arnold sums up the way Byron's critics have usually adopted the poet's own rhetoric to talk about the kind of physical necessity writing entailed for him when he found that Byron wrote "to relieve himself" ("Byron," *Poetry and Criticism of Matthew Arnold,* ed. A. Dwight Culler [Boston: Houghton Mifflin, 1961], p. 349).

2. Michel Foucault, "What Is an Author?" in *Textual Strategies,* ed. Josue V. Harari (Ithaca: Cornell University Press, 1979), pp. 141–60, 160.

3. In *The Madwoman in the Attic* (New Haven: Yale University Press, 1979), Sandra Gilbert and Susan Gubar define women's "anxiety of authorship" as a more primary version of Bloomian "anxiety of influence": "[The female writer's] battle, however, is not against her (male) precursor's reading of the world but against his reading of *her*" (p. 49). Implicitly, my discussion turns from Gilbert and Gubar's elaboration of "the secret sisterhood" of women's literary subculture to argue that the male writer experiences a similar anxiety about being read by others and that at crucial moments these others take the literal and figurative form of the woman.

4. See Nancy Armstrong, "Feminine Authority in the Novel," *Novel* 15, no. 2 (1982): 127–45, on "modes of conducting courtship and commerce" as "interdependent parts of an ongoing cultural discourse" (p. 128).

5. I want to express my indebtedness to others here. I am grateful to many,

especially to Gillian Brown, Frances Ferguson, Steven Knapp, Morton Paley, Lynn Wardley, and Susan Wolfson for conversations and comments throughout.

6. See Ian Watt, *The Rise of the Novel* (Berkeley and Los Angeles: University of California Press, 1957), pp. 35–59; Irene Tayler and Gina Luria, "Gender and Genre: Women in British Romantic Literature," *What Manner of Woman*, ed. Marlene Springer (New York: New York University Press, 1977), pp. 98–123; also, "Introduction," p. xvii of the same volume. Also see Richard D. Altick, *The English Common Reader: A Social History of the Mass Reading Public, 1800–1900* (Chicago: University of Chicago Press, 1957).

7. Mary Poovey, *The Proper Lady and the Woman Writer* (Chicago: University of Chicago Press, 1984), p. 35.

8. "By the end of the eighteenth century there was a burgeoning tradition of women writers," Poovey, p. 36. See also Eva Figes, *Sex and Subterfuge: Women Novelists to 1850* (London: Macmillan, 1982); Judith Lowder Newton, *Women, Power, and Subversion: Social Strategies in British Fiction, 1778–1860* (Athens: University of Georgia Press, 1981). In his "Aristotle's Sister: A Poetics of Abandonment," *Critical Inquiry* 10, no. 1 (1983): 61–81, Lawrence Lipking qualifies his (not unproblematic) formulation of the specifically feminine poetics of passion in an endnote:

> It might be objected that what I have characterized as a *woman's* poetics is merely a branch of *Romantic* poetics. There is obviously some truth in this; nor could there fail to be, since only in the Romantic period did women begin to construct a poetics. But one should note also that Romanticism itself emerged only at the point when women began to play an important role in literature as writers and readers. (p. 81)

In investigating how women function at the ground of masculine conceptions of authorship in the Romantic period, my discussion explores some of the lines of connection between the emergence of women as a force in literary culture and the emergence of a professionalized literary culture generally.

9. From its inception, the circulating library was associated with both sexual promiscuity and the dangerous spread of literacy. In 1728, Robert Wodrow complained that books were "lent out, for an easy price, to young boyes, servant weemin of the better sort, and gentlemen, and vice and obscenity dreadfully propagated." Quoted in Thomas Kelly, *Early English Libraries: A History of Public Libraries in Great Britain before 1850* (London: The Library Association, 1966), p. 147. Also see Raymond Irwin, *The English Library* (London: George Allen and Unwin, 1966), esp. pp. 227–57.

10. Catherine Gallagher, "George Eliot and *Daniel Deronda:* The Prostitute and the Jewish Question," in *Sex, Politics, and Science in the Nineteenth-Century Novel*, ed. Ruth Bernard Yeazell (Baltimore: Johns Hopkins University Press, 1986), pp. 39–62, 40.

11. The phrase, "frighteningly sinister" is from an earlier version of Gallagher's essay read at The English Institute, Cambridge, Mass., Sept. 1983.

12. *English Bards and Scotch Reviewers*, in *The Complete Poetical Works*, ed. Jerome McGann (Oxford: Clarendon Press, 1980), vol. 1. On the wandering woman image see Nina Auerbach, *Woman and the Demon* (Cambridge, Mass.: Harvard University Press, 1982), pp. 150–84. Auerbach points to the prostitute's "uneasy implications for wives who stayed at home" (p. 159). Although the prostitute is excluded from the home, "the interchangeability of the bought woman and the possessed wife" suggests the fragility of the patriarchal domestic structure that seems to fortify the "sexual power" of men. Also pertinent here is Peter Brook's discussion of prostitution in the novel in *Reading for the Plot: Design and Intention in Narrative* (New York: A. A. Knopf, 1984); J. W. Saunders' discussion of Scott as a literary prostitute in *The Profession of Letters* (London: Routledge and Kegan Paul, 1964).

13. *The Letters of Sir Walter Scott, 1815–1817*, vol. 4, ed. H. J. C. Grierson (London: Constable, 1933), 10 Jan. 1817.

14. *Pamela* is again pertinent. See Mr. B's late letter to Pamela: "You cannot imagine the obligation your return will lay me under . . . I am all gratitude." *Pamela* (New York: W. W. Norton, 1958), p. 263.

15. See Romans 12:20 and Proverbs 25:21–22.

16. A. S. Collins, *The Profession of Letters, 1780–1832* (London: George Routledge and Sons, 1928).

17. In *The Poetical Works of Lord Byron*, ed. Ernest Hartley Coleridge (London: J. Murray, 1958).

18. Luce Irigaray, "Commodities among Themselves," *This Sex Which Is Not One*, trans. Catherine Porter (Ithaca: Cornell University Press, 1985), pp. 192–97, 193.

19. Mary Jacobus, "Is There a Woman in This Text?" *New Literary History* 14, no. 1 (1982): 117–54, 119.

20. I borrow this phrase from Eve Kosofsky Sedgewick, *Between Men: English Literature and Homosocial Desire* (New York: Columbia University Press, 1985). The configuration proposed in Byron's letter to Scott illustrates Sedgewick's point that "the hidden symmetries that Girard's triangle helps us discover will always in turn discover hidden obliquities" (p. 22). Like the background figure in Manet's painting, excluded from the cover of Sedgewick's book, the powerless woman in Byron's discourse (the "fresh-colored housemaid") whose marginality would seem to render her insignificant in fact reveals another power play.

21. Hélène Cixous and Catherine Clément, *The Newly Born Woman*, trans. Betsy Wing (Minneapolis: University of Minnesota Press, 1986), p. 150. In her discussion of Freud's *Dora*, Cixous also suggests that what connects the servant and the prostitute in the male imagination is the fantasy and fear of the seductress (pp. 150–54).

22. In the popular farce "High Life Below Stairs" (London: Oxberry's Edition, 1822), the servants take liberties with their masters' identities and property, and the master must become a servant in order to expose the masquerade and restore the proper domestic hierarchy—a hierarchy that, in Byron, allows the master to take liberties with the servants. Scott's reference to this play when he avows his authorship of the *Waverly* novels in 1824 also comments on the relationship between literary authority and class structure. For an intriguing discussion of the power of servants in literature see Bruce Robbins, *The Servant's Hand: English Fiction from Below* (New York: Columbia University Press, 1986).

23. Doris Langley Moore, *The Late Lord Byron* (Philadelphia: J. B. Lippincott, 1961), p. 212.

24. This is, of course, a transparent disclaimer. Though we don't know when he last seduced a housemaid, Byron's amours with lower-class women and his investment in their "cheapness" (versus the "expensiveness" of women of his own degree) were noted by Shelley, who wrote to Peacock in 1818, "Well, L. B. is familiar with the lowest sort of these women, the people his gondolieri pick up in the streets. He allows fathers and mothers to bargain with him for their daughters" (17 or 18 Dec. 1818); (*Letters of Shelley*, ed. Frederick L. Jones [Oxford: Clarendon Press, 1964]).

25. Unlike Katherine Rogers in "Richardson's Empathy with Women," *The Authority of Experience*, ed. Arlyn Diamond and Lee R. Edwards (Amherst: University of Massachusetts Press, 1977), pp. 118–36, I am not suggesting that *Pamela* is a feminist novel. Nor do I mean to press the claim that the novel is an allegory of the writer's condition. What I suggest here is that in Byron's imagination, the figure of Pamela as prototypical housemaid could complicate his assumptions about his "proper," that is, inherited, power. See also Ellen Moers, *Literary Women: The Great Writers* (1963; New York: Oxford University Press, 1985), esp. pp. 113–16, who finds *Pamela* at the root of women's literary professionalism in the nineteenth century (p. 121).

26. "John Polidori, the young Italian doctor who accompanied him [when he left England in 1816] reported that Byron, on arriving in Belgium, fell upon the chambermaid like a thunderbolt." From Louis Crompton, *Byron and Greek Love* (Berkeley and Los Angeles: University of California Press, 1985), p. 241.

27. Writing to Murray about his liaison with Margarita Cogni—"La Fornarina" (the Baker's wife)—Byron notes that one advantage of the affair was that "she could neither read nor write, and could not plague me with letters" (1 Aug. 1819).

28. On the significance of Byron's changing attitude toward the economics of literary production see Jerome Christensen, "*Marino Faliero* and the Fault of Byron's Satire," *Studies in Romanticism*, 24, no. 3 (1985): 313–33. Byron's later work reflects the tension he felt between the power and the constraints of the myth that writing has nothing to do with profit.

29. See Hazlitt, "The Aristocracy of Letters," *Table Talk*, number 21, in *The Complete Works of William Hazlitt*, ed. P. P. Howe (London: J. M. Dent and Sons, 1931), 8: 205–14. In "Visions of Success: Byron and Southey," *Studies in Romanticism*, 24, no. 3 (1985): 355–73, Peter T. Murphy suggestively characterizes Southey as Abel to Byron's Cain.

30. Lipking, "Aristotle's Sister," note, p. 81.

31. *Glenarvon*, 3 vols. (London: Henry Colburn, 1816), 3: 91.

32. See Frances Ferguson, "The Unfamiliarity of Familiar Letters," *The State of the Language*, eds. Leonard Michaels and Christopher Ricks (Berkeley and Los Angeles: University of California Press, 1980), pp. 78–88.

33. *The Letters of John Keats, 1814–1821*, 2 vols., ed. Hyder Edward Rollins (Cambridge, Mass.: Harvard University Press, 1958). All future references to Keats's letters will be by date in the body of the essay.

34. Figes, *Sex and Subterfuge*, p. 15.

35. "The Itch of Writing Universal," *The Adventurer* 4, no. 115 (Dec. 1753): 76–83, 78.

36. William Hazlitt, "On Great and Little Things," *Table Talk*, number 23. "If I know that she had read any thing I have written, I cut her acquaintance immediately. This sort of literary intercourse with me passes for nothing. Her critical and scientific acquirements are *carrying coals to Newcastle*. I do not want to be told that I have published such or such a work. I knew all this before. It makes no addition to my sense of power." The context of Hazlitt's remarks about bluestockings is, significantly, his preference for "humble beauties, servant-maids and shepherd girls, with their red elbows, hard hands, black stockings and mob-caps" over "women of quality" (who make no addition to his sense of power): "I admire the Clementinas and Clarissas at a distance: the Pamelas and Fannys of Richardson and Fielding make my blood tingle," (8: 236). The problematics of such a preference are the subject of Hazlitt's *Liber Amoris; or, The New Pygmalion*, ed. Gerald Lahey (New York: New York University Press, 1980).

37. William Pitt Scargill, *Bluestocking Hall*, 3 vols. (London: Henry Colburn, 1827). The "silly project" foreshadows George Eliot's mid-century critique of "Silly Women Novelists" who compromise literary standards to cater to public taste. According to Robert Halsband in "Ladies of Letters in the Eighteenth Century," *The Lady of Letters in the Eighteenth Century* (Berkeley and Los Angeles: University of California Press, William Andrews Clark Memorial Library, 1969), the bluestockings "bridged the gap between genteel amateurism and respectable professionalism by welcoming women who earned their living by their writing" (p. 47). They thus represented a threat to the Romantic model of composition by conjoining literature as a private, domestic pursuit and the public, commercial endeavors of the literary professional.

38. See Aileen Ward, "That Last Infirmity of Noble Mind: Keats and the Idea of Fame," *The Evidence of the Imagination*, eds. Donald H. Reiman, Michael C. Jaye, and Betty T. Bennet (New York: Gotham Library of New York University Press, 1978),

pp. 312–33. See also Wolf Hirst, "Lord Byron Cuts a Figure: The Keatsian View," *The Byron Journal* 13 (1985): 36–51 on Keats's rivalry with and admiration for Byron in the context of his description of the beautiful (i.e. ravishing) Jane Cox—"I should like her to ruin me" (14–31 Oct. 1818).

39. In *John Keats: The Making of the Poet* (New York: Viking, 1963), Aileen Ward recognizes the threat Fanny Brawne poses for Keats, and sees the poet's escape into writing as a viable strategy for restoring the self's power. See also Dorothy Van Ghent, *Keats: The Myth of the Hero,* ed. Jeffrey Cane Robinson (Princeton: Princeton University Press, 1983), esp. pp. 130–41. Van Ghent sees Fanny Brawne as one in a series of Lamian women Keats constructed in his imagination. In Steven Knapp's deconstruction of "negative capability" in "Keats and the Sentimental," MLA Convention, Washington, D.C., Dec. 1984, Keats's apparent self-effacement in his letters to Fanny (as when he claims that Brawne "dissolves and uncrystallizes" him) is really an attempt at more thorough appropriation of the other for the self's use. Knapp makes the connection between Keats's poetics and his relationship to his fiancée that I want to underline in my discussion by looking at the inevitable resistance of the other in contexts that are at once literary and erotic. Susan Wolfson remarks such resistance in Keats's final poems addressed to Brawne in "Composition and 'Unrest': The Dynamics of Form in Keats's Last Lyrics," *Keats-Shelley Journal* 34 (1985): 53–82: "the primary effect [of Keats's attempts at 'mastery of form'] is to render a world where lovers and poems alike remain vulnerable to the radical insecurities of experience" (p. 80).

40. "On Living to One's-Self," *Table Talk*, number 10, 8: 90–101.

41. "Ravishment," in *A Lover's Discourse,* trans. Richard Howard (New York: Hill and Wang, 1978), pp. 188–89.

42. In Maurice Blanchot, *The Gaze of Orpheus,* trans. Lydia Davis (Barrytown, N.Y.: Station Hill, 1981), pp. 91–113, 97. I use Davis's version instead of Ann Smock's excellent translation of this essay in Blanchot's *The Space of Literature* (Lincoln: University of Nebraska Press, 1982), pp. 191–97, because it allows for the double sense of "ravishment" I want to invoke here. Smock's translation of the phrase, "le ravissement ou se prononce l'oeuvre" into "the sheer delight whereby the work proclaims itself" doesn't suggest the threatening disempowerment that "ravishment" conveys, with different intensity, for both Byron and Keats.

WITCH OR PAWN

WOMEN IN SCOTT'S NARRATIVE POETRY

Nancy Moore Goslee

When Walter Scott reviewed Jane Austen's novel *Emma* in 1816, he praised it highly; but he also criticized Austen's overemphasis upon a mercenary lust for property, a prudence at odds with the sense of romance.[1] Not only is this unfair to Austen's biting analyses of the marriage market, but it obscures Scott's own portrayals of similar pressures within the plots of the romantic novels he had begun to publish two years earlier. Even in the narrative poems, far more explicitly romantic than his novels, Scott shows how women and their property all too often become pawns in male plots. Three of his seven major narrative poems—*Marmion* (1808), *Rokeby* (1813), and *The Lord of the Isles* (1815)—modify the usual romance pattern of hero rescuing and winning fair lady by showing the women as heiresses who become pawns in realistically portrayed struggles over money or land. Strikingly, these poems alternate with those in which the women are apparently far more dominant, but dominant within a romantic or even mythic, more than realistic, mode. In Scott's first, third, and fifth poems—*The Lay of the Last Minstrel* in 1805, *The Lady of the Lake* in 1810, and *The Bridal of Triermain* in 1813—the dominant female figures are witches or enchantresses who lure men into their isolated castles, either to alienate them from social responsibility in a stable culture, or to replace them in that culture. Usually the members of the second group associate themselves with the mysterious natural powers of the deep forest or of the lakes—and thus seem only slightly displaced nature goddesses. Yet in the first group, too, the woman whose land is so desirable appears alien to the male consciousness which, as Sherry Ortner and others have argued, tends to define culture.[2]

Scott's seventh and final narrative poem, the 1817 *Harold the Dauntless*, includes even more, and more clearly hostile, witches than do the earlier poems. More central to the reform of the sullen Danish hero, however, is a woman disguised as a male skald or minstrel. Such cross-dressing, as conventional in literature as it is unconventional in society,[3] also appears in *Marmion* and in *The Lord of the Isles*. Yet in *Harold,* and even more strikingly in the immediately preceding *Lord of the Isles,* it becomes a way to modify, if

115

not fully to abolish, the two extreme patterns of women as passive land to be possessed, or as active natural or supernatural powers. Nina Auerbach has described how, "as feminist criticism gains authority, its new sense of power involves not the denial of mythology but the impulse toward it. . . . The mythologies of the past have become stronger endowments than oppressions."[4] By looking at the changing status of enchantress, pawn, or woman dressed as mediating minstrel within three of these poems—two from the first group and one from the second—we can recognize Scott's own dramatic modification of those quasi-mythic patterns for his vast reading public, and ask whether those modifications move, for his women characters and for his women readers, from oppression toward endowment.

In both *The Lay of the Last Minstrel* and *The Bridal of Triermain*, Scott filters the magic of his enchantresses through several narrators.[5] In a scholarly note to *The Lay*, he carefully distinguishes between the intelligence of the historical Lady of Buccleuch and the "vulgar" view of her as a witch.[6] Yet in his seventeenth-century minstrel's lay, the lady successfully calls up spirits to avenge the death of her husband at the hands of a neighboring border clan, and to forestall her daughter's love for a member of that clan. Similarly, in *The Bridal of Triermain*, a modern narrator tells two intertwined, avowedly fantastic medieval romances, to charm an heiress into eloping with him. In the earlier of the soldier's two narratives, King Arthur himself spends an idyllic summer in an enchantress's wilderness castle. Like the Lady of Buccleuch, this enchantress seems closely associated with nature. Yet almost as soon as the women's power becomes manifested in these poems, it becomes limited.

At the center of the lay sung by Scott's "last" minstrel is a figure who struggles to control her world through both written and spoken magic. Analogous to the problematic powers and limits of the imaginative self confronted by Scott and his minstrel, the struggles of the Renaissance Lady of Buccleuch have a very immediate purpose: she deploys her magic to protect her family and border terrain after her husband has been killed. As the minstrel begins his lay, he contrasts the physical power of the waiting soldiers in the castle hall to the intellectual, visionary power of the lady in her isolated tower. His shudder of horror at the lady's solitary incantations echoes that of the narrator in *Christabel* but asks protection for himself and for his listening audience who may explore such topics, not for other characters: "Jesu Maria, shield us well!" (1. 1). Yet if the lady's incantatory magic is powerful in calling spirits from the vasty deep and having them answer her, the answer of river and mountain spirits to the lady is one that announces an ethical view opposing her own: "Till pride be quelled and love be free," she will receive no more help from them. The pride is her own, in her self, her art, and her immediate family; the love is her daughter's for a member of the family that has just killed her husband. Although the lady uses her magic to help her take on the male role of leadership her son is too young to assume, these nature spirits express what Carol Gilligan would call a more profoundly female vision: they urge a vital reconciliation instead of a killing revenge, a quelling of the lady's pride and a freeing of her daughter's love.[7]

Instead of listening to those vocal presences, however, the lady continues her proud and individual challenge to romantic and domestic love. She also continues her usurpation of male power: in order to defend her view of family integrity, she sends her retainer, Walter of Deloraine, for a book of spells buried in the grave of its author, the local but renowned male wizard whose name is also Scott. Even though usurping a male wizard's power, this further reliance on magic increases her resemblance to the witches or enchantresses of romance who may indeed have descended from fertility goddesses but who draw men away from the human, social, and domestic ordering of that fertility.[8]

The godlike powers of the book's written spells become manifest only through speech. Yet whoever reads the book may speak the spells. Freed from the dead hand of their author, spells can be either reinterpreted or redirected against his original intentions. Within the narrative, however, those powers are denied to the Lady of Buccleuch. Instead, the malicious goblin Gilpin Horner suddenly enters Scott's book, as the modern Lady Dalkieth, wife of his present chieftain, had requested.[9] Seizing the wizard's book, the goblin forces it to open. Thus forcing both the wizard's text and Scott's own text into disorder, the goblin seems an animate and demonic *aporia*. This "elvish dwarf," we suddenly learn at the end of canto 2, serves Margaret of Buccleuch's suitor Cranstoun. As shown by his entry into the baron's service, his defining characteristic is leaping playfully and disruptively from one realm to another. When Cranstoun was hunting in Redesdale's remote glens,

> He heard a voice cry, "Lost! lost! lost!"
> And, like tennis-ball by racket toss'd,
> A leap, of thirty feet and three,
> Made from the gorse this elfin shape.

Even though, as the minstrel drily comments, "Lord Cranstoun was some whit dismay'd," and rode "five good miles . . . To rid him of his company," the dwarf "was first at the castle door" and eventually finds employment. "Though small his pleasure to do good," his alertness and devotion have since then served the baron well.

Taken alone, this "marvel" might seem only an image of anarchic violence or of the id. Yet he is also a figure for some original imaginative energy or presence that breaks through the conventional patterns of understanding.[10] Arising from the goblin's arbitrary acts is a pattern of relationships that confirms this second interpretation: a pattern that links page, book, and lady. The goblin's spontaneous substitution of himself for the "Mighty Book" requested by the lady arises from his own quick study of its "gramarye," its magical text. Following a bloody encounter between Cranstoun and the returning Deloraine, the goblin discovers the book and reads "one short spell." This is just enough, evidently, for him to perfect the shape-changing skill of "glamour," in which "All was delusion, nought was truth." Through the glamour of the written spell, then, he enters the lady's castle and thus replaces the book's latent and ambiguous power with his own malicious and energetic presence.

In a further exchange, that presence is even more explicitly linked to the lady than is the wizard's book she waits for. In an apparently spontaneous maliciousness, the goblin disguises himself as a playmate and leads the lady's "fair young child," the heir of Branksome Hall, into the woods. There, after frightening the child with "his own elvish shape," he abandons him. A band of English invaders soon discovers him and holds him for ransom. When the aggressive boy declares his own identity first by fighting off their dogs and then by announcing that he is "the heir of bold Buccleuch," the English reiterate his heritage: "I think our work is well begun, / When we have ta'en thy father's son" (stanza 19). Meanwhile, the goblin takes on his appearance and his place in the Buccleuch family:

> Although the child was led away,
> In Branksome still he seem'd to stay,
> For so the Dwarf his part did play.
> And in the shape of that young boy,
> He wrought the castle much annoy. (3. 21)

The socially acceptable, masculine, and other-directed aggression shown by the real child is distorted by the goblin into a painful pinching and sudden outbursts of flame: his violence, like the lady's magic, is a violation of domestic peace because it dislocates acceptable roles. It is nevertheless the dark side of that society's socially accepted violence. This connection is suggested by the minstrel's sequence of images at the end of canto 2: from the dwarf's small bonfires to Margaret's musings on what she thinks is the evening star that "shakes its loose tresses on the night" to her recognition that the "star" is in fact the beacon-blaze of war, announcing the arrival of the English and rallying support as far as Edinburgh.[11]

In the fourth canto, because the disguised goblin's efforts to avoid detection by the lady lead to his temporary banishment from Branxholm to another castle, that banishment makes the English forces' possession of her biological son both explicable and threatening from the lady's viewpoint. Yet the goblin is in his rebelliousness and in his magic a child of the witchlike lady. In replacing her biological son, the goblin frees her temporarily from the social chain that makes her only the mother of the new child-chieftain. And like her, he expresses an anarchic, disruptive individuality through a transforming magic.

Though shaking the fabric of society, this rebellion does not, however, fully transform it. Instead, the wizard's "Mighty Book," left with Cranstoun when the dwarf enters the lady's castle, makes possible a larger change. Tutored by his now-returned goblin-page, Cranstoun uses the book's "gramarye" in canto 5 to enter Branksome, the Buccleuchs' castle. Although the goblin hopes that Cranstoun's presence in Branksome will lead to sexual anarchy, the lovers can control the fires of their own passion well enough to redirect both passion and magic. Disguised through gramarye as Deloraine, the Lady's knight whom he had earlier wounded, Cranstoun fights a second and more formal single combat. Substituting himself for Deloraine as family champion, he fights this time against an English champion, in order to free the lady's biological son. His disguise as a retainer of the Scott family, moreover, proves prophetic; once the lady learns of his generous service, she reluctantly quells her pride and gives love its freedom, allowing him to marry her daughter. Thus his interpretation of the book's spells completes and reorders the exchanges, almost the metaphorical substitutions, made by the maliciously energetic goblin and brings peace not only between the feuding Scottish border clans but even, temporarily, between Scots and English.

Unwilling to disturb this fragile peace, itself so nearly a kind of "glamour" or illusion in that normally violent society, both Cranstoun and the lady are discreet about the nature of their struggle. "Much of the story she did gain," the minstrel comments, his balanced lines including the pun that confirms the interchange in his own story between the energy of the goblin page and that of speech written on a page:

> . . . How Cranstoun fought with Deloraine,
> And of his page, and of the Book
> Which from the wounded knight he took. . . . (5. 27)

Cranstoun, however, leaves "half his tale . . . unsaid"—the half concerning his own use of the book—as if narrating his own experiment with magic might commit the baron too fully to its practice, or as if narrative itself is that commitment to magic.

Because the lady, too, "car'd not . . . to betray / Her mystic arts in view of day," her conversation with Cranstoun after the combat is constrained. Yet she planned "ere midnight came, / Of that strange page the pride to tame, / From his foul hands the Book to save, / And send it back to Michael's grave" (5. 27). Her attribution of "pride" to the dwarf comes right after her own painful and public relinquishing of pride as her chastising nature spirits had demanded. She associates the goblin's expression of pride with the supplementary power of the book; but "pride" seems in both cases to be an independent self-assertion that makes use of the wizard's neutral spells. Her intention to return the book to the grave suggests that she is beginning to relinquish such independence for herself—or, at least, that she now sees her family's identity as defined more by loving alliance than by hostile self-assertion.

As the minstrel carefully rejects the "false slander" of "some bards" who claim that the lady would not enter the chapel for her daughter's wedding, he confirms this turn from individual pride and imaginative energy toward a communal harnessing of that energy:

> . . . I trust right well
> She wrought not by forbidden spell;
> For mighty words have signs and power
> O'er sprites in planetary hour. . . . (6. 5)

Instead, she assents to the sacramental words of her daughter's wedding. Dwindled from magician into domestic mother of the bride,

> The Ladye by the altar stood:
> . . . .
> . . . On her head a crimson hood,
> . . . .
> A merlin sat upon her wrist,
> Held by a leash of silken twist.

Both she and the hawk are hooded; its allusive name confirms it as the emblem of her present state of submission.

Finally, she loses even the demonic distortion of her power. Her intention to leash not only her own magic words but also the gramarye of Michael Scott's book meets, like all her attempts, a reverse that proves more socially generous in its twist. Before she can return the book to the wizard's grave, yet another exchange confirms the interdependence of goblin-page and book: the wizard leaves his grave, stalks through the wedding feast, and claims the still-malicious goblin as his own. When the shadowy figure says, "Gylbin, come!" the elvish page mutters, "Found! found! found!" and vanishes. Though apparently chastised, the goblin thus gains a paternal recognition and control, more than a total repression. With the dramatically if skeptically described return of its male author from the grave, moreover, the written text of Michael Scott seems to lose its threatening moral ambiguity and confirms the lovers' goal of an harmonious, cooperative, and social world. The domestic, nurturing values traditionally desired in women dominate the end of the poem, but at the cost of leashing other powers women might exercise: the power of "mighty words and signs," the power of the book.

Almost overlooked in this dramatic epiphany, the book itself is apparently left behind when the wizard and goblin vanish together. If we look for further references to it in the minstrel's tale, we find instead another, more sublime vanishing of a book in the renewed presence of its creator. Through a pilgrimage to Melrose, the border clans try to quiet the restless soul of the wizard, and the minstrel's narrative concludes with a tribute to divine presence over text, the singing of the *Dies Irae*. In the face of an apocalyptic divine presence, "shrivelling like a parched scroll, / The flaming heavens together roll" (6. 31).[12] Scott as writer, however, has the last word. He is now free to circulate his own individual, private text, doubly validated by male wizard and minstrel. Yet because the minstrel's song has also shown not quite the interchangeability but the familial relationships of written text and goblin energy, he preserves his own anarchic originality of imagination and his own identity by defining his family origins. Even though he has distanced and delimited her power, he becomes like the dwarf-goblin a son of the witchlike lady whose magic he has chastised.

A male magician bursting from the earth also marks a radical censuring of female magic in *The Bridal of Triermain*. In this case the magician is the powerful Merlin. In *Triermain,* too, a mother's antisocial magic sharply contrasts to and is redeemed through a daughter's more docile and conventional behavior. In the later poem, however, the mother begins to lose control even before the child is born. Conversely, and surprisingly, the modern narrator accomplishes his purpose—charming an heiress to elope with him—before he has completed the part of his story that shows this redemptive domestication. In this brief yet complex pattern of interlocking narratives, the modern heiress is first told about a thirteenth-century border knight, Sir Roland de Vaux of Triermaine. Visited by a strangely beautiful huntress whom no one else sees, Sir Roland asks a local bard to explain who she is. The bard Lyulph's tale goes back 500 years, to reveal King Arthur's seduction by an enchantress; the visionary huntress now loved by Sir Roland is the daughter of that temporary union. Roland's journey to the dark tower where he can find and free the daughter, now herself enchanted, is a morally instructive allegory. Yet the modern heiress, perhaps ironically named Lucy, chooses to elope with the narrator before he tells her that allegory; instead, her choice is prompted by the bard's Arthurian seduction narrative and its pendant, the daughter's arrival at Arthur's court fifteen years later. Although the serious social consequences of elopement appear fully in Jane Austen's novels,[13] the wonderful fantasy of the romance episodes in *Triermain* seems to have persuaded both Scott's fictional heiress Lucy and his readers to overlook such difficulties.

How, then, should we understand Lucy's response to the earlier stages of her suitor's narrative? Although his name is also Arthur, he seems to control his own powers of enchantment, not—like the king—falling victim to another's control. By examining more fully the steps backward into myth and then forward into the demythologizing of its enchantresses, we may understand more clearly the heiress's enthrallment by her Arthur-author's narrative imagination—and possibly her recognition and freedom from it.

Appropriately enough, Arthurian narrative then begins with the king's name and with a highly conventional romance motif: Arthur's yearning to escape his queen's bowers for "vent'rous quest . . . by wood or river." What is unconventional about this narrative is Arthur's active role in the quest and in the confrontation with a mysterious enchantress.[14] When this Arthur rides out into the "desert wild," the king places himself, rather startlingly, in the role of an imitator of traditional romance models: he "journey'd like knight errant" (1.10). In the isolated Vale of St. John he finds a mysterious, silent castle. Like Launfal, he is led by a "band of damsels fair" to their enchantress-queen. Once inside the castle, he finds himself ironically, if happily, enclosed in another bower.[15]

In canto 1 the queen's seductions appear entirely natural. She uses the

same human beguilements Guinevere uses on Lancelot (2. 15) and she is
entirely successful. Scott's multiple audiences, too, seem charmed into silence by the natural inevitability of this relationship. There is no sharp
narrative break between the formal divisions of canto 1 and canto 2, where
we might expect responses from the multiple internal listeners: from the
page listening to the bard Lyulph's tale, perhaps from Roland listening to
the page's report of that tale, or from Lucy listening to the modern
Arthur's. By refusing to describe the nearly mutual seduction of Arthur
and the enchantress Guendolen in detail and instead calling it a "common
tale," the bard Lyulph offers a distinctly moral commentary. Yet by linking
Arthur's "gliding" first into "folly" and then into "sin" with the way time
"glides away" as he lingers at the castle, Lyulph slides over the moral
problems his various audiences, known and unknown to him, might well
consider.

In canto 2, when the mysterious queen fears that the king's "hour of
waking" from his infatuation is "near," she must turn to her supernatural
powers. These powers connect her to an earlier world of myth: Lyulph
describes her as a sort of demi-nature-goddess, supernatural though closely
connected to the processes of an external natural world, "wood or river."
Although Guendolen's "mother was of mortal birth," "Her sire[,] a Genie of
the earth," presided over courtship and fertility rituals until the coming of
Christianity. Resentful of losing "his rights," "He trained to guile that lady
fair, / To sink in slothful sin and shame, / The Champions of the Christian
name" (2. 3).

Though he has lost territory to Christianity, the resentful genie has
neither vanished, like Plutarch's gods at the birth of Christ, nor lost all
power; the "guile" he teaches his daughter is described in stanza 4 as "Her
sire's soft arts the soul to tame." As stanza 3 describes Guendolen's practice
of those arts, it slides, like the transition between cantos, from natural
seduction to magical snare. It also glides, however, from a naively realistic
acceptance of the existence both of the genie and his daughter to a subtly
stated questioning of their actuality:

> Well skill'd to keep vain thoughts alive,
> And all to promise, naught to give;
> The timid youth had hope in store,
> The bold and pressing gain'd no more.
> As wilder'd children leave their home,
> After the rainbow's arch to roam,
> Her lovers barter'd fair esteem,
> Faith, fame, and honour, for a dream. (2. 3)[16]

Characteristically, however, Scott gives the visionary woman a motiva-
tion. Thus, even though her explicit if mythological family history would
seem to make her more obviously malevolent than Keats's and Shelley's
similar figures, its very explicitness makes her less mysterious and more
human. Further, it makes her failure to use her magic understandable. She

promptly forgets "each rule her father gave," and is "Sunk from a princess to a slave." As in *The Lay,* the lady has learned her magical skills from her father and thus does not draw her powers only from an originally female source in a fecund but alien nature. Scott's careful fathering of those mythic powers drawn from nature does not prevent but divides and thus controls the fusion of female and natural otherness so weirdly present in the powers both of Thomas the Rhymer's Queen of Elfland and of Keats's Belle Dame. Because of this weakening, Guendolen can keep Arthur, as Meleager captures Guinevere, only for a summer.[17] This is long enough to insure her own fertility (2. 6–7) but not to confirm her divinity. Instead of continuing as a receding goal for the dreamer and luring him to destruction as the dream-woman in *Alastor* will do only a year later, she herself becomes the pursuer who must seek to maintain her summer's dream of fulfillment, to keep the father of her expected child.

Only as the king actually leaves, having broken from her natural charms, does Guendolen remember enough of her magical art to set a trap. Yet her use of magic clarifies neither her powers nor Arthur's power to resist them. Like Comus or like his reputed mother Circe, she offers him a "cup of gold." To share the parting ritual, she drinks first. When the unsuspicious Arthur "lifted the cup," however, a "drop escaped the goblet's brink" and, "Intense as liquid fire from hell," burned his horse so severely that its leap carried the king out of the vale (2. 10). If Guendolen's ability to drink this fiery potion seems to confirm her own supernatural powers, Arthur's avoidance of it is less a moral or perceptual victory than a comic accident.

His judgment of the whole episode, like the audience's judgment, is made even more difficult by his retrospective view. When he "back on the fatal castle gazed," he sees only "A tufted knoll, where dimly shone / Fragments of rock and rifted stone" (2. 10). If Arthur had tasted the genie's drink, he might have been drawn permanently into Guendolen's Circe-like realm of enchantment and might himself have disappeared with the castle, folded into liminal elf-realm within, yet beyond, nature. On the other hand, the drink might simply have killed the king, preventing both his return and the fulfillment of his fantasy of a dallying escape into nature. As it is, the enchantress's power remains untested: he returns and follows the whole career told by the "history" of Geoffrey of Monmouth and the romances of later writers: giants captured, twelve battles won, and an almost-perfect kingdom established. In contrast to Keats's knight or the newly prophetic Thomas the Rhymer, Arthur seems not to have put on the enchantress' supernatural knowledge with her sexual power.

Again with no intervention from any later listener or narrator, Lyulph skips fifteen years or more, to focus in stanza 11 of canto 2 on the arrival of Arthur's hitherto unknown daughter at his Penrith court. Though one might expect the child of such a union to exercise her inherited magic and to pursue further the genie's vengeance against Christian culture, instead she pursues vengeance against Arthur's desertion of her mother. More aware of her mother as wronged mortal than as wrongdoing enchantress—

a view more justified by outcome than by her mother's intention—she turns the summer tournament meant to marry her off into an exposure of the decadence of Arthur's court. In contrast to her mother's earlier career as a receding visionary object, Gyneth and her new wealth become entirely too present. Abandoning their earlier commitments, all but three knights fight for her and for the two kingdoms Arthur promises with her. The sordidness of their motives is rewarded by the violence of their deaths. Though Arthur has given Gyneth his "leading-staff" to stop the tournament before it changes into such violence, she refuses to stop the slaughter and to restore the apparent order Arthur would have preserved in his court and in himself. Her destructive use of his phallic staff forms an appropriate revenge against Arthur's apparent seduction and abandonment of her mother.

Yet Gyneth does not complete her bloody quest for a husband among "the bravest, proved and tried." Instead, male magic intervenes with a claim to retaliate against her "mother's art." Arthur first uses this phrase in stanza 22, in response to her charge of "the faithlessness of men." In stanza 26, an angry Merlin arrives to avenge his nephew's death in the melee and repeats the charge: "they mother's art / Warp'd thine unsuspicious heart." Although Gyneth uses no magic but her beauty and her potential wealth, she now becomes the victim, or at least the object, of Merlin's own more powerful art. Even in his arrival on the scene, Arthur's enchanter usurps the powers of her mother's line:

> . . . rent by sudden throes,
> Yawn'd in mid lists the quaking earth,
> And from the gulf, tremendous birth!
> The form of Merlin rose! (2. 25)

Reborn from the earth, he has no use for women's powers of fertility; claiming the earth himself, he denies the power of the "Genie of the earth" who taught Guendolen her arts. Triply imprisoned by Merlin's spell—in sleep, in an enchanted chair, and in the mysterious castle hidden in the "Vale of Saint John," where she had come from—Gyneth is condemned to endure a more passive version of her mother's career.

Two slightly differing interpretations of this punishment are given at the end of the canto, one Christian and explicitly antifeminist, the second returning to the mythic pattern behind the romance to continue her guilt (2. 26). Because she has caused Arthur's knights to kill each other in a most un-Christian acting out of their greed, Merlin makes her an Eve causing a second fall—"all their woes"—of "the Red Cross champions" (2. 26). Even if it does recall her genie-grandfather's antagonism to Christianity, Merlin's condemnation is surely an elegiac whitewashing of the knights' behavior. Her "pride," moreover, has only mirrored Arthur's own. Claiming acknowledgment as his daughter, she plays upon his own too easy buying-off of her claims, so that the anarchic violence she creates is only too appropriate a dowry.

The second interpretation recalls the genie's intentions even more fully, yet returns sympathy to the prisoner. Completing his narrative to the page, Lyulph explains that Gyneth "still . . . bears her weird alone, / In the valley of Saint John." As a visionary image she has even more power than did her mother to draw knights astray: "her semblance oft will seem, / Mingling in a champion's dream, / Of her weary lot to plain, / And brave his aid to burst her chain." Her imprisonment creates a trial of solitary, not social bravery for the knights who are led either by her dream or by "her wondrous tale" to search for her (2. 28). Among those who see the castle, "few have braved the yawning door, / And those few return'd no more." As her story is gradually forgotten, Lyulph implies, her power to haunt dreams is also lessened, and thus "well nigh lost is Gyneth's lot" (stanza 28). Her very existence seems dependent upon the active imagination of narrator and dreamer.

To consider the active realization of the knights' dreams also implies a complex assessment of the functions of romance as a genre. With its "yawning door," the terrifying castle in the mysterious vale resembles a Lawrence-like nightmare of the absorbing, consuming womb, seen as alien, annihilating, tomblike. Once realized as an actual person and not as a vision, Gyneth in part shares the castle's role as a physical trap that threatens the separate consciousness, even the existence of the male questers. Yet she is in part freed from this role because in her sleep she too seems a virginal victim. Like the lady in *Comus,* imprisoned in her chair, she is immobilized. In sharp contrast to Comus, Merlin is trying to freeze, not to release, the natural fertility she represents. In greater fairness to Merlin, we might say that he is trying to reassert control over the lust and avarice that Gyneth has called out in the court. Daughter of a nature deity and a Circe, Gyneth has herself been a Comus, turning Arthur's ordered tournament into a brutal antimasque; but with Merlin's greater powers, she becomes the helpless Lady.

Bruno Bettelheim argues that the spell cast over the sleeping beauty is a necessary period of narcissism in puberty, for emotional development to catch up to physical maturity. He suggests that the old woman, the evil fairy, represents the feared yet necessary aspects of physical maturity for women.[18] In this version, however, Merlin's sleep punishes Gyneth for not denying the witchcraft of natural fertility and process. She must become a victim in order to be saved from her own maternal sources of power. In some sense, too, her purging from enchantment represents a purging of the women in Arthur's court, whose bowers have distorted the social structures of male chivalry or at least of military alliance.

When that Arthurian narrative ends, we expect to hear how one of those haunted knights, Sir Roland de Vaux, sets off to rescue the princess from her centuries-long sleep. Yet, surprisingly, the modern heiress does not wait for a happy ending at this point; she decides to elope with the soldier who is telling her both romances. She may see herself as a princess whose wealth makes her only the object of suitors' quests; or perhaps she is asleep,

charmed by this ambitious minstrel about whom we know little except his
rather cynical portrayal of the king for whom he is named. The conclusion
of the modern Arthur's story, however, suggests that the heiress has
gambled well. For the romance-quest of Sir Roland is a Renaissance moral
allegory. Each mysterious chamber of the magical castle houses women
whose temptations are both sexual and psychological.

At the center of these enclosures, the goal of Scott's knight differs from
those of Ariosto's, Tasso's, and Spenser's. Roland's attempt is closest to
Guyon's, for he is a rescuer. Yet he rescues not a preceding male quester
victimized by an enchantress, but a younger, less guilty version of the
enchantress herself. With great precision Scott uses these analogues to
earlier Renaissance romantic epics to recall Gyneth's parentage and to
distinguish her from her mother. Rogero has adopted "wanton, womanish
behavior . . . An Atys or Adonis for to be / Unto Alcina" (canto 7, p. 164);
Rinaldo's "sword, that many a pagan stout had shent, / Bewrapt with
flowers hung idly by his side" (16. 30); Verdant has cast aside his sword (2.
12. 80).[19] Although Scott's poem echoes these lines closely, they do not
describe Roland. Instead, the lines (2. 1) come from Lyulph's tale, the first
narrative, and they describe King Arthur. Even more dramatically than
Spenser shifts the balance of Tasso's narrative by making his main protagonist the rescuer instead of the victim, Scott shifts the balance of these
sources by dividing them into two parts. Thus Rogero, Rinaldo, and Verdant are models for Arthur, and, even more strikingly, the Circean enchantresses Alcina, Armida, and Acrasia are models for Guendolen. In all
four cases, these dominant enchantresses unman their lovers by embower-
ing them in passive enjoyment. The sword hanging unused is both an
abandonment of social responsibility and evidence of their impotence in
the personal, if not the physical relationship.

Far less effective than the other three, Scott's Guendolen is also more
sympathetic. As we saw, Arthur eventually decides to rescue himself, and
she even spills the Circean cup that might have enchained him more
permanently. Alcina, Armida, and Acrasia are indeed conquered, but only
with superior magic beyond the power of their passive victims. Even with
that superior magic, only Spenser's Acrasia is firmly conquered. Though
these Renaissance parallels surely make Guendolen's career as an enchantress seem less terrifying than those of the earlier Circes, they nevertheless
make firmer the association of female sexuality, demonic enchantment, and
a dangerously contagious, yet isolated and antisocial domesticity. If remote
from normal society, the bower is feminizing for the heroes. Also, since
these parallels with Ariosto, Tasso, and Spenser become far clearer in the
third canto of *The Bridal,* we not only share the modern Arthur's tendency
to interpret Roland's quest allegorically, but we also reread or recall the
earlier Arthurian story of the first two cantos in a different way. In this
retrospective process Guendolen's significance, if not her actions, seems
more terrifying and thus the need for Gyneth's purgation seems stronger.
Through this network of allusions both to the preceding Renaissance

poems and to the preceding parts of this one, Gyneth is trapped in a kind of sedimented, hermeneutic guilt.[20]

Just as the elemental functions of romance heroes—those of errant dallier and of rescuer—are split between Arthur and Roland, so the function of witch and passive "damsel" to be "from danger freed" (*Marmion*, 4. 4) are split between Guendolen and Gyneth, between mother and daughter. This generational distinction between the female figures should remind us of *The Lay,* in which the Lady of Buccleuch relinquishes her powers of witchcraft to make way for her daugher's conventional domesticity. Both through contrast with the now more moralistic and more misogynist reading of the Arthurian narrative and through his return to analogues of *Comus* and "The Sleeping Beauty," Scott works out Gyneth's purification. Roland, a somewhat more charming Guyon, brushes off all temptation. Purified by this testing, he finds the sleeping Gyneth also purified by her long sleep: "Doubt, and anger, and dismay, / From her brow had pass'd away" (3. 37). No longer the Circean enchantress whose refusal to use the warder created brute chaos in the tournament, she releases the warder into Roland's hands as she wakes up. As mentioned earlier, she now resembles the lady in *Comus,* temporary victim of a son of Circe (3. 38). Like Milton's lady, she seems far younger than all the Circean arguments or the furor at the tournaments had led us to expect. Though a pun only in French, the "ivory chair" in which her life has been suspended seems almost to symbolize the suspended processes of her own sexual development. That suspension redeems her from being condemned as an enchantress.

Further, Roland's trials have made him wary of holding her in thrall. Instead of the earlier bluff, forthright egotism that we might have expected from him, he plays neither Comus nor even the gently aggressive prince in tales of the sleeping beauty:

> Motionless a while he stands,
> Folds his arms and clasps his hands,
> Trembling in his fitful joy,
> Doubtful how he should destroy
>   Long-enduring spell.
> Doubtful, too, when slowly rise
> Dark-fring'd lids of Gyneth's eyes,
>   What those eyes shall tell.

At first reading the elided grammar of the line suggests that Gyneth wakes up, given the freedom to do so. Yet in a sense his hesitation does lead to that result. In his willingness to wait for her response, he reaches out "gently" to grasp her hand and kiss her. As he does so, "the warder" that had been in her hand "leaves his grasp." Neither the newly educated Sir Roland nor Gyneth, then, keeps that power over male aggression, which was in Arthur's hands civic rule and in Gyneth's became, in both Arthur's and Merlin's view, "her mother's art." As Roland inadvertently parallels Prospero's breaking of his wand, the last magic of the poem becomes a release

from magic. When "the warder leaves his grasp," the "magic halls / Melt . . .
away,"

> But beneath their mystic rocks,
> In the arms of bold De Vaux,
> > Safe the princess lay.
> Safe and free from magic power,
> Blushing like the rose's flower
> Opening to the day. . . .

Although the phrase "beneath their mystic rocks" suggests for a moment
that both Roland and Gyneth have been swallowed up into the magic castle,
Arthur's conclusion places them firmly in this world, far less haunted than
Keats's wan knight on the cold hill's side. Arthur wraps up his fiction with a
flurry of conventional phrases, as if afraid to confront their entrance into
ordinary time too closely:

> Our lovers, briefly, be it said,
> Wedded as lovers wont to wed,
> > When tale or play is o'er—
> Lived long and blest, loved fond and true,
> And saw a numerous race renew
> The honours that they bore.

"Safe and free from magic power," Gyneth apparently retains none of
her mother's art. One could say, in an extension of Virginia Woolf's thesis,
that even though she was trapped in that castle, unconscious for five
centuries, she had a room and a power of her own. Now this second-
generation enchantress has neither. The image of the castle, Arthur tells
Lucy, still occasionally haunts a lost traveler. Yet he attributes the power of
making it more than illusion to the male quester, not to the in-house female
magician: "Never man since brave De Vaux / The charmed portal won."
Thus the menacing power of an independent female imagination or an
independent, aggressive female sexuality is redefined. The first now becomes the creation of a male moral and aesthetic criterion so compelling
that Roland has in a sense realized his own fantasy by finding Gyneth; and
the second becomes a passive blossoming out of sleeping innocence. Thus
in both poems the independent enchantresses are simultaneously domesticated and demythologized. Even the love that one might expect to draw
men into the lawless, alien, antisocial aspects of their magic is revised in
both poems into a domesticating force made manifest through a younger
generation.

In a second group of poems, Scott makes the chief woman character an
heiress who is far more obviously a powerless pawn, a victim of male plots
for ownership. Two of the three poems in this group I will mention only
briefly; the tangled web of the plots spun by their villains would take more
space than I have here. In *Marmion* and *Rokeby,* the villains plot to trick

unwilling heiresses into marriage in order to control their land. They are thwarted not only by the heiresses themselves, but also by the men the heiresses love. In both cases the successful lover proves his character while in disguise. In the third of these "pawn" poems, *The Lord of the Isles*, it is the woman who assumes the disguise. By doing so, she succeeds, paradoxically, in bringing about the family-arranged political marriage that she had wanted all along. It was one, however, that her brother and her fiancé had tried to break off, the brother from changed political loyalties and the fiancé from changed personal loyalties. Thus Scott uses a conventional literary topos—a woman disguised as a boy, pursuing her lover—to correct an all-too-conventional social situation, the woman as pawn.

Yet in this poem both the heroine's venturesome experiment in transexual dressing and her final success in marriage are nearly undermined by her extreme passivity, even in her disguise. Shakespeare's disguised heroines in the romantic comedies manipulate both the language of the play and the entire plot. Scott's heroine quite explicitly denies herself even that control of language. Presumably to avoid being recognized, she disguises herself as a harp-playing but vocally mute minstrel. For Scott, as his last minstrel says in *The Lay,* the medieval minstrel who relied on music alone abdicated his true vocation in shaping, through language, a culture's vision of itself. His heroine Edith of Lorn, then, seems to free herself from her role as pawn—only to have her assumed role express an even stronger denial of female power to develop either a self or a supporting culture. Cultural self-definition, moreover, is central to the poem's historical milieu, the struggle of Robert the Bruce to restore Scottish independence from England.

As the poem moves from castle to wilderness, then back to civilization, that journey leads, as in many romances, to the education of the hero— here, both Robert the Bruce, the would-be king of Scotland, and Mac-Donald of the Isles, the would-not-be bridegroom. In a further use of romance convention, the disguised Edith travels for weeks with Bruce and Ronald. Unidentified as a woman, she is—even more outrageously—unrecognized by her former fiancé. Reading the situation literally and realistically, at least one reviewer was scandalized by what he saw as impropriety.[21] In the civilized settings of the first two cantos Scott does indeed treat the earlier relationship between Edith and Ronald realistically, though a part of that realism involves the effect of romantic circumstances upon the characters. From canto 3 on, this realism is modified, but not fully transformed, by the roles of women in two different romance conventions—the medieval quest, suggested in part by Edith's green clothing, and Elizabethan comedy, suggested by her male clothing. The specific nature of her disguise as minstrel adds still further complexity to this use of romance conventions.

In canto 1 her foster mother gently chides Edith for the "cold demeanor" that seems so inappropriate to the wedding clothes she already wears. Reminding her of "many a tower" that "Owns thy broad brother's feudal power" (1. 18), Morag reminds her how "auspicious" the morning is that will unite "the daughter of high Lorn" with "the heir of mighty Somerled." Only adding to this appropriateness is "Fame's heroic tale" (1. 10) of Ronald's military success. Yet while Edith, betrothed to him since childhood by family arrangement, is prepared to love him by those "lays" of his "achievement," Ronald has not been equally prepared for her; his response is "cold delay" (1. 11). Although arranged marriages of this sort often enough led to indifference on both sides,[22] Edith's readiness to love leaves her doubly vulnerable. A willing pawn in the arrangements for the marriage, she wants it to be more than an arrangement and thus becomes an emotional victim. Although the early betrothal and the vast landscapes involved in the negotiations are characteristic of the medieval period, Edith's poignant demand for love—though surely not unknown earlier— also reflects the growing emphasis placed upon woman's sentiments and the frequent conflict of such sentiments with the economics of the marriage market in the late eighteenth and early nineteenth century.[23]

With Bruce's storm-driven arrival and then his recognition, the realism of larger political conflicts and actual historical characters breaks in upon the realism of Edith's typical characterization. First defending the still-anonymous Bruce by the laws of hospitality, Ronald responds to a "long-suppress'd . . . spark" of nationalism, then defends him even more hotly when he recognizes Bruce's sister as a woman he had admired at an English tournament.[24] When he speaks to Isabel Bruce, his language eclipses the place of Edith—his possessives, even his term "bride," are addressed confusedly to both women (2. 19). Further, once Lorn sees that Ronald and his Islesmen are no longer his allies against Bruce but now the king's supporters, he threatens to marry Edith to another, more reliable ally—and he also reveals how unfeelingly he had pressed for the earlier marriage in spite of seeing Ronald's obvious indifference:

> Was't not enough to Ronald's bower
> I brought thee, like a paramour,
> Or bond maid at her master's gate,
> His careless cold approach to wait? (2. 25)

Her vanishing, then her reappearance, disguised and silent, in a near-wasteland are only the outward correlatives of her status at the end of this scene.

Her choice of a minstrel's disguise makes a further ironic protest against her situation. During the first two cantos, the minstrels at Ardtornish have distinguished themselves by their readiness to sing the socially and politically appropriate, if emotionally inappropriate, aubades for her wedding day. In canto 2, Lorn supplies a "lay" for the resident minstrel to sing; its narrative is so insulting to Bruce that he virtually reveals himself to correct his own history. Sardonically, Bruce praises the minstrel who has "framed thy strains / To praise the hand that pays thy pains" (2. 14). Edith's disguise of a voiceless minstrel seems an effective criticism of the politically compromised art she has just heard.

Further, her role as disguised minstrel on Skye enables Bruce to work toward the kingship that will be fully confirmed, undisguised, at Bannockburn. Effective for others, however, her silent minstrelsy is not a disguise that lends her strength, as does Flora MacDonald's disguising of Bonnie Prince Charles on Skye in 1746, a narrative much in the minds of Scott's readers.[25] Instead, confirming a variant of Sandra Gilbert's thesis about cross-dressing,[26] her weakness becomes a way to teach others a way to regulate their strength.

When Bruce and MacDonald pursue a stag to the edge of the bleak Loch Corriskin on the Isle of Skye, they encounter there the mute minstrel-page, dressed in green as if a kind of nature spirit. Though disguised as a boy, Edith acts like one of the more benevolent ladies of the lake in Arthurian romance, a myth Scott has already used playfully in his own *Lady of the Lake*.[27] When Edith warns the men of an ambush by her own brother's forces, their successful struggle becomes an omen for the long guerilla struggles that lead toward independence. Though a human and not a magical nature-spirit, Edith mediates between these men and the landscape as if to prophesy that its sublimity is an image of the moral grandeur of their cause, and thus an image of their claim upon the land of Scotland as a whole. Scott's supplement to history—Bruce's detour to Skye—converts romance into a cause of actual history.

One reason for her failure to gain male strength through her disguise is that Scott reshapes and relocates episodes from Barbour's *Bruce* to draw out their resemblance to medieval romance.[28] As he does so, he modifies the freedom of male cross-dressing available to the heroines of Elizabethan comedy with a more conventional, even archetypal woman's role from romance. For Edith, however, the role of the elfin queen or wilderness enchantress carries no radically transforming "gramarye." Instead, it emphasizes—yet, paradoxically, in a constructive way—her passivity as object.

Unlike Ellen Douglas in *The Lady of the Lake*, the disguised Edith by no means thinks of herself, even teasingly, as a nearly supernatural lady of the lake. With her "cap and cloak of velvet green" (3. 22), she wears fairies' clothing. She thus shares with the elfin world and with traditional ladies of the lake that border-figure role of mediating between the natural and the supernatural. Because of her male disguise, however, she does not assume the sexual power of a Circean fertility goddess, or even of a Guendolen in *The Bridal of Triermain*. Unlike the ladies of the lake, she is also a border figure between the sexes. As Ronald later recalls, the men who brought her to Skye and who plan to ambush Bruce call her "Amadine . . . (In Gaelic 'tis the Changeling)" (5. 18). Alluding to the tradition that the fairies steal human children and leave behind their own "changelings," these men half-consciously recognize her disguised sexual identity. Thus they do not quite credit her with male power, nor does she possess, except associatively or iconically, the powers of a Nimue or a Morgan le Fay. Instead, she preserves only the half-natural, half-supernatural otherness of both changeling and enchantress.

She does indeed function as a guardian spirit. Though she gives neither sword nor the gift of prophecy, she protects the heroes from ambush by warning them with an inarticulate cry. Yet the help she offers Bruce and MacDonald in the camp on Skye emerges not through any strength she gains or is freer to exercise in her masculine page's disguise. Nor does it emerge even through the sort of cool-headed, articulate, and yet ladylike manner apparently shown by Flora MacDonald. Instead, it works through the double weaknesses of womanhood and muteness. Unlike the militant Britomart or the highly articulate Rosalind, she reveals in her apparent androgyny only a passivity. Yet her passivity awakens others, literally on Skye and more figuratively in two later episodes, to the possibilities of tenderer emotions and attitudes than those normally shown in war. Her disguise works, then, not to make her more masculine but to make her companions recognize more domestically feminine and thus more compassionate human values in themselves.

In the second of the three episodes in which the changeling minstrel-page acts as an almost supernatural guardian for Bruce's cause, her vulnerability becomes a test of character for the men she encounters. When Edward Bruce sends the page "Amadine" ashore as an advance scout before their landing at Carrick, he explains the double advantage presented by the physically frail and apparently mute boy:

> Noteless his presence, sharp his sense,
> His imperfection his defence.
> If seen, none can his errand guess;
> If ta'en, his words no tale express. (5. 10)

Ironically, of course, the "imperfection" is not of tongue but of phallus; and because Edith is not in fact physically mute but is physically weak, she requires enormous courage to resist the pressures once she is captured. That resistance, however, passive as it is, both creates the delay needed by Bruce's forces and intensifies the sympathetic bond growing between her and MacDonald. Isabel continues to educate her brother in the task of honoring vows as a positive, if sometimes painful, way to stabilize and unify society. He in turn can educate Ronald, made more susceptible to tenderness by his guardianship of the nearly helpless page. Because Ronald has grown fond of the young minstrel-page who joined their forces on Skye, he can eventually accept the undisguised Edith as person more than as political pawn. Because Scott's Bruce also eventually supports the betrothal vows, he develops a higher morality than the historical king.

The question of what final freedom Edith has gained for herself is left deliberately and ironically ambiguous. When Bruce now urges MacDonald to honor his original engagement to Edith, he seems to base the political loyalties of his supporters upon personal honor and loyalty—an important unifying theme for the public and private plots of the poem. Yet as the narrator points out, "King Robert's eye / Might have some glance of policy"; for his military campaign had destroyed Edith's brother, and now

> Ample, through exile, death, and flight,
> O'er tower and land was Edith's right;
> This ample right o'er tower and land
> Were safe in [MacDonald's] faithful hand.

So much for "Edith's right"; in reassuming her woman's clothing, she reassumes her role as pawn, though a happy one even as she loses "ample right o'er tower and land." Scott's repetition neatly and deliberately confirms the irony.

Before this return to a woman's clothing and identity becomes known to more than Bruce and his sister, however, Edith reassumes her minstrel's disguise and intervenes for a third time to act as guardian spirit for the king and for the Lord of the Isles. Here the problem of interpreting the role of the minstrel becomes even more acute. This intervention, like the earlier two, supplements history. When she sees the Scottish forces wavering at Bannockburn, Edith cries out in warning. Because the unarmed camp followers still believe her the mute minstrel page, they think her suddenly restored speech is a miracle—and they charge so vigorously that they shift the momentum of battle. The charge of camp followers comes from history—but the double fiction of the minstrel's miraculous speech is again Scott's own. This miraculous speech is in one way the full assertion of the more active male role that Edith's disguise as a minstrel page had promised her. Yet because that speech is effective only in the context of its earlier denial, its miraculousness seems an elegant fraud that has in reality defrauded Edith—and all other women—of audible speech. Women's speech, women's abilities, women's leadership—like Edith's leadership of the camp followers—will seem miraculous when freed from the apparently voluntary constraints society has placed upon their exercise. Or further, once we consider the "miracle" of the page regaining his voice a false miracle, then the articulate speech and the leadership may themselves be seen as only fictional possibilities, not real, if belatedly recognized, accomplishments. As mediating symbolic object in and of the landscape, the green-clad, silent minstrel takes on great power for the development of the male figures in the poem. As a woman in her own right, she subsides into a domestic silence, relinquishing her rights in marriage, and becomes identified with the silence of the land she no longer holds in her own name. A poem that Scott first called *The Nameless Glen*,[29] an appropriate metaphor for the unappropriated and silent woman as well as for Loch Corriskin, he finally inscribes as *The Lord of the Isles*, to preserve that and other patriarchal titles.

In all of these poems, then, we can see a movement toward the center, from the extreme stereotypes of witch or pawn. The pawns gain some power through the virtues of domestic morality, and the witches must lose their power in order to share the same domesticity, whether they want it or not. This center of domestic morality, moreover, is the realm toward which the novel had been developing, especially in the hands of the women novelists writing in the genre from the 1790s through the following twenty years.[30] So in some sense Scott's turn toward the female minstrel may reflect his own role as a male taking on the female role of novel-writing, and the female values of domestic morality. No wonder Jane Austen, when she heard the strong rumor that Scott had turned from his best-seller poems to novel-writing, said, "Walter Scott has no business to write novels, especially good ones. It is not fair. He has fame and profit enough as a poet, and should not be taking the bread out of other people's mouths."[31] Yet, finally, it is fair to say that even in his poems Scott employs the patterns of witch and pawn not simply for fame and profit, but in order both to criticize and to modify these half-stereotypical, half-mythic categories. If that modification costs his more interesting women too much independence, and especially too much power over "mighty words and signs," he at least seems more sensitive to the cost than one might at first have suspected.

NOTES

1. *Quarterly Review* 14, no. 27 (October 1815): 200–01.

2. See Sherry B. Ortner, "Is Female to Male as Nature Is to Culture?" in *Woman, Society, and Culture,* ed. Michelle Zimbalist Rosaldo and Louise Lamphere (Stanford: Stanford University Press, 1974), pp. 67–87.

3. See Thomas Crawford, *Scott,* Writers and Critics Series (London: Oliver and Boyd, 1965), p. 42.

4. In *Woman and the Demon: The Life of a Victorian Myth* (Cambridge, Mass.: Harvard University Press, 1982), p. 12. Because Scott fused medieval and Renaissance social history with his own revision of romance as a genre, we cannot easily make generalizations about either the past he wrote of or the present he wrote for. A useful introduction to the place of women in Scottish society can be found in Rosalind Marshall, *Virgins and Viragos: A History of Women in Scotland 1080–1980* (Chicago: Academy Chicago, 1983).

5. Three recent critics of Scott's poetry have greatly advanced our understanding of his artistry in these poems: Jill Rubenstein, "The Dilemma of History: A Reading of Scott's *Bridal of Triermain,*" *SEL* 12, no. 4 (Autumn 1972): 721–34; Ruth Eller, "Themes of Time and Art in *The Lay of the Last Minstrel,*" *Studies in Scottish Literature* 13 (1978): 43–56; and J. H. Alexander, *The Lay of the Last Minstrel: Three Essays,* Romantic Reassessment, no. 77 (Salzburg: Institut für englische Sprache und Literatur, 1978).

6. Scott, *Poetical Works,* ed. J. Logie Robertson, Oxford Standard Authors Edition (1904; reprint ed., London: Oxford University Press, 1967), p. 58. All quotations from Scott's poetry are taken from this edition and will be cited by canto and stanza. For a discussion of the witch as literary archetype for creative women, see Sandra Gilbert and Susan Gubar, *The Madwoman in the Attic* (New Haven: Yale University Press, 1979). For historical studies of British witchcraft, see Christine Larner, *Enemies of God: The Witch-hunt in Scotland* (London: Chatto and Windus, 1981); and Alan Macfarlane, *Witchcraft in Tudor and Stuart England: A Regional and Comparative Study* (New York: Harper, 1970). Harold Wimberley, *Folklore in the English and Scottish Ballads* (1928; reprint ed., New York: Ungar, 1959), notes that

witches in the ballads were almost always women, and that male conjurors acted "under instructions from" them (p. 219).

7. Carol Gilligan, *In a Different Voice: Psychological Theory and Women's Development* (Cambridge, Mass.: Harvard University Press, 1982).

8. Modern studies of witchcraft, particularly those of Larner and Macfarlane, have challenged the earlier twentieth-century theory of Margaret Murray, who argued that witches were members of ancient fertility cults still practicing their old religion. Nevertheless, the literary mythology of the Circe figures and the Arthurian enchantresses reaffirms such a connection. For suggestions of such a connection, see Scott's *Letters on Demonology and Witchcraft*, intro. Henry Morley, 3rd ed. (London: George Routledge, 1887), pp. 76–80, 85–88, and 111ff.

9. See *The Letters of Sir Walter Scott*, ed. H. J. C. Grierson, 12 vols. (London: Constable, 1932), 1:166, 1:174–75, and 1:242–43. See also Edgar Johnson, *Sir Walter Scott: The Great Unknown*, 2 vols. (New York: Macmillan, 1970), 1:197–98.

10. For a slightly different interpretation, see Judith Wilt, *Secret Leaves* (Chicago: University of Chicago Press, 1986), p. 190; and Ruth Eller, "The Poetic Theme in Scott's Novels," in *Scott and his Influence: The Papers of the Aberdeen Scott Conference, 1982*, ed. J. H. Alexander and David Hewitt (Aberdeen: Association for Scottish Literary Studies, 1983), pp. 79–80.

11. See Alexander, *"Lay,"* pp. 77–78.

12. See Frank Kermode, *The Genesis of Secrecy: On the Interpretation of Narrative* (Cambridge, Mass.: Harvard University Press, 1979), for a distinction between book and scroll as ways of looking at apocalypse and prophecy (p. 88).

13. *Mansfield Park* presents these consequences most seriously; see also *Pride and Prejudice;* and Rosalind Marshall, *Virgins and Viragos*, pp. 182–85.

14. See, for example, E. K. Chambers, *Arthur of Britain* (1927; reprint ed., New York: October House, 1967), p. 155.

15. See *Launfal* in *Ancient English Metrical Romances*, ed. Joseph Ritson, rev. Joseph Goldsmid, 3 vols. bound in 1 (Edinburgh: E. and G. Goldsmid, 1885), pp. 11–12, 28–33.

16. See the Pierpont Morgan Manuscript 44351; these lines were added after that manuscript, as if Scott reevaluated his theme.

17. See Richard Robinson, *A Learned and True Assertion of the original Life, Actes, and death of the most Noble, Valiant, and Renowned Prince Arthure, King of great Brittaine* . . . collected and written of late yeares in Lattin, by . . . John Leyland (London, 1582), ed. William Edward Mead for E.E.T.S. (Oxford: Oxford University Press, 1925), pp. 62–65 (Cap. xiii).

18. Johnson points out the fairy-tale parallel (1:478) but does not explain it. See Bruno Bettelheim, *The Uses of Enchantment: The Meaning and Importance of Fairy Tales* (1975; reprint ed., New York: Vintage, 1977), pp. 232–33. For a criticism of Bettelheim that resembles my protest at Gyneth's punishment, see Nina Auerbach, *Woman and the Demon*, pp. 41–43.

19. My references are to *Ariosto's Orlando Furioso, Selections from the Translation of Sir John Harington,* ed. Rudolph Gottfried (Bloomington: Indiana University Press, 1963); Torquato Tasso, *Jerusalem Delivered,* trans. Edward Fairfax, intro. John Charles Nelson (New York: Capricorn, 1963); and Edmund Spenser, *The Works of Edmund Spenser, A Variorum Edition,* ed. Edwin Greenlaw, Charles Grosvenor Osgood, and Frederick Morgan Padelford, *The Fairie Qveene,* book 2, ed. Greenlaw (Baltimore: Johns Hopkins University Press, 1933).

20. See Fredric Jameson, *The Political Unconscious: Narrative as a Socially Symbolic Act* (1981; reprint ed. Ithaca: Cornell University Press, 1982), p. 140; and Paul Ricoeur, *Time and Narrative,* vol. 1, trans. Kathleen McLaughlin and David Pellauer (Chicago: University of Chicago Press, 1984), pp. 68–70.

21. See *Eclectic Review,* n.s., 3 (May 1815): 473.

22. See Rosalind Marshall, *Virgins and Viragos,* chaps. 1 and 8.

23. See Mary Poovey, *The Proper Lady and the Woman Writer: Ideology as Style in the Works of Mary Wollstonecraft, Mary Shelley, and Jane Austen* (Chicago: University of Chicago Press, 1984), chap. 1; Jane Austen, *Northanger Abbey* in particular; and Rosalind Marshall, *Virgins and Viragos,* chap. 8.

24. See C. I. Rothery, "Scott's Narrative Poetry and the Classical Form of the Historical Novel," in *Scott and His Influence,* pp. 63–74, for a discussion of the relationship between private and public in *The Lord of the Isles.*

25. For Scott's consciousness of Boswell's and Johnson's visit to Skye, see *Letters* 2:357 (3 July 1810). Boswell's journal contains at its center the narrative of Charles Edward's escape across Skye, helped by Flora MacDonald and her woman's clothing: see *The Journal of a Tour to the Hebrides with Samuel Johnson, L. L. D.* (London: Henry Baldwin for Charles Dilley, 1785). *Waverly,* published just before *The Lord of the Isles,* does not trace the prince as far as Skye but certainly presents his rebellion to a wide audience.

26. Sandra M. Gilbert, "Costumes of the Mind: Transvestism as Metaphor in Modern Literature," *Critical Inquiry* 7, no. 2 (Winter 1980): 391–417.

27. See my essay, "Romance as Theme and Structure in Scott's *The Lady of the Lake,*" *TSLL* 27, no. 4 (Winter 1976): 737–57.

28. See *Barbour's Bruce,* ed. Matthew P. McDiarmid and James A. C. Stevenson, 3 vols. (Edinburgh: Scottish Text Society, 1985), book 7; 2:162–88. Scott moves the episode to Skye, inserting that fictional journey before Bruce reenters documented history to land at Carrick on the mainland. In Barbour's episode, there is no deer but a slaughtered sheep as bait for the ambush of the hungry guerilla-fighters, no minstrel-page or lady of the lake but a "howswyff" who helps Bruce after the ambush. The editors of this recent edition newly assess the fourteenth-century Barbour's historical reliability.

29. See Johnson, *Scott,* 1:417, 419, 438.

30. See Margaret Kirkham, *Jane Austen, Feminism, and Fiction* (Sussex: Harvester, 1983), Introduction; and Jane Spencer, *The Rise of the Woman Novelist from Aphra Behn to Jane Austen* (Oxford: Basil Blackwell, 1986); see also Scott's review of *Emma* cited above, p. 189.

31. To Anna Austen, 28 September 1814, in *Scott: The Critical Heritage,* ed. John O. Hayden (New York: Barnes and Noble, 1970), p. 74.

IV.
The Women Respond

INDIVIDUAL IN COMMUNITY

DOROTHY WORDSWORTH IN CONVERSATION WITH WILLIAM

Susan J. Wolfson

I

Dorothy Wordsworth is known primarily as a writer of journals and recollections, and though passages in these works have impressed readers such as Virginia Woolf with "the gift of the poet," her actual poetry has attracted little critical attention and even less acclaim.[1] The usual remark is that it lacks literary merit, especially when compared to that of the other writer and chief poet of the household, William Wordsworth. More recently, her poems have been read as documents revealing the inhibitions of "a literary tradition that depends on and reinforces the masculine orientation of language and of the poet"[2]—an approach that has renewed interest in her poetry, but sometimes at the expense of confining its significance to that interpretive matrix alone. In this essay I want to suggest how some of Dorothy Wordsworth's poems, and one of her narratives, are not always so restricted, but reveal efforts to test modes of experience and self-representation different from those privileged, practiced, and promoted by her brother. While these projects are clearly affected by William's example and William's success, they also engage acts of imagination that show Dorothy indirectly questioning her brother's favored tropes and figures, and speculating about alternatives. This essay focuses on the play of such equivocation, both as it informs Dorothy's sense of what makes a poet and as it affects the poetry she makes.

The differences that emerge bear not only on the composition of the Wordsworth circle, but also focus attention on the larger diversity of Romantic writing, both in and beyond the familiar canon. That these differences within a shared historical circumstance, and sometimes within a shared generic practice, are ones also marked by gender affords us an additional opportunity to consider the relation of both writers to "the masculine tradition." This tradition is typically characterized as deriving from the performative Logos of a paternal deity and is discerned in poetic

subjectivity that simultaneously advances a male center and writes the
female as the "other"—necessarily represented without her own subjectivity
or power of self-representation, and inscribed in political and epistemic
hierarchies alike as the object of appropriation, instruction, or mastery.[3] We
can see the effect of this tradition on both Wordsworths. If William's poetic
mode is conspicuously self-enacting, Dorothy "detest[s] the idea of setting
myself up as an Author"—even of prose—so she says to friends who were
urging the publication of a narrative she had written on behalf of the
Grasmere community about its care for a large family of suddenly orphaned children. Dorothy nominally deflects her aversion to setting herself
up as such a figure into a concern about the "injurious effect" of bringing
the orphans "forward to notice as Individuals," and so making them "objects of curiosity" before their "Characters . . . are formed"; but her reticence may also reflect her discomfort with one kind of notice she herself
had gained, namely, that of a figure in William's poetry. She can imagine
her narrative published only "Thirty or forty years hence," and then, only
as a "service" to others, and only "without a name"—no "thought of me."[4]
As if to prescribe this self-effacement, the title page of her manuscript
announces merely:

A NARRATIVE
Concerning George and Sarah Green
of the Parish of Grasmere
addressed to a Friend

———

1808[5]

It is William's Preface, in fact, that gives the *Narrative* prestige, and,
under his authority, this is only one of two places in the document in which
his sister's name appears: "The following Narrative was drawn up by
Dorothy Wordsworth at the request of her Brother, William Wordsworth:
he entreated that she would give a *minute detail* of all the particulars which
had come within her notice; thinking that the end for which the account
was written would be thereby better answered, viz. that of leaving behind a
record of human sympathies, and moral sentiments, either as they were
called forth or brought to remembrance, by a distressful event, which took
place in the course of the month of March, 1808, at Grasmere in the
County of Westmoreland" (p. 41). William's underscored phrase accommo-
dates Dorothy's reticence about setting herself up for notice, for it is the
record rather than the recorder that is stressed; the sympathies and sentiments in question are not so much personally as socially important; they are
understood to reflect communal response. This construction of authority is
quite opposite to what habitually obtains in William's own self-inscribing
projects, and for Dorothy it is an enabling compromise: she writes as
service and in assignment, the recorder for the community and its reporter
to others. The second instance of her name in this manuscript fulfills this
role. She merely signs and dates the end, as if the designated scribe. This

resistance to individual notice, along with her inclination to subscribe her literary activity to acts of service authorized by William, also has a more domestic register. Dorothy manages his household and literally manages the production of his texts, at times equating her subjectivity with his: "After Tea I wrote the first part of Peter Bell," she notes; "I wrote the Pedlar"; "I wrote the Leech Gatherer for him which he had begun the night before"—meaning, of course, she wrote out fair copies of these poems, but the effect of her syntax is to conflate her activity as a writer into William's authority, as if she were absorbed into his "I" and operating as the technological extension of his imagination.[6]

Correspondingly, Dorothy discredits her own poetic aptitude, especially if measured against William's. Of a nighttime spectacle that animated "many very exquisite feelings," she says, "it made me more than half a poet"; yet she struggles to complement the event with her own poetic making: "tried to write verses but alas! I gave up expecting William"[7]— "expecting William," that is, from a visit with Coleridge, but her syntax as well as the proximity of this note to her record of defeat have the uncanny effect of relating his absence to absence of poetic power in herself. William, too, wrestles with moods of frustration, and Dorothy's journals are quite informative about the flux of success and failure in his labors; but he retains his sense of vocation, even on occasion turning doubts of capability into his subject and theme, as in the introduction of *The Prelude*. Dorothy, by contrast, says she is amazed that anyone "would persuade *me* that I am capable of writing poems that might give pleasure to others besides my own particular friends!! indeed, indeed you do not know me thoroughly," she exclaims to Lady Beaumont, who had admired some poems of hers she had heard William read along with his own.[8] The prescriptive force of William's model and methods is critical to her low self-estimation: "I have made several attempts," she explains,

> and have been obliged to give it up in despair; and looking into my mind I find nothing there, even if I had the gift of language and numbers, that I could have the vanity to suppose could be of any use beyond our own fireside, or to please, as in your case, a few partial friends; but I have no command of language, no power of expressing my ideas, and no one was ever more inapt at molding words into regular metre.

Her implicit equation of poetry with formal regularity, "command" of language, and "power" to express subjective ideas derives from exercises William has perfected, and, not coincidentally, these are the terms in which critics tend to dismiss Dorothy's poetic ability.[9] This is not the only model for poetic production, of course, yet Dorothy's commitment to it is so complete that she even emulates its inspiration: "I have often tried when I have been walking alone (muttering to myself as is my Brother's custom) to express my feelings in verse; feelings, and *ideas* such as they were, I have never wanted at those times; but prose and rhyme and blank verse were jumbled together and nothing ever came of it." It does not occur to her that the jumble itself might be a productive result, indeed a worthy literary form.

In a late poem, a set of self-described *Irregular Verses,* Dorothy takes up the issue in retrospect, writing a myth of negative vocation in response to a question: why in the "jocund time" of youth did she "not in jingling rhyme / Display those pleasant guileless dreams / That furnished still exhaustless themes?"[10] As she recalls how she *"reverenced* the Poet's skill, / And *might have* nursed a mounting Will / To imitate the tender Lays / Of them who sang in Nature's praise" (60–63), the capital *P* she attaches to the word "Poet" already betrays the otherness she associates with the term, for this is the figure of William's ideal. His self-confidence about his credit as "Poet" may waver, but he and Dorothy accept such identity as his vocation and destiny. Dorothy declines such aspiration, not even calling her work "poetry" or "poems"—merely "verses" or "rhyme." The origin of this slightly deauthorizing manner may be read in the girlhood history she recounts, for she writes, in effect, a countertext to the growth of a poet's mind:

> . . . bashfulness, a struggling shame
> A fear that elder heads might blame
> —Or something worse—a lurking pride
> Whispering my playmates would deride
> Stifled ambition, checked the aim
> If e'er by chance "the numbers came."
> —Nay even the mild maternal smile,
> That oft-times would repress, beguile
> The over-confidence of youth,
> Even that dear smile, to own the truth
> Was dreaded by a fond self-love;
> " 'Twill glance on me—and to reprove
> Or," (sorest wrong in chidhood's school)
> " 'Will *point* the sting of ridicule." (64–77)

The two voices in quotations are important pressures of imagination in this story of stifled ambition. One is maternal reproof, a negative muse all the more compelling for being fictional, since in the era recounted—her childhood friendship with Jane Pollard—Dorothy's mother was no longer alive. That the "mild maternal smile" remains, Cheshire-cat-like, is a significant trace, for it encodes the judgments that "repress" her poetic impulse, implying that the informing motions—"pride," "ambition," "overconfidence" and "self-love"—are inappropriate for girls to exercise, however normative to "masculinist" poetics they may be.[11] Tellingly, Dorothy has the adult speaker of *Lines intended for my Niece's Album* refer to that book as one inscribed by male poets, in homage to a male author, Dora's "gifted Sire": "A wreath for thee is here entwined / By his true Brothers of the Lyre" (27–28). Even if she does not directly link the gender of this company to the question she writes three stanzas later—"But why should *I* inscribe my name, / No poet I—no longer young?" (37–38)—the issue is surely relevant, for as Susan Levin reports, women writers such as Felicia Hemans and

Maria Jane Jewsbury also contributed poems to Dora's album (p. 143). Dorothy's *Lines* suppress this information, with the effect of enhancing the impropriety of her name and poem appearing among the "true" society of male inscribers and the "Sire" they honor.

Not surprisingly, the other voice quoted in her account of childhood inhibition is that of the "gifted Sire" himself. This is the phrase "the numbers came," cited in *Irregular Verses* in an attitude of irony and self-mocking—for in the Wordsworth circle, at least, it is a clear allusion to that master-document of poetic vocation itself, the "glad preamble" of *The Prelude*: "To the open fields I told / A prophesy; poetic numbers came / Spontaneously, and clothed in priestly robe / My spirit, thus singled out, as it might seem, / For holy services."[12] William's voice poses a stark contrast to the *"might have"* and "if e'er" with which Dorothy's "I" designates the limits of her own ambition. Not only is his statement energized by the pride, ambition, over-confidence, and self-love denied to her, but it is resonant with echoes of one of the chief precursors in the masculine tradition, the poet of *Paradise Lost,* who claims to "feed on thoughts, that voluntary move / Harmonious numbers," and whose "Celestial Patroness" "inspires / Easy . . . unpremeditated Verse."[13] It is significant that Dorothy's irregular verse cites only William's voice of high inspiration, with no indication that what follows this charged moment in his poem is a record of prolonged struggle with doubts of self-worth and vocation, confessions to defeated hopes and thwarted ambition. Along with her distancing and discrediting of her own ambition as a merely juvenile love of "jingling rhyme," the force of Dorothy's decidedly partial reading of her brother's compositional processes (which she knew full well were rarely spontaneous, rarely easy) allows her to project "the Poet's skill" as radically "other," and so define herself as disabled and deluded from the start.

Having declined a claim to the title of "Poet," Dorothy finds another vocation in writing recollections and journals—prose works, as Elizabeth Hardwick puts it, that "are not so much an ambition as a sort of offering" (p. 3) to William and the circle around him. This mode may be more psychologically amenable, but Dorothy also regards such writing as trivial, something "to fill a Lady's bookshelf" (*LDW,* 159), and she never entirely revokes the ambitions expressed by and recorded within her poetry. Her ardent protests to Lady Beaumont, notwithstanding, the very length and energy of her disclaimer imply interest in the question; indeed, despite her accounts of inhibition and poor skill, Dorothy continues to write and revise poetry into the early 1830s and rework the narrative of *George and Sarah Green.* Even when she contests her identity as "poet," she may resort to the medium itself: "why should *I* inscribe my name, / No poet I . . . ?" And responding to a request for "some Christmas verses" (*LY* 2:176), she begins *Irregular Verses,* "Ah Julia! ask a Christmas rhyme / Of *me* who in the golden time / Of careless, hopeful happy youth / Ne'er strove" beyond "simple prose" (1–4, 9). Though the tone and stressed first-person pronouns in both texts affect modest self-appraisal, the name still gets inscribed, and the rhyme—"irregular" though it is deemed—gets written, suggesting that Dorothy felt able to modulate modesty into a poet's modesty topos. The behavior of the poetry itself applies further contradictions to these acts of poetic self-denial. The syntax of the response to Julia, for instance, verges on (as if to test) a gentle imperative—the poet's soft request for encouragement by a potential reader. That tonal ambiguity is enhanced by the play of the rhymes: though Dorothy pairs the word *rhyme* with the fancies of a past *time,* and her present response to Julia reports prose—"To her I told in simple prose / Each girlish vision, as it rose / Before an active busy brain / That needed neither spur nor rein" (9–12)—the form of telling is still rhyme, a form, moreover, that reins the alternative, *prose,* into its pairings. Though Dorothy evades this curious contradiction as she elaborates her girlish visions and recalls the matrix of thwarted ambition, the fact that her medium throughout remains rhyme keeps the issue alive.

II

In *Women Writers and Poetic Identity,* Margaret Homans argues that the aspiration of writers such as Dorothy Wordsworth is checked by a sense of felt exclusion from the male authority of poetic tradition. Both William and Dorothy are undeniably affected by the force of this tradition, as we have seen, yet before we allow the evidence to assume interpretive priority for them or to support general arguments about poetry and gender, we need to attend to complex energies and vulnerabilities on both sides. Can Dorothy Wordsworth be read fully or exclusively with the premises of the masculine tradition? Is her situation only—or primarily—that of someone whose "dislocation from the phallogocentric community causes [her] great difficulty in creating a central sense of self in poetry," thus thwarting ability to imagine "other structures with which to replace that centrism, so completely does it occlude her view of the possibilities for writing"?[14] Homans is one of the first, and still one of the few, to offer an extensive reading of Dorothy Wordsworth's poetry, giving us welcome relief from the dubious but widely accepted view—renewed as recently as 1978—that her writing is not "in any sustained way interesting as literature, no matter how beguiling it is."[15] Even so, readers such as Homans, partly because of their polemical commitments, may miss the alternation in Dorothy's own writing between her self-baffling attempts to write William's kind of poetry and her tactful departures from, or equivocations about, some of the imaginative values associated with his agenda. Thus, if in the following pages I question some of Homans's readings, it is not to challenge the value of her interests, but to suggest how her concern to demonstrate the force of a culturally inherited paradigm has difficulty recognizing and speaking about forms of equivocation within that paradigm. In Dorothy Wordsworth's case, these emerge in quite subtle poetic registers—contrasting figures and different verbal emphases, paths not taken, situations filtered through alternative modes of imagination, or intertextual conversation with the language and informing circumstances of William's poetry.[16]

A brief example will focus the issue. The speaker of *Floating Island* recounts a vision granted by Nature's "Harmonious Powers": "Once did I see a slip of earth / (By throbbing waves long undermined) / Loosed from its hold; how, no one knew, / But all might see it float, obedient to the wind" (5–8).[17] This is "a latent figure for the dissolving self," Homans proposes: "The 'I' . . . casts loose . . . and becomes similarly diffuse" (p. 83). But is dissolution the sole alternative to egocentricity such as William's? The full range of the poem's pronouns suggests otherwise, for it does not so much diffuse first-person vision as extend it to the potential access of any "one," and then to "all." This expansion of individual subjectivity into visionary community is important, because this is the context within which the consequence already revealed parenthetically—the vision "undermined"—may be accepted and integrated into a larger vision of natural process. Dorothy's verse turns to include even her readers in this expanding community: "Perchance when you are wandering forth / Upon some vacant sunny day, / Without an object, hope, or fear, / Thither your eyes may turn—the Isle is passed away" (21–24).

The contrasts with William's visionary poetics are significant. When the speaker of *The Thorn* makes a similar proposal to his auditors, "perhaps when you are at the place / You something of her tale may trace," he means to seek validation for a private and deeply traumatic event and his discourse remains self-concentrated right up to the final lines: "I cannot tell how this may be, / But . . . this I know . . . That I have heard her cry."[18] If the speaker of *Floating Island* is not so obsessed, the tenuousness even of her cherished vision is a circumstance shared with many of William's speakers, and, in these terms as well, important divergences may be noted. William's tendency is to want to lodge perishable visions in shrines that may preserve them (typically lamenting their inadequacy); Dorothy avoids elegy by blending the passing of her vision into a suggestion that what has passed away from one may be renewed by others: the isle is not so much lost as invisible, "Buried beneath the glittering Lake." And unlike the corpse beneath the lake recalled in book 5 of *The Prelude*, Dorothy's burial promises renewed life: "Yet the lost fragments shall remain / To fertilise some other ground." The absence of an "I" in this process does not have to denote a "vanished self"—indeed the disappearance of "both subject and object"—that Homans reads (p. 85), but may signify Dorothy's deliberate turn from those modes of imagination, such as William's, which stake their value solely on self-inscription and individual privilege. The title in her Commonplace Book, *Floating Island at Hawkshead, An Incident in the schemes of Nature,* signals this plural value, for the terms with which it scans this event in nature, instead of writing a language of self, ponder a relationship that abides in a text outside and beyond the self. Dorothy is aware of William's habitual concern to read terms of relation between an impressive incident and a purposeful design, and her poem, like many of his, concerns such acts of interpretation. There is a difference, however, for she has no special investment in confirming her own privileged place in Nature's schemes or in promoting the authority of her poetic "I" as the designated reader of Nature's designs. Thus the "fragments" of her particular seeing do not challenge the poetic self with purposes obscured, projects uncompleted, or unities disintegrated, as they tend to in William's poetry—recall, for instance, the "Tree," "single Field," and "Pansy" that repeat a tale of absences in *Ode: Intimations of Immortality;* or the unfinished sheepfold in *Michael;* or the broken bowl and ruined cottage in book 1 of *The Excursion;* or *The Excursion* itself. The potency of Dorothy's fragments has precisely to do with their release from the burdens of self-reference that oppress the speakers of William's poems; though "lost" to her, they abide to "remain" as potential elements of "other ground," other visions, other envisioners.

These revisions of William's poetics are in part strategies of evasion, but they are not just that, for Dorothy's motions around William, as *Floating Island* suggests, yield oblique conversations with his favored imaginative values, especially his habitual turns and returns to moments of individual confrontation and solitary reflection. Nor are these always inscriptions of difference, for they often work to amplify ambivalences and dialogues already active in William's poetry. To read Dorothy's poems in secondary and defeated relation to William's is to neglect not only her reevaluations of his risky preoccupation with the power of self, but to neglect his own equivocations. It is suggested that William would insist on publishing *Floating Island* in his 1842 edition, as if he wanted to accommodate its poetics of democratic integration. For the alternative poetics of confrontation, appropriation, subjection, and mastery, as he clearly knows, require demonstrations of power and assertions of success. Indeed the hierarchical order of masculinist poetics demands that the mind emerge as lord and master, or acknowledge itself bewildered and engulphed—and William Wordsworth, at least, frequently writes in ways that show him uneasy about his place in this economy; he is not the sure, secure figure of logocentric performance and egocentric confidence abscribed to him in some feminist (and older masculinist) readings of Romanticism.[19]

If at times he writes nature as "feminine" in order to take advantage of traditional sexual politics, to imply, as Homans does, that this "feminization of nature" is the whole of his imagination (p. 13), and to privilege as a "usual tendency" those moments in William's poetry when he strives "to dominate in subject-object relations" (p. 23) is to attend to only half the evidence. For just as typically, and with a full range of investigation, this poet may represent male consciousness as passive, itself inscribed by voices of the "other": "the changeful earth . . . on my mind had stamped / The faces of the moving year" (*Prelude* 1.586–88); the "common face of Nature spake to me . . . impressed / Collateral objects and appearances, / Albeit lifeless then, and doomed to sleep / Until maturer seasons call them forth / To impregnate and to elevate the mind" (1.615–24). Here the self is not just passive but feminine, and imaged, implicitly, with the potential of female (re)productivity. At other times, of course, sensations of passivity are not so elevating, but inhabit dramas of a male self dominated by a nature not only of distinctly masculine aspect, but of supernatural potency—as in his recollection of that "huge cliff" that, "as if with voluntary power instinct . . . growing still in stature," loomed up against the boy who has stolen a shepherd's boat (1.372–426). That this trauma remains a trouble even to the mind of the adult poet is due in part, surely, to the apparent collaboration of nature perceived as female, and not at all passive: "—surely I was led by her—" he reflects. Even the domestic influence of such devoted feminine allies as Dorothy herself may erode the poet's sense of strong self and strong language, the very foundation of "masculinist" poetics. As William and she were both aware, his poems owed her numerous verbal and imaginative debts, and he reflects his quiet agitation over this in strategies that suppress, disguise, or deny her influence—usually by representing experiences they shared as solitary ones or, if not, acknowledging her influence with statements that seem as condescending as they are affectionate.

Dorothy's poetry does not deliberately exploit these issues, but she renews our attention to them by conceiving the alternatives her brother is intent to contain or reject altogether. The argumentative priorities of reading in relation to "masculinist poetics" not only obscure this view of William but, furthermore, apply a paradigm that fails to account for the wayward evidence of Dorothy's own poetry. Her speakers are not always, or even usually (for instance), thwarted or dominated by the passive, feminized nature of the masculine tradition: some poems show an enabling and energizing vision of nature as a world of female voices, female builders, female authority, female community: " 'Twas nature built this Hall of ours, / She shap'd the banks, she framed the bowers, . . . From her we hold our precious right. . . . She rules with mildest sway" (*A Holiday at Gwerndovennant, Irregular Stanzas*, 11–16). At other times, nature is not even feminine, but a masculine other whom she figuratively governs, as in *Address to a Child*, whose speaker domesticates a winter storm by casting it into the imagery of a rambunctious and merely mischievous boy: "He will suddenly stop in a cunning nook, / And ring a sharp 'larum;—but, if you should look, / There's nothing to see but a cushion of snow / Round as a pillow, and whiter than milk, / And softer than if it were covered with silk."[20] These two poems, and others, show Dorothy not written by external authority, but instead writing the self into the figure of a community—whether this is the domestic one of hearth and family, the social one of the village, or the world of natural events that shape and flow through these human communities.

III

If the clearest divergence of Dorothy's imagination from William's poetry is to be read in her repeated figurings of a community in which the self has a place, but not the privileged place, and in which shared lives and values shape and sustain individual desire, she is also aware of how dependent this ideal is: it assumes both the availability of a community as a home for the self and the accessibility of that community to the self as its ground of security and focus of activity. Two works from her first decade in Grasmere show the flux of her negotiations with this ideal, each revealing the degree to which its conditions are not given, but must be achieved and are not always achievable. *A Winter's Ramble in Grasmere's Vale* (about her first days there in early 1799)[21] recalls her desire to imagine and write herself into potentially supportive figures of community, playing this against certain alternative figures in William's Grasmere poetry. *George and Sarah Green* (1808), her most sustained literary work, continues this dialogue, crediting the achievements of community life in Grasmere's Vale, but also wrestling with the psychic pressures and vulnerabilities these values would contain. Both works engage tentative conversations with William's turns of imagination, for the very process of elaborating her ideal of community involves Dorothy with his antithetical figures of solitude or isolation.

William's greetings to Grasmere are informed by individual purpose. With epic invocations for nature's blessing on his chosen career, he claims his place, and reads the vale itself as a receptive field for his endeavors:

> What dwelling shall receive me, in what vale
> Shall be my harbour, underneath what grove
> Shall I take up my home, and what sweet stream
> Shall with its murmurs lull me to rest?
> The earth is all before me. . . . (1805 *Prelude* 1.11–15)

The allusion to the close of *Paradise Lost* ("The World was all before them, where to choose / Thir place of rest, and Providence thir guide" [12.646–47]) has long been noted; less often remarked is the deft conversion of Milton's *them* to a singular pronoun that rewrites Adam and Eve's community as self-absorption and solitary labor: "Enough that I am free, for months to come / May dedicate myself to chosen tasks" (33–34). This self-concentration is no less pronounced in *Home at Grasmere:* "On Nature's invitation do I come, / By reason sanctioned. Can the choice mislead / That made the calmest, fairest spot of earth, / With all its unappropriated good, / My own . . . ?"[22] He begs the question of entitlement, even more emphatically so in an earlier draft: "The unappropriated bliss hath found / An owner, and that owner I am he," the poet simply asserts; "The Lord of this enjoyment is on Earth / And in my breast. What wonder if I speak / With fervour, am exalted with the thought / Of my possessions, of my genuine wealth / inward and outward?" (B. 85–91). Writing himself as the center, he assumes all as his imaginative property, a resource ordained for his use. Even when he thinks of himself in community, one of "a happy Band" (D. 663), he is provoked to differentiate himself: "Why do *They* shine around me, whom I love? . . . Possessions have I that are solely mine, / Something within, which yet is shared by none" (679, 686–87). And while he acknowledges that Grasmere is "not mine only" (75), the way he elaborates his network of social relations typically returns community to the language of solitary self-sufficiency: "a genuine frame / Of many into one incorporate" (615–16); "A Whole without dependence or defect, / Made for itself and happy in itself, / Perfect Contentment, Unity entire" (149–51).

The image of community conceived in William's poetry is, moreover, a noticeably embattled one, shaded with vulnerability and defensiveness: it is a "Society" established in urgent retreat "Far from" that larger community of "the thronged World" and its "multitude / Human and brute" (D. 613–14, 621–22). What "must be looked for here," he insists, is "One family and one mansion; to themselves / Appropriate and divided from the world" (617–20). It is not surprising that such assertions (as readers of William's poetry know) habitually interact with darker moods: obsession with tales of loss and disunion, with grief unredeemed by art, with fears of "Ill neighbourhood," or at best, a place where the heart "may . . . Breathe in the air of fellow suffering / Dreadless" (356, 368–69). As the poet lectures his sister, "No, we are not alone; we do not stand . . . here misplaced and desolate" (427–28), the excess of instruction, as in *Nutting*, suggests that the attitudes imputed to the auditor also need assimilation in the self. William's poetry conveys the sense that its emphatic charter is framed more by desire than informed by the confidence of lived fact, that its repeated assertions and exhortations are laboring to contain anxiety and defend against adverse influence.

The figures of community in Dorothy's *Ramble* are not imposed by such rhetorical assertion, but emerge as the poem's speaker discovers their possibility. Dorothy unfolds that drama in part by testing her alignment with the modes of imagination that characterize her brother's Grasmere poetry. She evokes certain of his images and circumstances, but does so to discover alternatives—ones to be read in the way she recasts his habitual figures, recontextualizes key words, and substitutes for his speakers' fascinated solitary converse with alien presences her speaker's impulse to read signs promising community. Although she opens her poem in near alignment with William's early mood—"A Stranger, Grasmere, in thy Vale, / All faces then to me unknown . . ." (1–2)—her present perspective contains its figures of strangeness all in the past: casting the past self as archetypal "Stranger" marks that self, rather than the world that awaits its exploration, as strange. The sense of present familiarity is enhanced by the apostrophe, especially in the way it tropes on the convention itself. For if, as Jonathan Culler puts it, apostrophe derives its evocative power from countermanding a temporal sequence through which "something once present has been lost or attenuated," and depends for effect on the absence of the apostrophized object, Dorothy's pretext is different:[23] she does not summon an absent object, but addresses the Vale as a conversational presence at the moment of composition. Her second line enhances the effect of this rhetorical maneuver by implying that the community of faces is now known, familiar as the vale.

The chief movement of Dorothy's *Ramble* in fact dramatizes her emergence from her initial status of "Stranger" to her present identity as "Inmate of this vale." This is something she senses in retrospect that she needed to accomplish on her own: "I left my sole companion-friend / To wander out alone" (3–4)—wander, that is, without his mediations, exhortations, and expectations. That separation from William's experience—and William's urgencies—may be seen in the departure of her *Ramble* from his habitual poetic routes. In his "glad preamble," William does not so much "wander out alone" as look to wandering objects for portents and signs: "a wandering cloud" seems an apt "guide" (1.17–18); he reports that later he "made a choice / Of one sweet vale whither my steps should turn . . . nor did I fail / To add meanwhile assurance of some work / Of glory there forthwith to be begun" (81–88); he longs to "brace [him]self to some determined aim" (124), and though he reports obstacles, frustrations, and self-doubt, these are ultimately contained by a prospect in the mind that conceives a chart of action: "The road lies plain before me" (668). This aim also guides the course of *Home at Grasmere* toward the famous statement of vocation that William will later incorporate as the Prospectus for his epic, *The Recluse*.

Home at Grasmere will ultimately remain a fragment, as is the poem from which Dorothy adapts her *Ramble, Grasmere—A Fragment*, but William casts himself as beginning a major project, while Dorothy's exploration seems as tentative as her designation. If he proceeds home to Grasmere map in hand, she represents herself as not quite knowing how to read. Even with the vantage of retrospect, her drama seems less calculated in its motions of inquiry than do his egocentric assertions and self-absorbed musings, the very interrogatives of which seem presumptuous. Instead of lofty blank-verse declarations, she writes a humble ballad, whose oblique, generally unaccented rhymes and rhythmic irregularity yield a jauntily explorative poem, a ramble that converts the metaphoric amble of William's "preamble" into dramatic action. Her speaker does not stand and invoke, but sets out without agenda—either of poetic form or poetic project—on a walk to acquaint herself with her world:

> Lured by a little winding path,
> Quickly I left the public road,
> A smooth and tempting path it was
> By sheep and shepherds trod. (5–8)

The interplay of "wander," "lured," "winding," "tempting"—as well as the departure from the public road—wittily reimagines the prospect of error William would shun, by revealing it to be the insider's way through the vale, smoothed from familiar traffic and inviting for that very reason. When the poet of *Michael* exhorts his reader to leave "the public way" (1), his posture is one of superiority: he knows something about the "hidden valley" (8) we do not; an object unintelligible to us—one that we might even "pass by, / Might see and notice not" (15–16)—is the marker of a full story for him.[24]

This poetic habit of making the strange path a figure in a predetermined scheme—the chosen way in the "glad preamble" or the way known to the poet of *Michael*—suggests in its very schematism the risk of pathlessness. Indeed, the darkest moments of *The Prelude* tend to be marked by the way lost, or the path obscured. The master trope is given in the Conclusion as the poet refers to those passages of life and text when the stream of imagination was lost, "bewildered and engulphed" (13.178); but the figure is everywhere—from the boy who, having lost his path, "encourager and guide," confronts haunting vestiges of murder and execution (11.278 ff.), to the adult poet who can scarcely remember his course of life after the death of his mother: it "is a path / More difficult before me, and I fear / That in its broken windings we shall need / The chamois' sinews and the eagle's wing" (2.287–90), or who worries about the course of his poetry, "My drift hath scarcely / I fear been obvious" (5.290–91). Even a path seen can betray—such as the "beaten road" that seemed to promise the high sensation of crossing the Alps, only to lead William and his companions downward to "dejection" (6.491–524).

The voices William hears on his first walks through Grasmere bear these burdens, imposing private pressures of mission and misgivings of purpose:

> Bleak season was it, turbulent and bleak,
> When hitherward we journeyed, side by side . . .
>   The naked Trees,
> The icy brooks, as on we passed, appeared
> To question us. "Whence come ye? To what end?"
> They seemed to say. "What would ye?" said the shower,
> "Wild Wanderers, whither through my dark domain?"
> The sunbeam said, "Be happy." When this Vale
> We entered, bright and solemn was the sky
> That faced us. . . . (*Home at Grasmere*, D. 152–3; 165–71)

William's verb for the alien voice of nature, *appeared,* carries the contrary impulses of his imagination: it suggests an illusion of speaking nature about which he is softly ironic, but it also implies a felt challenge to himself an intruder. The excessive simplicity of the sunbeam's voice is the thinnest of retreats—so thin that the brightness of the sky seems part of its solemnity.

Dorothy's *Ramble* enters unmapped terrain with different expectations: not intent on a course, she does not risk failure, error, or betrayal. And thus released from William's urgencies, she can test his imaginative tendencies without being overwhelmed by them. This renegotiation of William's terrain can be seen in her study of a figure that recalls the focus of one of his more vexed poems of strange encounters—*The Thorn*—but with a difference:

> This pathway led me on
> Until I reach'd a stately Rock
> With velvet moss o'ergrown.

> With russet oak and tufts of fern
> Its top was richly garlanded;
> Its sides adorned with eglantine
> Bedropp'd with hips of glossy red. (10–16)

This image is critical in Margaret Homans's assessment of Dorothy's plight as poet, for it reveals "the adverse psychic effects" of an encounter with that "feminized or maternal nature" already written by William: she can only read his figures, which, "instead of provoking poetry . . . arrest it" (pp. 50–51); this rock, "gorgeous and domineering," blocks her "speaker's spiritual and physical progress" with his "experience of nature and of maternal origins," and so imposes "difficulties in sustaining poetic voice" (p. 53). Homans has *Nutting* in mind as the countertext, but the imagery of *The Thorn* seems not only more visible, but of different import for Dorothy's poetic adventures. Covered in "splendid moss . . . More rich its hues of various green, / Orange, and gold & glittering red" (29–32), Dorothy's rock palpably evokes that "fresh and lovely sight, / A beauteous heap, a hill of moss" on the mountain ridge of William's poem—a feminine figure whose "network" of "olive-green and scarlet bright" seems "woven" by "hand of lady fair" (35–46), in a spot perhaps haunted by an actual woman, Martha Ray. Yet the spectral shimmer of William's figure in Dorothy's image seems not to block her imagination; indeed she seems to be reading against it. For one, her pronouns are not feminine, but neuter: "Its top . . . Its sides . . . its hues." To Homans, these spell Dorothy's alienation from William's feminized nature—revealed as nature refuses her gender—but it is just as possible that her neuters mark an effort to explore a world free from ascriptions of gender and the social politics so implicated. The "stately Rock" has attracted her speaker's eye and stayed her course, but nothing in Dorothy's poem shows her "I" usurped or silenced by the force of William's prior figurings. When, in fact, Dorothy has her speaker apply a gender to nature, it is masculine: "Here winter keeps his revelry . . . Hath pleasure gardens of his own" (24, 28). This denizen, moreover, is of a different character from William's masculine figures of nature, those stern paternal presences he writes into various psychological agons: if there is a certain lordly demeanor in Dorothy's "Winter," it is not one implicated with exercises of dominance, but one instead equated with play and pleasure. Indeed, "Winter" inhabits the world of her poem as a kind of absent benefactor—a happy counterpart to the absent "companion friend" from whom Dorothy's speaker has consciously departed: unlike that poet (who is not quite at home in Grasmere), this one is able to evoke a sense of communal joy amid an adverse season.

That sense of community is reinforced by the way Dorothy uses her *Ramble* for a tacit restaging of the central confrontation reported by the speaker of *The Thorn*. William's dramatic experiment in representing the conversation of a mind under stress has a different imaginative project from her sentimental retrospect; even so, Dorothy's interest in evoking

William's extremes of circumstance and imagery is significant, for she means to test the possibility of community against the strain of increasing isolation that grips the discourse of *The Thorn*. Her engagement with William's figures suggests that she is not oblivious to the power of isolation against community; she does not repress his attraction to figures of isolated consciousness, but tries to work through them in order to imagine a more self-sustaining alternative. Like *The Thorn*, the *Ramble* concerns a strange encounter in a new world. Dorothy's speaker greets the Rock in terms expressing interest in and potential for relationship: "Thou wear'st," said I, "a splendid garb" (23)—a stark contrast to how the speaker of *The Thorn* reacts. Less savvy about figures, he believes the spot into which he has rambled is actually inhabited, or haunted, by "A woman in a scarlet cloak" (63), and he recoils from his discovery. The colors he reports suggest his agitation—though of nature, the tints seem super- or unnatural, repelling relationship even as they fixate attention—and the story of maternal grief he attaches in retrospect to this sight doubles this fixation. The encounter Dorothy stages involves more remediable psychic pressures. The Rock at once elicits the confession, "I griev'd when summer days were gone," but immediately turns that thought of grief into a prospect of recompense: "No more I'll grieve; for Winter here / Hath pleasure gardens of his own" (26–28). Her pastoral impulse is no naive delusion (she in fact revised a softer verb, *sigh*, to the more challenging *grieve*); Dorothy represents this as a conscious effort to take advantage of the resources at hand: "What need of flowers? The splendid moss / Is gayer than an April mead" (26–30). Her speaker then projects a voice welcoming her to a new community, as if in confirmation:

> —Beside that gay and lovely Rock
> There came with merry voice
> A foaming streamlet glancing by:
> It seemed to say 'Rejoice!'

The speaker of *The Thorn* hears only "Oh misery! oh misery!" (65)—a moan as bleak as "the stormy winter gale" (24) that carries it, and one that sends him running "Head-foremost" for cover (193–95). His incorporation of that voice of misery becomes the poem's last word. In *Home at Grasmere*, "icy brooks" challenge the wanderers, and William ends the poem less with a resolution of isolation into community than with the poet's translation of isolation into individual visionary purpose. The streamlet of the *Ramble* is given a more social character, its voice seeming to encourage a sensation of community that will sustain and nurture daily life, and Dorothy responds in the poetic present by repeating that voice as her own, using it to close her poem.

> My youthful wishes all fulfill'd,
> Wishes matured by thoughtful choice,

> I stood an Inmate of this vale,
> How could I but rejoice? (37–40)

The final identification of the self as "Inmate" is worth comment, for in William's poetry the word usually implies an untenable ideal—only the blessed infant babe is "An inmate of this *active* universe" (*Prelude* 2.266)—or it carries a dark reflex of that ideal: "inmate" as an exile from one world imprisoned in another. The image of the birds in *Home at Grasmere* as "inmates . . . Of Winter's household" bears some of this sense (D. 194–95), one carried forward into the poet's claim of refuge from the "jarring world," wherein all may be "Inmates not unworthy of their home" (D. 632, 647)—the litotes further weakening the claim. "Prisoner" is not listed in the 1901 *NED* as a synonym for "Inmate," but the sense is latent in the entry, "an occupant along with others,"[25] and is implied by William's usages above still more forcefully so in the "Intimations" Ode, wherein a feminized nature—a "homely Nurse" with "something of a Mother's mind"—does "all she can / To Make her Foster-child, her Inmate Man, / Forget the glories he hath known, / And that imperial palace whence he came" (79–84).[26] Dorothy uses "inmate" in quite another register—to suggest the condition of a familiar resident, even a mate or productive partner, "one of the family or company . . . Indweller, inhabitant" *(NED)*. That sense of belonging achieves a deft formal correlative in her closing rhymes—*voice / Rejoice / choice / rejoice*—which not only stress the responsive joining of her choice to rejoice with the voice she was willing to hear in her new world, but underscore that responsiveness with a community of sound and sense: as the most emphatic set of rhymes in the *Ramble,* they mark an emphatic evolution from the state implied by the initial, and oppositely marked pair of the poem: *unknown / alone.*

If the social sensibility animating this joyous welcome avoids the risks attending William's more solitary poetics, Dorothy's vision still engages other risks and other anxieties. Her representation of the self in community is no mere sentimentality, for she is fully alert both to advantages and liabilities, and, as in the case of William's deepest imaginings, her writing discloses the shadows involved in any complex engagement with an ideal.

Dorothy's initiating figure of the self as an inmate of a community is the enabling muse of *George and Sarah Green.* It is significant that she frames this narrative for and addresses it "to a Friend," for whatever her actual referent—her brother, Mrs. Clarkson, or Joanna Hutchinson—the rhetorical construction writes her reader into a general community of concern, a potential sympathizer who welcomes her narrative service. The "distressful events" concern one family of the Vale, the Greens. The parents, George and Sarah, went to the village of Langdale on the morning of March 19, 1808, to sell butter, attend a sale, and visit one of Sarah's daughters "in service" there. They perished the same night on their return home across a mountain: baffled by a snowstorm, George fell down a precipice; Sarah, not realizing he died instantly of a fractured skull, tried to assist him, but unable to reach him, climbed back, tripped, and also fell. Six children at home, the oldest age eleven, waited in vain for them to return; they concluded that their parents stayed in town to avoid the weather and would arrive Sunday. On Monday, after the oldest child asked a neighbor for a cloak so that she might retrace her parents' steps, an alarm went out for a community search, and the bodies were found two days later. A public subscription was organized at once—the *Narrative* helping to "promote this benevolent design" (17)—and the children were placed with various families in the parish, among them the Wordsworths, who accepted the daughter they were already boarding. The *Narrative* not only reports the immediate disaster, but offers images and recollections of the Green family, and details the aftermath of their tragedy—in particular, the community's concerted care for the orphans.

The community is Dorothy's theme, and her presence both as author of and figure in her *Narrative* is communal and social. Levin's remark that the "I" of Dorothy's journals is "a facilitating rather than a competitive presence . . . nonaggressive rather than ego-dominant" (p. 36) also describes the social integration basic to the idealism of the *Narrative*. Dorothy herself acts as an alternate (standing in for Mary Wordsworth) on the "Committee of six of the neighbouring Ladies . . . appointed to overlook the Children and manage the funds." And as chronicler of the whole for the larger community of sympathy focused on their cause, her attitude is generally one of self-effacement before the events at hand. Even when she speaks in the first person, she does so on behalf of all: "I am happy to tell you . . . our united efforts have been even more successful than we had dared to hope" (pp. 61, 62). Not only does Dorothy not engage those contests of self and other that occupy and preoccupy William, but her poetics of community, in being nonhierarchical, are materially threatened by exercises of egotism. It is, significantly, a spectacle of individual assertion against community that provokes her rare ire. One unnamed lady, "sullen and dissatisfied that she had not had the whole management of the concern," did not hesitate to show the committee early on how "galled" she was that the entire matter "had not been entrusted to her guidance." Her behavior in turns galls Dorothy, for her "true interest in the Children's well-doing" is less apparent than her pride of self (p. 72). This lady, Dorothy hotly reports, "had before (without any authority) herself (though only recently come into the country and having no connection with Grasmere) engaged to place all the Children with an old Woman in indigent circumstances, who was totally incapable of the charge" (p. 63).

Dorothy's obsession with "the irregular interference," "cabals and heart-burnings" of "Mrs. _____" (p. 63) underscores not only the modesty of her own assumption of any "authority," but its credit in her long-standing "connection with Grasmere." It is such connection, for instance, that authenticates the metaphor she summons to report how poverty impelled the

Greens to sell "a few peats in the summer, which they dug out of their own hearts' heart, their Land" (p. 49); the image of self-mutilation bears a knowledge of local values, what "passion" attaches to the legacy of a "few fields" and "ancient home" (p. 75). Knowing how this "Family were bound together by the same cares and exertions," Dorothy never doubts the children's value to their new families; indeed, she reports, "already one of them has proved that she maintained this spirit after she had quitted her Father's Roof" (p. 76). "I am convinced from observation that there is in the whole Family a peculiar tenderness of Nature . . . an uncommonly feeling heart" (p. 77)—a conviction that is not sentimental, but credited, Dorothy emphasizes, by first-person witness and acquaintance. The authority that enables her to speak of "how closely the bonds of family connection are held together in these retired vallies" (p. 65) also lies behind the tendency of her narrative to modulate the dispersal of the orphans among several households into a sense of the way the vale itself abides as foster parent and fosters a family bond; one of the girls was even accepted by descendants of George Green's first wife, not blood relatives.

Dorothy's intimacy with the textures that bind the community is not just self-authorizing, but gives her access to the several voices that she weaves into the texture of her narrative: "It is, when any unusual event happens, affecting to listen to the fireside talk in our Cottages; you then find how faithfully the inner histories of Families, their lesser and greater cares, their peculiar habits, and ways of life are recorded in the breasts of their Fellow-inhabitants of the Vale." The veracity of such records depends on the register of individual life in the life of the family, and in the life of the larger community of the Vale: as Dorothy goes on to remark, records in the hearts of "Fellow-inhabitants" can "much more faithfully . . . be preserved in remembrance" than "the lives of those, who have moved in higher stations and had numerous Friends in the busy world . . . even when their doings and sufferings have been watched for the express purpose of re-cording them in written narratives" (pp. 52–53). This last comparison is striking, for its implication that the truest record of self is familial, commu-nal, and social has the effect of recalling William's markedly opposite commitments—not only his dedicated self-regard for the express purpose of recording his doings and sufferings in written narrative, but also the way his manner of accounting for "distressful events" serves a set of interests quite different from those that guide the composition of her *Narrative*. William's focus is primarily a private one. In *The Prelude* of 1799, for example, having related a boyhood discovery of a drowning, he tells his "Friend" that he "might advert / To numerous accidents in flood or field, / Quarry or moor, or 'mid the winter snows, / Distresses and disasters, tragic facts / Of rural history," because all such events "impressed [his] mind / With images to which in following years / Far other feelings were attached" (1.279–86). William's record is individual rather than social; its primary information is for "my mind" and of my "feelings"; its deepest significance applies to the self, not others.

Dorothy's notably different orientation affects rhetorical strategy as well. Where William begins his various autobiographies at a high pitch of self-concern, she begins her *Narrative* with an address to her readers that writes them into the world of her story. This approach may recall William's prologue to *Michael*, in which the poet exhorts us to leave the public way and discover the valley hidden behind an apparently forbidding facade; but Dorothy's tone is different. She assumes community rather than supposes an adversarial reader, and invites us in: "You remember a single Cottage at the foot of Blentern Gill—it is the only dwelling on the Western Side of the upper reaches of the Vale of Easedale, and close under the mountain; a little stream runs over rocks and stones beside the garden wall, after tumbling down the crags: I am sure you recollect the spot: if not, you remember George and Sarah Green who dwelt there" (p. 43). "I" enters her prose only as a voice of encouragement and assurance, in solidarity with a most generously construed "you," whose powers of recollection are solicited as a prelude to sympathy. The "minute detail of all the particulars" to which she was asked to attend assists this purpose, for her introduction does not treat these details as alien signs needing interpretation, as does the prologue to *Michael;* she produces them as markers for a memory she assumes is efficacious. She even supplies her own point of reference: the Greens were last seen "at the top of Blea Crag above Easedale Tarn, that very spot where I myself had sate down six years ago, unable to see a yard before me, or to go a step further over the Crags. . . . A mist came on . . . and I wandered long, not knowing whither. When at last the mist cleared away I found myself at the edge of the Precipice, and trembled at the Gulph below." It is this memory, she says, that made her think that even though "The neighbourhood of this Precipice had been searched," she "could not help believing that George and Sarah Green were lying somewhere thereabouts" (pp. 45–46)—as indeed they were.

This quality of sympathetic meditation also checks Dorothy's inclination to judge events, assess liability, or offer instruction. An impulse is there—"perhaps formerly it might be said, and with truth, the Woman had better been at home" (p. 50)—but equally strong is Dorothy's effort to restrain judgment with sympathy, and to evoke that sympathy in her readers with a question requiring our animation of the particulars of her narrative: "who shall assert that this same spirit which led [Sarah] to come at times among her Neighbours as an equal, seeking like them society and pleasure, that this spirit did not assist greatly in preserving her in chearful independance [sic] of mind through the many hardships and privations of extreme poverty?" (p. 50).[27] Judgment is applied only against those who accept orphans merely to gain payment from the parish and access to cheap labor, with neither love nor care for the welfare of such children, Dorothy laments. It is primarily to avoid such a fate for the Greens that all, "From the moment we heard that their Parents were lost . . . anxiously framed plans for raising a sum of money for the purpose of assisting the Parish in placing them with respectable Families; and to give them a little school-learning" (p. 61).

This commitment to communal effort and its informing values appears in the way Dorothy's penultimate paragraph misquotes, perhaps deliberately, a passage from William's as-yet-unpublished story of Margaret's ruined cottage:

> I may say with the Pedlar in the "Recluse"
> > "I feel
> > > The story linger in my heart, my memory
> > > Clings to this poor Woman and her Family,"
> and I fear I have spun out my narrative to a tedious length. I cannot give *you* the same feelings that *I* have of them as neighbours and fellow-inhabitants of this Vale; therefore what is in my mind a full and living picture will be to you but a feeble sketch. (p. 86)

The lines she has in mind are addressed by the Pedlar to the poem's Author, and are about the effect of his last visit with Margaret, by then clearly deranged and hopeless. Unlike Dorothy, the Pedlar, authorized by powerful feeling, confesses no lack of confidence in the power of his narrative:

> > > > It would have grieved
> > > Your very heart to see her. Sir, I feel
> > > The story linger in my heart. I fear
> > > 'Tis long and tedious, but my script clings
> > > To that poor woman: so familiarly
> > > Do I perceive her manner, and her look
> > > And presence, and so deeply do I feel
> > > Her goodness, that, not seldom, in my walks
> > > A momentary trance comes over me;
> > > And to myself I seem to muse on one
> > > By sorrow laid asleep or borne away. . . . (MS. D. 361–71)[28]

As readers often remark, the Pedlar's concern seems equally divided between care for Margaret and care for his own equanimity. Both in his actions at the time and in subsequent narrative action, he works to contain the pressure of disturbing emotion: having left Margaret "With the best hope and comfort I could give," he says he was perplexed only that, having thanked him "for his will," she seemed not to thank him for the hope so tendered (389–92). He himself managed by modulating sympathetic grief into a compensatory fantasy of Margaret consoled by forces beyond nature and human life. Such motions, as students of *The Excursion* know, are crucial and controversial in assessments of the poem's chief didactic spokesman, for from De Quincey on, many note the contradiction Wordsworth has introduced between the Pedlar's expressions of sympathy and his manner of action, which is one of detachment, retreat, even abandonment. The modest withdrawal from full identity with this figure given by Dorothy's "I may say" is suggestive, for the theme of her *Narrative* as a whole more emphatically refuses his mode of behavior. The involvement of

Grasmere—the men who organize to search for the bodies and the women who organize to assist the orphans—manifestly contrasts the wanderer's departure. That difference is underscored by Dorothy's revision of William's verse: her version ("My *memory* / Clings to *this* poor Woman and her family") alters the Pedlar's line ("my *spirit* clings / To *that* poor woman") to convey the ethical attachment of someone still in the community. The Pedlar's *that* issues from wandering spirit that identifies itself with no community and clings to Margaret only at an imaginative distance; Dorothy's *this* expresses a sense of continuing relationship and responsibility, even though her poor woman, like the Pedlar's, is dead at the time of the narration.

Dorothy's alternative to the Pedlar's self-concern can also be read in her care for the "family" victimized by these events. The Pedlar may speak of a "bond / Of brotherhood . . . broken" by Margaret's death—she never failed, he says, to give "A daughter's welcome . . . And I loved her / As my own child" (D. 81–85, 94–96)—but his metaphors describe relations he has honored more in absence than in presence. Dorothy, by contrast, has not only participated in a united effort to secure the material welfare of the orphans, but prays that they may remember "the awful end of their Parents . . . in such a manner as to implant in their hearts a reverence and sorrow for them that may purify their thoughts and make them wiser and better" (pp. 86–87). These terms write a different economy from the one that impels the actual and imaginative distance sought by William's Pedlar from his "daughter," for they are enabled and empowered by community responsibility. William's Pedlar, a solitary wanderer whose livelihood and composure depend on remaining unfixed and uninvolved in any one particular set of events, is concerned to restrict grief, banish sorrow, and suppress even the elegiac remnants that "steal upon the meditative mind." In one version he counsels his listener in the "purposes of wisdom" thus: "enough to sorrow have you given . . . Be wise and chearful" (D. 508–10); and as a model, he cites his own psychological processes: through meditation, he found that all "the uneasy thoughts which filled my mind, . . . what we feel of sorrow and despair / From ruin and from change, and all the grief / That passing shows of being leave behind, / Appeared an idle dream that could not live" (D. 519–23). Dorothy imagines otherwise for the children who survive to remember their parents' death and their subsequent dislocation from the only home they had known: not only is there is no question that sorrow will remain, but she is confident that the children's acceptance of it will ultimately make them wiser and better. The mediation and sympathy of the community is integral to this faith. At the funeral, "Many tears were shed by persons who had known little of the Deceased; and all the people who were gathered together appeared to be united in one general feeling of sympathy for the helpless condition of the Orphans" (pp. 56–57). Isolated from community, William's Pedlar and his auditor (the Author of the poem) are committed to a different plot, one in which sorrow has to be suppressed or mediated into something else in order for

wisdom to be achieved. Though the Author is at first a reluctant student—
overcome by "a brother's love" and "the impotence of grief" (D. 499–500)—
William fortifies him with the Pedlar's instruction. Another manuscript
shows him busily sketching out various curricula: "The trouble . . . sent
into my thought / Was sweet, I looked and looked again, & to myself / I
seemed a better and wiser man"; "for the tale which you have told I think / I
am a better and a wiser man."[29] Dorothy prays for the Greens' children to
become purer, wiser, and better through sorrow; William's figures, even
with the mediation of a tale, treat sorrow as an impure excess that needs to
be curtailed if one is to think himself wiser and better.

Dorothy's sensitivity to a community of sorrow has its risks, however, and
she suggests these in her peripheral obsession with figures of isolation and
abandonment. Such attitudes are subordinate in the *Narrative* proper, but
they are as clearly marked in their fixations as are the Pedlar's in his
compulsion to escape. One early indication is the peculiar manner in which
she writes herself across the Greens' path—namely, her report of "that very
spot" where they disappeared. This account does more than corroborate
their confusion; it obliquely associates her "dreadful situation" there with
her wandering in separation from the family member to whom she is
closest: "I left W. at Stikell Tarn. A mist came on after I had parted with
him, and I wandered long, not knowing whither. When at last the mist
cleared away I found myself at the edge of the Precipice, and trembled at
the Gulph below, which appeared immeasurable." Recalling a separation
from William, Dorothy also recalls a world of mist and danger that seems
internal as well as external, psychological as well as natural, threatening
self-destruction with an intensity hardly dispelled by the matter-of-fact
conclusion she applies: "Happily I had some hours of daylight before me,
and after a laborious walk I arrived home in the evening" (pp. 45–46). The
Greens' fate was otherwise, but Dorothy's spectral layering of their loss of
home and family over her terror away from home and William, once
revealed, remains a potential point of reference throughout the course of
her narrative, casting a shadowy map of self-interest across the Greens'
tragedy and its terms of resolution.

That plane of interest remains suppressed until the *Narrative*'s close, but
it reappears there, again in the imagination of alternative fates, alternative
circumstances: "There is at least this consolation, that the Father and
Mother have been preserved by their untimely end from that dependence
which they dreaded. . . . and perhaps, after the Land had been sold, the
happy chearfulness of George and Sarah Green might have forsaken them,
and their latter days have been tedious and melancholy" (p. 87). This is
Dorothy's last sentence: a dark fantasy of dependency, of being a burden,
of living out one's life in poverty and bereft of the history preserved in the
Land. Not only is it a stark departure from her optimistic and idealizing
story of life in the Grasmere community, but it is sufficiently odd to suggest
the pressure of private authorial concerns in this story of a family scattered.

One wonders to what degree Dorothy's own experience—first as an orphaned child fearing the prospect of being "destitute of the means of
supporting myself" (*LDW,* 11), and then as an adult feeling abandoned by
her brother's marriage—haunts about the shape of this conclusion. "How
we are squandered abroad!" she laments as her brothers return to school
and John sails for Barbados.[30] She imagines, alternatively, that the "Day of
my Felicity" will be "the Day in which I am once more to find a Home under
the same Roof with my Brother" (16 June 1793; *EY,* 93); "the idea of a
home" is basic to her happiness (2–3 Sept. 1795; *EY,* 146). It seems clear
enough that her misfortune in being orphaned as a child and a fear of
being left without family, or a burden to others, are felt pressures in the
stiffly formal letter she writes to her brother Richard, in which she attempts
to come to terms with William's impending marriage and the disruption it
bodes (10 June 1802; *LDW,* 51–52). Though she claims full confidence in
"the affection of my Brothers and their regard for my happiness" and
knows she "shall continue to live with my Brother William," she is concerned not to strain affection with a necessary dependence: William, "having nothing to spare nor being likely to have, at least for many years, I am
obliged (I need not say how much he regrets this necessity) to set him aside,
and I will consider myself as boarding through my whole life with an
indifferent person"—a resolve, in effect, to convert her status as intimate
inmate of a household into a social and psychological correlative of her
brother's intimation of man as the "inmate" of a world to which he does not
originally or properly belong. Dorothy wants only to be minimally comfortable without dependence: she asks Richard to arrange a per annum so that
she "should have something to spare to exercise my better feelings in
relieving the necessities of others," and she insists that it is "absolutely
necessary, to give it any effect," that her stipend "be independent of accidents of death or any other sort that may befal [sic] you or any of my
Brothers, its principal object being to make me tranquil in my mind with
respect to my future life. . . . I should be very loth to be oppressive to you,
or any of my Brothers, or to draw upon you for more than you could
spare."

The bleak conclusion of Dorothy's *Narrative* not only bears the imprint of
these concerns, but is made bleaker yet by notes she added to it. One attests
to the literal truth of her "account of the stock of provisions in the House at
the time of [the Greens'] Death," remarking that this list is really one of
absences, "all the things that were wanting even to the ordinary supply of a
poor house" (p. 88). These absences impinge in the next paragraph of the
note, which details the sale of the "household goods" and the prices they
fetched—repeating the distribution of the children to new families, but
with marketplace values replacing the bonds of connection. What seems to
play in Dorothy's mind as she writes these addenda and supplements are
figures of dissolution, dispersal, and the reduction of a shared life to a
mere list of properties. The bleakness of these details is extended by a

series of dreadful associations Dorothy feels compelled to append, and which, in ending her manuscript, acquire the quality of a summary gloss on the *Narrative* itself.

The first is a report of the frantic reaction of the daughter with whom Sarah Green had been visiting before her death: in her "distraction" over the Greens' disappearance, "she thought that *she* should surely find them" and had to be restrained from going to the mountains to look for them herself (p. 90). This distraction operates as a bond of connection in Dorothy's imagination to the story of Mary Watson, who expressed the same poignant confidence in her ability to find a son who had drowned in the local lake six years before. "I never shall forget the agony of her face" (p. 90), Dorothy says, acknowledging in effect the order of memory she hopes the orphans will be spared, for this unforgettable agony not only lacks meliorating thoughts, but focuses on the reciprocal tragedy, a mother bereft of a child. This tragedy recalls a further connection to "the end of Mary Watson herself . . . murdered a few years ago in her own cottage by a poor Maniac, [another] Son, with whom she had lived fearlessly though everyone in the vale had had apprehensions for her." And if this inward collapse of the family were not enough, Dorothy's last sentence reports that the estate "fell to a grandson" who "had been sent to Liverpool to learn a trade, came home a dashing fellow, spent all his property—took to dishonest practices, and [like William's Luke] is now under sentence of transportation" (p. 91). In assessing these peculiar addenda, Margaret Homans proposes that the "arbitrary cruelty inflicted on Mary Watson by circumstances is a corrective" to the too "positively framed" and "saccharine ending with which Dorothy felt compelled to close" the narrative proper (pp. 59–60). These notes are correctives, however, only if one finds that ending saccharine. The *Narrative* has meliorating motions, to be sure, but its final words suggest that Dorothy's addenda may fill out, rather than counter, something definitely not saccharine in her final sentence, which broods over circumstances in which "the happy chearfulness of George and Sarah Green might have forsaken them, and their latter days have been tedious and melancholy." Though this is only a fantasy alternative that Dorothy is glad they have been spared, her manuscript in effect creates it for them, first in the note that details the breakup of their estate, and then more starkly, in the story of the complete disintegration of Mary Watson's family and estate.

If William's egocentric poetics depend on asserting self over circumstance or, alternately, confronting the impotence of self in the face of circumstance, Dorothy's poetics of community generate their own countertexts and spectres of defeat. Having written the *Narrative* in service to the community, and having stressed throughout the sustaining and restorative identification of individual lives with the ongoing life of the vale, Dorothy is captured by thoughts and recollections that compete with and threaten to subvert the tradition of writing in which she hoped to locate herself. These impulses suggest that the "otherness" of Dorothy Wordsworth's imagination may not so much be the imperatives of an alienating masculine tradition, as an "otherness" in the mind itself, which inevitably, and perhaps naturally, contests its own most cherished compositions.

NOTES

To avoid the condescending and implicitly sexist practice of referring to "Dorothy" among the company "Wordsworth," "Coleridge," and "De Quincey," and to avoid the stylistic encumberment of "Dorothy Wordsworth" and "William Wordsworth," I shall at times refer only to "Dorothy" and "William."

1. Woolf, "Dorothy Wordsworth," *The Second Common Reader* (1932); rpt. *Collected Essays* (London: Hogarth, 1967), 3:199–206. For general dismissals of Dorothy Wordsworth as writer, see Richard Fadem, who not only rules out the possibility of any legitimate interest, but claims that by "inflating Dorothy's stature as a critic and writer, we in fact do her a disservice" ("Dorothy Wordsworth: A View from 'Tintern Abbey,'" *TWC* 9 [1978], p. 17); for specific dismissals of her poetic ability see: Ernest De Selincourt, *Dorothy Wordworth: A Biography* (Oxford: Clarendon Press, 1933), p. 388; Elizabeth Hardwick, "Amateurs: Dorothy Wordsworth & Jane Carlyle," *NYRB* 19, no. 9 (30 Nov. 1972): 3–4; Rachel Mayer Brownstein, "The Private Life," *MLQ* 34 (1971): 48–63; Pamela Woof, "Dorothy Wordsworth, Writer," *TWC* 17 (1986): 95–110.

2. Margaret Homans, *Women Writers and Poetic Identity: Dorothy Wordsworth, Emily Brontë, and Emily Dickinson* (Princeton: Princeton University Press, 1980), p. 3. Homans gives an account of this tradition in her first chapter and of its effect on Dorothy Wordsworth in her second. A still more recent study by Susan M. Levin (*Dorothy Wordsworth and Romanticism* [New Brunswick: Rutgers University Press, 1987]) offers a reading of Dorothy Wordsworth's poetry that finds her less disabled by the "masculine tradition" and more fully engaged in a tradition of "feminine romanticism." My work is indebted to these two strong interpretations and the questions they raise.

3. In addition to the studies of Homans and Levin, cited in n. 2 above, see Irene Taylor and Gina Luria, "Gender and Genre: Women in British Romantic Literature," *What Manner of Woman: Essays on English and American Life and Literature*, ed. Marlene Springer (New York: New York University Press, 1977), pp. 98–123, and Anne K. Mellor, "Teaching Wordsworth and Women," *Approaches to Teaching Wordsworth's Poetry*, ed. Spencer Hall with Jonathan Ramsey (New York: Modern Language Assocation of America, 1986), pp. 142–46.

4. *Letters of Dorothy Wordsworth*, ed. Alan G. Hill (Oxford: Oxford University Press, 1981), p. 113; hereafter cited *LDW* with page number.

5. *George & Sarah Green: A Narrative, By Dorothy Wordsworth*, ed. with a preface by E. De Selincourt (Oxford: Clarendon Press, 1936), p. 39. Hereafter, references to page numbers are given parenthetically in my text.

6. *Journals of Dorothy Wordsworth*, 2nd ed., ed. Mary Moorman (Oxford: Oxford University Press, 1971); Grasmere Journal is cited GJ. My quotations, in order, are from 20 Feb. 1802 (GJ, 93), 6 March 1802 (GJ, 98), 4 May 1802 (GJ, 120). There are numerous other examples of this incorporation: "Writing all the morning for William" (17 Dec. 1800; GJ, 54); "still at work at the Pedlar, altering and refitting. . . . William left me at work altering some passages of the Pedlar. . . . I worked hard, got the backs pasted the writing finished, and all quite trim" (13–14 Feb. 1802;

GJ, 90); "I wrote the 2nd prologue to Peter Bell. . . . After dinner I wrote the 1st Prologue" (21 Feb. 1802; GJ, 93); "I stitched up the Pedlar—wrote out Ruth" (7 Mar. 1802; GJ, 98).

7. 8 March 1802 (GJ, 104).

8. 20 April 1806 (*LDW*, 75–77).

9. For example, Hardwick's unquestioned formalist and essentialist standards lead her to deem the poems "not good": Dorothy "did not understand meter and wasn't, in any case, really happy with formal constructions. Most of all she lacked generalizing power" and ability to articulate "the meaning of her life" (p. 3). Brownstein repeats this second point: finding a crucial liability in Dorothy's failure to "say how she felt, how a poet must feel, and what she thought," she invokes an unexamined idea of "a poet" to discredit Dorothy's divergent practices—the "absence of interpretation or explanation, her failure to connect, explicitly, her own feelings with what she observes and finds important enough to write down" (p. 51). Woof points to a tendency to "helpless and passive" responses to visual stimuli to conclude that Dorothy's sense of poor poetic worth is the "correct" judgment (p. 101). Only Levin (p. 66) suggests that Dorothy's terms of self-evaluation reflect assumptions about literary form that are open to debate; she reminds us, in fact, that Dorothy's "jumbled" modes of literary expression anticipate the celebrated experimentalism of certain post-Romantic male writers (p. 108).

10. *Irregular Verses* (1827), 56–59; references are to line numbers. Unless otherwise indicated, my texts for the poems follow Levin, *The Collected Poems of Dorothy Wordsworth*, published as Appendix One of *Dorothy Wordsworth and Romanticism*, cited in n. 2 above.

11. For a discussion of the poem in these terms, see Homans, pp. 67–69. It should be noted, however, that there is a second mother in this poem, the adult Jane Pollard Marshall, whose assumed responsiveness to Dorothy's verses counters the maternal smile that discourages childhood ambitions: the poet assures her auditor (Jane's daughter, Julia Marshall) that if this present "strain, / Breathed from the depth of years gone by, / Should touch her Mother's heart with tender pain, / Or call a tear into her loving eye, / She will not check the tear or still the rising sigh" (96–100), but will value the emotions stirred by these verses—merely "irregular" and "poor memorial" though they be. Dorothy herself becomes an encouraging literary mother to Julia's own poetic efforts: see *The Letters of William and Dorothy Wordsworth: The Later Years, Part 2: 1829–1834*, ed. Ernest de Selincourt; 2nd ed., ed. Alan G. Hill (Oxford: Clarendon Press, 1979), pp. 332, 349, 424. Cited hereafter *LY* 2, with page number.

12. Book 1.59–63 (1805). Quotations follow *The Prelude: 1799, 1805, 1850*, ed. Jonathan Wordsworth, M. H. Abrams, and Stephen Gill (New York: Norton, 1979). All citations, by book and line, are to the text of 1805, unless otherwise indicated.

13. Books 3.36–37 and 9.21–24, respectively. Quotations follow John Milton, *Complete Poems and Major Prose*, ed. Merritt Y. Hughes (New York: Odyssey, 1957). Citations are given by book and line. The particular context in which Dorothy summons the phrase "the numbers came," aided by her couplet form, also suggests a second, half-bitter allusion to the brief account of poetic vocation Pope renders in *An Epistle from Mr. Pope, To Dr. Arbuthnot:* "Why did I write? what sin to me unknown / Dipt me in Ink, my Parents', or my own? / As yet a Child, nor yet a Fool to Fame, / I lisp'd in Numbers, for the Numbers came. / I left no Calling for this idle trade, / No Duty broke, no Father dis-obey'd" (125–30). Dorothy's account of maternal discouragement offers a pointed contrast to the cooperation of Pope's father with (indeed his relentless insistence on) his son's writing poetry: for a relevant anecdote, see vol. 6, p. 376 of *The Twickenham Edition of the Poems of Alexander Pope*, 7 vols., ed. John Butt (London: Methuen, 1939); my quotation follows this edition. I am grateful to the Press's reader for calling my attention to this text as another possible reference for Dorothy's phrase.

14. Homans, *Women Writers*, p. 36; a local version is Woof's view that "Dorothy progressively absorbed rather than challenged Wordsworth's critical stance" (p. 97).

15. Fadem, p. 78. Equating the fictions of the "Sister" in William's poetry (especially "Tintern Abbey") with the historical Dorothy Wordsworth, Fadem claims that "Dorothy was spontaneous, intuitive, emotional" (p. 17), and "like any number of Wordsworth's characters who are oracularly banal . . . not thoughtful" (pp. 24, 26); "at twenty-six she is what William was at seven. She is splendid but rudimentary and incomplete. . . . she has not become an adult" (p. 28). One could not guess from his account that Dorothy Wordsworth had an inner life, read (if eclectically) German, Italian, and English literature, was fluent in French, valued as an intelligent companion by her brother, De Quincey, and Coleridge (among others), and successfully managed several households. Fadem's attitude is perpetuated even by the Modern Language Association: *The English Romantic Poets: A Review of Research and Criticism* (New York: MLA, 1985) offers no review of the critical and scholarly work on Dorothy Wordsworth (nor on any of the *publishing* women poets of the age).

16. Homans's more recent study, *Bearing the Word: Language and Female Experience in Nineteenth-Century Women's Writing* (Chicago: University of Chicago Press, 1986), revises the thesis of her first; here she argues that passages of Dorothy's journals operate as oppositional texts to William's "apocalyptic tendencies": by "privileg[ing] the literal meaning inherent in appearances over symbolism that requires absent signification" (p. 59), Dorothy emphasizes, in ways that William's transcendental and symbolizing imagination subverts, "the lack of distance between object and meaning, signifier and referent" (p. 62). This is a provocative argument but, like its predecessor, may polarize William and Dorothy too exclusively, for many of the passages Homans summons in evidence show Dorothy's imagination also engaged in that "subordination of nature to meaning" attributed only to William (p. 58).

17. Levin reports that this poem "was probably written in the late 1820s" (p. 208) and prints the version of the Commonplace Book. I use the version published by William in *Poems, Chiefly of Early and Late Years* (1842); my text follows *The Poetical Works of William Wordsworth*, ed. Ernest de Selincourt and Helen Darbishire (Oxford: Clarendon Press, 1956), *Miscellaneous Poems*, (vol. 4, pp. 162–63), this edition is cited hereafter *PW*.

18. Quotations of *The Thorn* follow *Wordsworth & Coleridge: Lyrical Ballads, The text of the 1798 edition with the additional 1800 poems and the Prefaces*, ed. R. L. Brett and A. R. Jones (1965; London: Methuen, 1971).

19. Homans and Levin are intelligent sponsors of the more recent procedures to which I refer. Although Levin remarks briefly that what she calls "Dorothy's 'feminine consciousness' inheres in the writing of her male contemporaries" (p. 7), her chief concern is to differentiate and polarize in relation to issues of gender. Thus, like Homans, she stresses the oppositional relation of Dorothy's writing to William's modes of imagination and self-definition and to the "male romanticism" these are taken to exemplify: "Dorothy's work represents the suspension of male romanticism as well as the suspension of its literary forms. . . . the quality and emphases of [her] romanticism are as different from those of the men around her as is her writing from theirs" (pp. 7–8).

20. This poem was written in 1806 and published in William's *Poems* of 1815 as *Address to a Child, During a Boisterous Winter Evening. By a female Friend of the Author* and placed with "Poems Referring to the Period of Childhood"; my quotation follows that text as given in *PW* vol. 1, pp. 229–30.

21. Appearing in Dorothy's Commonplace Book (1826–32) under the title *A Winter's Ramble in Grasmere's Vale*, this is a slightly revised, independent version of the last ten stanzas of *Grasmere—A Fragment*, a twenty-two stanza poem probably written some time during or after 1805. Levin does not date *A Fragment* beyond stating that it is "an early composition" (p. 187); in volume 8 of *The Poetical Works of William Wordsworth* (London: Macmillan, 1896) William Knight refers to a "MS. of

1805" from which he prints his text of the poem and ascribes a date (p. 259). This is the copy Catherine Clarkson made in 1805 of Dorothy's *Recollections of a Tour made in Scotland* in which she also transcribed *A Fragment* and four other poems, three of which certainly date from that decade. I treat the ten-stanza version only because it suits my immediate subject, the Wordsworths' initial explorations of the vale. *A Fragment* is a revealing origin: in that context, the retrospective *Ramble* stanzas are preceded by ten present-tense stanzas celebrating the peace of the vale and the security of Dove Cottage (also made into an independent poem in the Commonplace Book), then two stanzas recalling the winter's day when the Cottage was first beheld. My quotations are based on the last ten stanzas of Levin's edition of *A Fragment,* incorporating the Commonplace Book variants. For a report on texts and dates, see Levin, pp. 176–77, 187–88.

22. *Home at Grasmere. Part First, Book First of The Recluse,* ed. Beth Darlington (Ithaca: Cornell University Press, 1977): MS. D. 71–75. Citations hereafter are given parenthetically, noting manuscript and line.

23. Culler, "Apostrophe," *Diacritics* 7, no. 4 (Dec. 1977), p. 67.

24. Quotations of *Michael* follow Brett and Jones, cited in note 18 above.

25. Relevant to the sense of estrangement or alienation in William's use of *inmate,* the 1901 *NED* gives the following definitions: "In relation to other persons: One who is the mate or associate of another or others in a house. In early use, one admitted for a consideration [i.e., fee] to reside in a house occupied or rented by another. . . . In the 16th and 17th c. there were stringent by-laws against the harbouring of poor persons as 'inmates,' subtenants or lodgers, a practice which tended to increase the number of paupers locally chargeable; . . . Sometimes, One not originally or properly belonging to the place where he dwells; a foreigner, stranger" (5:307).

26. My text follows *Poems, in Two Volumes and Other Poems, 1800–1807 by William Wordsworth,* ed. Jared Curtis (Ithaca: Cornell University Press, 1983) lines 79–84, p. 273.

27. For a different view, see Levin, who reads Dorothy's affirmation of "a certain mode of social assistance" as qualified by a palpable narrative intent to show a "wicked mother and the destructive world of nature conspiring to bring about unforgettable loss and devastation" (pp. 41–52).

28. MS. D (1799); I follow the "reading text" in *The Ruined Cottage and The Pedlar,* ed. James Butler (Ithaca: Cornell University Press, 1979). Citations are to manuscript and line.

29. B. 43v and 45r respectively. See Butler's edition, pp. 256–59.

30. 27 Jan. 1788; *The Letters of William and Dorothy Wordsworth: The Early Years 1787–1805,* ed. Ernest de Selincourt; 2nd rev. ed., ed. Chester Shaver (Oxford: Clarendon Press, 1967), p. 16; cited hereafter *EY* with page number. Dorothy's exclamation is an echo of *Merchant of Venice* (1.3.21): with Antonio's "ventures . . . squandered abroad," Shylock imagines "his means are in supposition"; the editors cite the echo, noting this is a "favourite phrase" of Dorothy's (*EY,* 26; see also 25 Jan. 1790). Levin reads such pressures of imagination in the Grasmere Journal as well, where Dorothy's attention to "people affected by the economic pressures of the time, dislocated from the land . . . become[s] a means of focusing ideas about communal charity, about her own center at Grasmere and the possible disintegration of her chosen manner of life. For even as the . . . journals describe community, unity, and coherence, they also detail breakdown and discontinuity" (p. 21; see also pp. 38–41).

"ON NEEDLE-WORK"

PROTEST AND CONTRADICTION IN MARY LAMB'S ESSAY

Jane Aaron

On 22 September 1796 Mary Lamb, in a sudden outbreak of violent mania, brought about the death of her mother. According to a contemporary newspaper account of the incident, while preparing a meal that day

> the young lady seized a case knife laying on the table, and in a menacing manner pursued a little girl, her apprentice, round the room; on the eager calls of her helpless infirm mother to forbear, she renounced her first object, and with loud shrieks approached her parent. The child by her cries quickly brought up the landlord of the house, but too late—the dreadful scene presented to him the mother lifeless, pierced to the heart, on a chair, her daughter yet wildly standing over her with the fatal knife.

In concluding its report of the coroner's verdict, *"Lunacy,"* the newspaper added: "It seems the young Lady had been once before, in her earlier years, deranged, from the harassing fatigues of too much business."[1]

In 1796 Mary Lamb was working as a self-employed mantua-maker, a needlewoman making ladies' cloaks. In 1815, having been spared permanent confinement as a criminal lunatic by the intervention of her brother Charles, she published, under the pseudonym "Sempronia," an article entitled "On Needle-Work" in the new *British Ladies' Magazine.* The purpose of the article, which is published in the form of a letter to the magazine's editor, is to beg his affluent female readership no longer to take money out of the mouths of their needy sisters, "never so much in distress for want of employment," by "needle-work *done at home.*"[2] Unusual for the directness with which it tackles the economic situation of women, it also concerns itself with the problematic issues of female aptitude for occupations conventionally pursued by men, of women's role in marriage, women's education, and the value of a woman's time generally. And yet, for all the major changes in women's employment Sempronia proposes, she also desires to bring about the necessary reforms "without affronting the preconceived habits of society" (p. 178). A deferential decorum veils the anger of the

167

piece and muffles its protesting voice. As a contradictory and self-divided protest, it shares what are now regarded as characteristics common to much nineteenth-century women's writing.[3] The aim of this paper is to explore the social and psychological factors that lie behind the composition of Mary Lamb's essay as one representative example of such writing, in an attempt to gain insights into both its strengths and its contradictions.

Sempronia begins her letter by informing the editor of the personal experience that provides her with the authority to speak on "the state of needlework in this country": in her youth, she tells him, she passed eleven years "in the exercise of my needle for a livelihood." Now addressing readers "among whom might perhaps be found some of the kind patronesses of my former humble labours," she is writing from a changed social position, one approximating more closely parity with that of her earlier employers. Emphasis is laid upon the reality of this change, and therefore on her capacity to speak to the conditions of the upper classes as well as to those of the class of which she was originally part: "among the present circle of my acquaintance," she stresses, "I am proud to rank many that may truly be called respectable." But her loyalties, she confesses, still lie with the less fortunate group she has left, and her "strongest motive" in writing the letter "is to excite attention towards the industrious sisterhood to which I once belonged" (p. 176).

Nevertheless, the article concerns itself more with the daily lives of Britain's ladies than with that of its seamstresses, for Sempronia wishes to persuade her readers that it would be in their interest, as well as in that of their laboring sisters, to desist from needlework *"done in the family."* Her main argument is that time spent upon needlework is time lost from a new goal amongst upper- and middle-class women, that of "intellectual progression": "needlework and intellectual improvement," she asserts, "are naturally in a state of warfare" (p. 176). She is writing to the *British Ladies' Magazine* precisely because it has allied itself to the cause of women's intellectual development. This progressive movement must have already, Sempronia believes, done much to help needlewomen, in that it provided more affluent women with occupation other than the making of their own clothes. But its effects have not been far-reaching enough: needlewomen are still underemployed and insufficiently remunerated for the work they do obtain, and women of the higher classes are still laboring under the intellectually impoverishing conviction that to fulfill their own and their family's sewing needs is their moral duty. Only if needlework were "never practised but for a remuneration in money" might it become possible for women's lot to equal that of men "as far as respects the mere enjoyment of life." "As far as that goes," Sempronia adds, "I believe it is every woman's opinion that the condition of men is far superior to her own." And she presses home her argument with an extended account of the impoverishment of women's time, and therefore of their way of life, in comparison to that of men:

"They can do what they like," we say. Do not these words generally mean, they have time to seek out whatever amusements suit their tastes? We dare not tell them we have no time to do this; for, if they should ask in what manner we dispose of our time, we should blush to enter upon a detail of the minutiæ which compose the sum of a woman's daily employment. Nay, many a lady who allows not herself one quarter of an hour's positive leisure during her waking hours, considers her own husband as the most industrious of men, if he steadily pursue his occupation till the hour of dinner, and will be perpetually lamenting her own idleness.

Real business and *real leisure* make up the portions of men's time—two sources of happiness which we certainly partake of in a very inferior degree. To the execution of employment, in which the faculties of the body or mind are called into busy action, there must be a consoling importance attached, which feminine duties (that generic term for all our business) cannot aspire to. (p. 177)

As an indictment of the early nineteenth-century English matron's situation, in which she ceaselessly wastes her time on an array of undervalued, and in themselves trivial, tasks, in which needlework figures obsessively, these paragraphs are painful and convincing. But they are immediately followed by one of the abrupt ideological swerves that characterize this text, as if the writer feared her protest had taken her too far. For in the next paragraph, women's subordination to men is accepted as inevitable and even just, and accommodated as such within the writer's argument. Sempronia goes on to proclaim that in the pursuance of these "feminine duties" the highest praise women *rightly* look for is "to be accounted the helpmates of *man:* who, in return for all he does for us, expects, and justly expects, us to do all in our power to soften and sweeten life." And her argument now proceeds through presenting the intellectual improvement of a woman as a means for improving the home life of her husband rather than of herself: it is her duty to "fit herself to become a conversational companion," and laudably to exert herself in study, not so much to develop her own mind as to contribute to the "undisturbed relaxation of man." If she fulfills this function then she ought to have satisfied her sense of duty, and be in a position cheerfully to lay aside her needle-book, contributing her part instead "to the slender gains of . . . all the numerous classifications of females supporting themselves by *needle-work,* that great stable commodity which is alone appropriated to the self-supporting part of our sex" (p. 178).

But as if in recognition here of the injustice inherent in the fàct that needlework does indeed constitute one of the very few means of subsistence available to the unmarried woman, whose parents' income "does not very much exceed the moderate," Sempronia in accounting for this situation, is aroused to anger again. Needlework is represented as the only profession open to women, not because they lack the capacity for acquiring new skills, or the robustness for furthering them, but because they have

never been in any way trained or educated for other tasks. She argues that
the male of the species, were he in the same position, could fare no better:

> Even where boys have gone through a laborious education, superinducing
> habits of steady attention, accompanied with the entire conviction that the
> business which they learn is to be the source of their future distinction, may
> it not be affirmed that the persevering industry required to accomplish this
> desirable end causes many a hard struggle in the minds of young men, even
> of the most hopeful disposition? What then must be the disadvantages
> under which a very young woman is placed who is required to learn a trade,
> from which she can never expect to reap any profit, but at the expence of
> losing that place in society, to the possession of which she may reasonably
> look forward, inasmuch as it is by far the most *common lot,* namely, the
> condition of a *happy* English wife? (p. 179)

This elucidation of the importance of the psychological preparation for
work that education, and social expectation, provides for men but denies to
women, according to the nineteenth-century gender-role system, is striking
and perceptive. Nevertheless, the author's stance in the essay as a whole
prevents one from interpreting in an ironic light her concluding reference
here to "the *happy* English wife." Although she argues that only their lack of
education stops women from sharing in the occupations of men, and that as
a result of this deprivation they suffer both materially and in terms of
thwarted potential, Sempronia would not have the status quo essentially
changed. On the contrary she asks her reader "to contribute all the assistance in her power to those of her own sex who may need it, in the
employments they at present occupy, rather than to force them into situations now filled wholly by men." No arguments sustain these reversals: they
are interjected abruptly into the protesting body of the text, to be accounted for only by unspecific references to the writer's "many years of
observation and reflection." In order to explore what lies behind
Sempronia's insistence upon such retrograde conclusions in an article that
raises so many essentially radical issues, the circumstance of Mary Lamb's
personal and social experience, her "cultural locus," as Elaine Showalter
would have it,[4] needs to be examined more closely.

Foremost of that undisclosed, yet relevant, experience upon which her
"years of observation and reflection" were based must have been the actual
conditions of life under which she, as a former needlewoman, had labored;
she takes her readers' knowledge of the dire situation of nineteenth-
century needlewomen for granted. Contemporary records did, in fact,
draw the attention of the more affluent classes to the plight of "thousands
of young females of respectable parents" who, "necessitated by the pecuniary misfortunes of their parents to earn a livelihood from needlework,"
found that employment so precarious and the profit so small that they were
driven through "sheer want" to resort "to prostitution and its concomitants,
misery, disease and death!"[5] And a needlewoman who managed to survive
on selling her labor rather than herself hardly seems to have enjoyed a less

miserable, or healthier, existence. As an apprentice learning her trade, she worked extortionately long hours for no pay, and once trained, a mantua-maker, attempting to make an independent living in a hopelessly over-stocked and consequently underpriced market, could consider herself lucky to find work that kept her plying her needle from 9 A.M. to 11 P.M. for very little gain.[6] As the *Morning Chronicle* account of her mother's death suggests, the "harassing fatigues" of her employment had much to do with the onset of Mary Lamb's madness. Given her firsthand experience of the hazards of the trade, she may well have felt that to describe its conditions in more detail in her essay would have been to shatter the ostensible purpose of her plea completely. For if her affluent female audience had been reminded more graphically of the sufferings of those who earned their living by the needle they might well have preferred to force the penurious of their sex into situations "filled wholly by men" rather than to perpetuate through their commissions the sweatshop trade. And yet Mary Lamb's sympathies clearly lie with the struggling needlewomen; why she chose to argue for so little change in their apparently hopeless position, which was in fact rapidly to deteriorate even further as the century progressed, remains problematic. Her essay suggests that she did know of the proposals then being put forward that work opportunities for women be extended. A "Ladies Committee for Promoting the Education and Employment of the Female Poor" had, for example, proposed in 1810 that women should at least be allowed to regain those occupations, such as midwifery and other branches of medical practice, that had traditionally been theirs, but that had been wrested from them by the demand for more specialized training, not available to women.[7] Such employment would at least have detracted from the prevalent concept of women's labor, and therefore of their time, as essentially worthless by comparison with that of men. And Mary Lamb's essay does indicate that she was vividly aware that the lack of female education and training meant that all women's labor, not only that of those forced to be self-supporting, brought them little pecuniary reward and therefore no independent social status. Their occupations, such as they were, could not bring them the "consoling importance" acquired by male labor but only either a precarious and unrespected subsistence or, at best, the approval of masculine protectors. Whether it belonged to the strug-gling or more affluent classes, women's time was never in fact self-val-idatingly their own. Her account delineates the female condition with a perspicacity, and an awareness of the consequence of its material depen-dence, much in advance of the general ideology of her time, but she does not begin to propose any of the revolutions in the gender roles of nine-teenth-century women that would be necessary to bring about any real amendment in their situation.

One indication of why she does not feel able to take this strategic step lies in the conclusion to her account, quoted above, of the impossibility of preparing oneself adequately for the nineteenth-century entrepreneurial job market without appropriate educational and psychological training. For a woman to receive such necessary preparation, according to the essay, would be to endanger the possibility of her arriving at the condition "of a *happy* English wife." A woman's chance of marriage, as her best hope of happiness, is to be protected at all costs, even at the risk of her subsequent destitution were she to remain, like Mary herself and very many of her contemporaries, unwed, and even though her situation in that marriage has previously in the essay been forcefully shown to be much inferior to her husband's. The *"happy* English wife" of Mary's description is clearly a middle-or upper-class spouse, of the same social grouping as the readers she addresses; a working-class wife's lot would hardly be presented in such firmly positive terms.

Historical studies of the period do indeed indicate that a practical education would have detracted from a woman's opportunities in the upper- and middle-class marriage market: to be trained for any profession would have entailed a loss in status and marital appeal in an age in which it was considered an "affront against nature," and an indication of "moral and spiritual degradation," for a woman to earn her own wages.[8] Needlework, along with the one other occupation open to women of this class at the time, viz., a teacher or governess who educated girls and small children, were the only forms of remunerative employment for which a "genteel" upbringing could have prepared a woman. Hence the glutting of the seamstresses' market with an endless supply of unfortunate daughters struggling to retain a foothold in the middle classes, and the possibility of marriage within that class, even though they were thus reduced to worse material circumstance than they would have endured had they sought factory employment or domestic service. The tragic irony of their situation was that the difficulty of ensuring a subsistence as a needlewoman meant that many were forced, through lack of employment, from the lower middle-class status of an independent milliner or mantua-maker to the working-class position of a plain sewer or "slop-worker" employed by a mistress, and often from thence, particularly in the middle years of the century, to prostitution and its concomitant entire and irremediable loss, in their society's eyes, of all character and status. It is in the attempt to prevent this degradation of the lower middle-class needlewoman that Mary is writing her article.

And yet marriage, as the hoped-for goal toward which this deliberate curtailment of female potential was aimed, does not in itself ever seem to have had a very potent appeal for Mary Lamb. In her correspondence with her close friend, Sarah Stoddart, which often concerned itself with Sarah's frustrations in the marriage market, she generally attempts to tease Sarah out of her overriding preoccupation with finding herself a husband. In one letter of 1806, she invites Sarah, instead, to set up house with herself and her brother:

> I think I should like to have you always to the end of our lives living with us, and I do not know any reason why that should not be except for the great

fancy you seem to have for marrying, which after all is but a hazardous kind
of an affair . . . very few husbands have I ever wished was mine which is
rather against the state in general that one never is disposed to envy wives
their good husands, So much for marrying—but however get married if you
can.[9]

But the ideological pressure on upper- and middle-class women at this time
to find in marriage the end of their existence, even though both their
inclination and their perception of the condition of women inside marriage
might be against it, was, of course, extraordinarily strong. The belief, held
as established through religious doctrine, that Providence had created
woman as the helpmate and comfort of man, and by doing so had fully
indicated her function, served as a central foundation of the patriarchal
bourgeois social system. Mary, then, in accepting a married woman's lot as
unquestionably *"happy"* in "On Needle-Work," even though she has just
previously described its circumscriptions, is accommodating inside her
argument the established nostrums of her period.

Such an act of accommodation, though it involved a contradiction of
what was perceived as the reality of the situation, no doubt helped "On
Needle-Work" gain the sympathies of its readers, and thus furthered its
plea; accommodation also, and more significantly, seems to have been an
habitual characteristic of Mary Lamb's psychological makeup. Eyewitnesses
to her behavior testify to its extreme mildness and selflessness. Writing to
Coleridge immediately after the death of their mother, her brother Charles
stressed that:

> Of all the people I ever saw in the world my poor sister was most &
> thoroughly devoi[d] of the least tincture of selfishness—. . . . if I mistake not
> in the most trying situation that a human being can be found in, she will be
> found (I speak not with sufficient humility, I fear, but humanly & foolishly
> speaking) she will be found, I trust, uniformly great & amiable.[10]

Less close acquaintances than her brother were also much impressed by
Mary Lamb's gentle and conciliatory disposition: Wordsworth, for example,
in his elegy to Charles Lamb, describes Lamb's sister as "the meek, / The
self-restraining and the ever-kind."[11] Charles's contemporary biographers
all emphasized Mary's gentle mildness: P. G. Patmore testifies to her "universal loving-kindness and toleration,"[12] and Barry Cornwall recalls her
habitual reconciliatory placidity.[13] Thomas Noon Talfourd in his *Final
Memorials of Charles Lamb* records in some detail the "remarkable sweetness
of her disposition": this "most quiet, sensible and kind of women" was "to a
friend in any difficulty . . . the most comfortable of advisers, the wisest of
consolers." He adds to his own account Hazlitt's testimony to her good
sense; Mary, alone of all her sex, becomes the exception that proves the
misogynist's rule: "Hazlitt used to say, that he never met with a woman who
could reason, and had met with one only thoroughly reasonable—the sole
exception being Mary Lamb."[14] De Quincey, in his account of his first

meeting with the Lambs, maintains that the manner in which Charles teased him for his idolatrous worship of Coleridge's poetry would have led to a quarrel between them had it not been for the "winning goodness" of "that Madonna-like lady," Mary, "before which all resentment must have melted in a moment."[15]

In so acting as mediator, Mary was, of course, fulfilling her society's accepted ideal of female virtue. Interestingly, recent socio-psychological analyses of female as opposed to male development have suggested that the structure of a female child's relation to her parents in a conventional family situation might indeed make it more in keeping with women's psychological development generally, in contrast with that of men, to identify with and accept a number of different sources of authority rather than experience them as conflicting. For a girl's identification with her mother, being more formative and longer-lasting than that of a male child, is not relinquished when the father also becomes important: she "retains her preoedipal tie to her mother . . . and builds oedipal attachments to both her mother and her father upon it."[16] In the late eighteenth and early nineteenth century, a popular genre of conduct tracts, designed to inculcate in its readers appropriate morals and values for a developing bourgeois society, stressed the need for women to accept a structure of external authorities, and emphasized that it was inherent in female nature to accomplish such an accommodation. Women were informed by their male advisers that since "Nature has not given you that unlimited range in your choice which we enjoy, she has wisely and benevolently assigned to you a greater flexibility of taste on this subject."[17] Thomas Gisborne in his influential *Enquiry into the Duties of the Female Sex* (1797) similarly pronounced that "Providence had deliberately "implanted" in women "a remarkable tendency to conform to the wishes and example of those for whom they feel a warmth of regard."[18] The success of such preaching may indeed have been facilitated by the psychological consequences of the conventional allocation of childcare to women, though, of course, it is a particular, if all too well-established, aspect of the manmade gender-role system that leads to this stereotypical childrearing pattern, and not an ordinance of "Nature" or of "Providence."

Mary Poovey, in her critical study of Romantic women writers *The Proper Lady and the Woman Writer,* lists a series of effective acts of accommodation that she sees the novelists on whom she writes as having incorporated into their texts. Nevertheless, she also points out that such strategies could, of course, represent an evasion on the part of the author of the tensions inherent in the life of a nineteenth-century woman writer.[19] Similarly, the central thesis of Sandra M. Gilbert and Susan Gubar's work *The Madwoman in the Attic: The Woman Writer and the Nineteenth-Century Literary Imagination* is that a nineteenth-century woman's attempt to contain the paradoxes of the gender role-model into which she was required to fit resulted in a psychological conflict that manifested itself in the literature of the period in the doubling of a virtuous and self-controlled heroine with a "bad," insane doppelganger character, Brontë's *Jane Eyre* presenting the most striking example of this configuration.[20] In Mary Lamb's case, however, the impossible pressures involved in requiring the self to live entirely selflessly were clearly signified not so much in her writing as, much more devastatingly, in her life. From her early thirties on, her "thoroughly reasonable" self-restraint was interrupted by the virtually annual onset of her periodic manic-depressive attacks. One of her brother's biographers, Talfourd, in his *Final Memorials,* gives a vivid account of Mary's double life. Recording her response to Hazlitt's praise, quoted above, he adds:

> She did not wish, however, to be made an exception, to a general disparagement of her sex; for in all her thoughts and feelings she was most womanly—keeping, under even undue subordination, to her notion of a woman's province, intellect of rare excellence, which flashed out when the restraint of gentle habit and humble manner were withdrawn by the terrible force of disease.

During her insanity, he remembers:

> her ramblings often sparkled with brilliant description and shattered beauty. She would fancy herself in the days of Queen Anne or George the First; and describe the brocaded dames and courtly manners, as though she had been bred among them, in the lost style of the old comedy . . . the fragments were like the jewelled speeches of Congreve, only shaken from their setting.

It is surely significant that even in her madness Lamb could not imagine herself as living freely in the nineteenth century but had to project herself back in her imagination to an earlier period of less strenuous gender-role restraint. For all his apparent sympathy, Talfourd concludes his account with approbation of the strait jacket of propriety with which Mary constrained herself when "well," and makes a moral lesson of her struggle. He informs his readers that

> not for the purpose of exhibiting a curious phenomenon of mental aberration are the aspects of her insanity unveiled, but to illustrate the moral force of gentleness by which the faculties that thus sparkled when restraining wisdom was withdrawn, were subjected to its sway, in her periods of reason.[21]

His earlier recognition of the excessive constraint under which she lived is lost when he considers the effect of his account upon his audience, and "undue subordination" becomes "wisdom."

A close reading of Mary's letters, as much as her acquaintances' records of her behavior, also conveys the impression of a mind under such severe self-restraint that it could allow itself very little freedom, particularly when it came to expressing the merest hint of criticism, or what she interpreted as criticism, of her friends. One striking incident of her epistolary restraint, and of her anguish when she feared she had lost control of it, bears movingly upon her own experience as a mental patient. In offering advice to Sarah Stoddart with regard to the treatment of Sarah's mother, suffering from senile dementia, Mary, in a letter of November 1805, writes:

> do not I conjure you let her unhappy malady afflict you too deeply—I speak from experience & from the opportunity I have had of much observation in such cases that insane people in the fancy's they take into their heads do not feel as one in a sane state of mind does under the real evil of poverty the perception of having done wrong or any such thing that runs in their heads.
>
> Think as little as you can, & let your whole care be to be certain that she is treated with *tenderness*. I lay a stress upon this, because it is a thing of which people in her state are uncommonly susceptible, & which hardly any one is at all aware of, a hired nurse *never*, even though in all other respects they are a good kind of people. I do not think your own presence necessary unless she *takes to you very much* except for the purpose of seeing with your own eyes that she is very kindly treated.[22]

This would appear most compassionate and humane advice, from the point of view of both mother and daughter; even the hired nurse's unkindness is remembered with a forgiving parenthetical qualification. But "the perception of having done wrong" in writing it was soon running in Mary's head. In her next letter she tells Sarah that she has been distressed ever since:

> that which gives me most concern is the way in which I talked about your Mothers illness & which I have since feared you might construe into my having a doubt of your showing her proper attention without my improper interference. God knows nothing of this kind was ever in my thoughts, but I have entered very deeply into your afflictions with regard to your Mother, & while I was writing, the many poor souls in the kind of desponding way she is in whom I have seen, came afresh into my mind, & all the mismanagement with which I have seen them treated was strong in my mind, & I wrote under a forcible impulse which I could not at that time resist, but I have fretted so much about it since, that I think it is the last time I will ever let my pen run away with me.[23]

Such an extreme sensitivity to the possibility of having her words construed as a critical attack by her audience, similarly evinced in many other episodes in her correspondence,[24] indicates the extent of Mary's concern to restrain her spontaneous responses to her experience lest they should contain some hint of anger or protest against others. No doubt her anxiety was intensified by the events of 22 September 1796, and the manner of her mother's death; if her unleashed anger could result in such traumatic violence then clearly she must tether it at all costs. The consciousness of herself as a potential lunatic must always have weighed upon Mary during her periods of sanity, and exacerbated any tendencies she had toward voluntary self-suppression.

The treatment afforded to the mad during the early nineteenth century cannot but have increased her diffidence, and made forceful self-expression more dangerous. As the recent work of social historians has established, during this period a fundamental change took place in the general concept of madness, and therefore of appropriate ways of dealing with the mad.[25] Throughout most of the eighteenth century, madness was still considered caused either by demonic possession or by a physical inflamation of the brain or body;[26] the madman either way was considered a monster, inhuman and beyond any treatment except that of physical restriction, in chains, cages, and strait jackets, or the application of leeches, cupping, strenuous purging, and other such practices intended to drain away the tainted physical substances. While such methods were still very much in use at the beginning of the nineteenth century, influential innovative institutions, such as the York Retreat, established in 1792, had successfully shown that the insane could respond satisfactorily to a system that inculcated self-restraint, rather than using external corporeal bondage, through offering its patients greater freedom and esteem as a reward for greater self-control.[27] According to this so-called moral treatment the insane were to be considered not so much monsters as recalcitrant children, who needed to be retaught, by persuasive means rather than overt coercion, how to function adequately as members of society; conditioned to fear all signs of lapses from conformity in their behavior, Blake's internalized "mind-forg'd manacles" rather than literal bonds now became the means recommended for their treatment. Although promoted as a humane and enlightened reform, which would correct the atrocities of the past, this development in the history of the treatment of insanity also functioned as a more efficient means of social control of the insane than had their earlier neglect. As recent feminist critics have pointed out, "moral treatment" corresponds interestingly to the ideological methods by which women also as a group were persuaded into accepting, and internalizing, a restricted view of themselves during this period.[28] It would appear that this correlation was evident to contemporary observers too, for while it was generally considered a serious disadvantage for a man to be certified as insane, one physician, at least, suggested that it could qualify as part of the attractions of a marriageable woman. "Humility," Thomas Bakewell wrote in his popular *The Domestic Guide in Cases of Insanity* (1805), "is a quality which men wish for in a wife. This complaint [insanity] cannot be said to teach humility, as to implant it in the very nature."[29]

Owing to a fortunate combination of her brother's concern and the date of her attack on her mother, Mary was spared the worst possible consequence of her psychosis. In 1796, persons found guilty of committing an act of manslaughter while mentally impaired were not required to suffer permanent incarceration provided that sufficient surety could be given that they would be taken care of as potentially unstable for the rest of their lives. This pledge Charles gave, much to the disapproval of his older brother, who thought it wiser to leave Mary to her fate in Bethlehem Hospital.[30] By 1800, however, owing to the public outcry over the attempted murder by a lunatic of the king, George III, himself suffering from insanity, a parliamentary act had been passed enforcing the detention of the criminally insane "in strict custody" in a jail or asylum "during the king's pleasure."[31] From this date on, given her past record, any action of Mary's that drew renewed public attention to her case could have had very serious consequences. Whenever possible she was cared for at home during her periodic breakdowns, by the hired nurses, whose failings her letter quoted above indicates, and taken to private asylums only when an attack seemed particularly grave or violent. Even so, her treatment as a mental patient must indeed have often been deeply humiliating and damaging to her self-esteem. A recent investigation of asylum records has shown, for example, that she was once, in 1831, an inmate of Brooke House asylum in Clapton.[32] An official report of Brooke House in 1841 found it dilapidated and seriously deficient in amenities for its patients: according to the report, the female quarters in particular "were most wretched furnished with old-fashioned lattice windows, letting the wind in so as to defy all attempts at keeping them warm."[33] In her letters, she refers to the periods she spent in asylums as her "banishment," and to herself generally as "an useless creature." "I have lost all self confidence in my own actions," she writes to Sarah Stoddart in 1805, and continues: "a perception of not being in a sane state perpetually haunts me. I am ashamed to confess this weakness to you, which as I am so sensible of I ought to strive to conquer."[34] Given the ceaseless struggle of her life, and her perpetual concern to maintain herself in obscurity, the intensity of sympathy she must have felt for the seamstresses in order to publish such a protesting article as "On Needle-Work," even under its necessary pseudonym, now becomes more evident. The erosion of her ability to believe in the justification of her own perceptions when they were contrary to those of received opinion must have made the pressure to conform to conventional ideology much stronger in her case than even in that of the more ordinarily circumscribed nineteenth-century woman.

For all that, a concern, such as that which is implicit in the arguments of "On Needle-Work," for the maintenance of self-employed working women, such as she herself had been, inside a middle-class as opposed to a working-class social grouping has led those few critics who have commented upon Mary Lamb's writings in the past to accuse her of snobbery. She is held to be much more anxiously aware of class and social status than her brother Charles, and much more protective of their position.[35] Yet her situation as a potential inmate of asylums for the insane during this period provides an explicatory context for such anxiety; loss of middle-class status would have had disastrous consequence for Mary Lamb. The segregation of mental patients into "private" and "pauper" groupings was rigidly enforced, "pauper" patients being categorized as those who received some or all of the cost of their treatment from the parish authorities. Not only were the conditions for lower-class inmates much worse than for private patients, but paupers were also, apparently, much more readily certified as insane, and much more likely, statistically, to be retained in the asylums as incurables.[36] Rationalizations were put forward to account for the discrepancy in their treatment. Francis Willis, for example, in his *Treatise on Mental Derangement* (1823), professes himself as of the opinion that "the man of fortune . . . will require a greater nicety in our moral treatment of him than the poor and illiterate; for he that serves, will not feel so acutely, even under his derangement, as he that is served."[37]

The vulnerability of Mary Lamb's status lay in the fact that her hereditary social position placed her amongst those who "served" rather than "were served," for both her parents belonged to the upper ranks of domestic service. The Inner Temple chambers in which she had been reared were the property of her father's employer, Samuel Salt, a barrister of the Temple and a Whig member of Parliament. Her father, John Lamb, after a period of early employment as a footman in Bath, had established himself as a waiter at the Inner Temple Hall, and had become Salt's personal "man," his valet and secretarial assistant. Salt had probably to some degree been an agent in his servant's marriage, for John Lamb's wife Elizabeth was the daughter of a housekeeper to one of his master's friends and colleagues at Westminster, Wiliam Plumer; Elizabeth likely assisted in the housekeeping of Salt's establishment after her marriage. It was Salt's influence that secured for the two Lamb boys their schooling at Christ's Hospital, and enabled them to find subsequent employment as trading-house clerks. He also allowed his servant's children access to his large library, which no doubt did much to enhance Mary's otherwise elementary dame's school education.[38] Her apprenticeship in her teens to a mantua-maker does not necessarily imply that her parents intended her for a career outside domestic service, for such an apprenticeship was commonly considered suitable preparation for a post as a lady's-maid.[39] Protected by Salt's benevolent paternalism during his lifetime, the family's situation changed suddenly and drastically with his death in 1792; required to leave the Temple, with the father sinking into senility and the mother physically ailing, the family was dependent, during Charles's apprenticeship of 1792–95, on the legacies bequeathed to it in Salt's will and on Mary's earnings, her elder brother having apparently, even before the death of his mother, detached himself from any responsibility for the family's precarious financial position. One of Charles's biographers describes the Lambs at this time as "helpless and poor, and all huddled together in a small lodging, scarcely large enough to admit of their moving about without restraint."[40] It was only Charles's decision to spare a great part of his meager earnings for Mary's maintenance in private care that saved her from the fate of a pauper lunatic. Given her act of matricide, it is highly unlikely that had she been so categorized she would ever have been restored to anything resembling a free and self-respecting existence.

But as well as a precarious material social standing, Mary must also have inherited from her parents, and from the conditions of her upbringing, an ideological sense of her relation to the sources of power and authority in her society that would also have increased the difficulty of her sustaining a coherent protest against its established hierarchies. For the ethos of domestic service under which she was reared still retained, in the eighteenth century, much of the characteristic flavor of the old feudal system. Conduct books written for servants during this period stressed the need for an entire self-subordination on the part of the servant to the requirements of his role. A servant's identity was considered as merged with that of his employer, as if he possessed no independent existence; "you will be known by your master's rank and fortune," the anonymous author of the *Servant's Pocket-Book* (1761) declares.[41] Complete obedience and deference was due to the master, as to a patriarchal parent. Anthony Heasel's *Servant's Book of Knowledge* (1773), for example, reminded those in service that "as we are commanded to honour our parents, so it is necessarily implied that we also honour and respect all those who have authority over us."[42] The late eighteenth century in England is regarded, in general, as a transitional period, in which, owing to the rapid growth of industrialization, the old master-servant relation, with its traditions of patronage, deference, and dependence, was swiftly eroded as an essentially capitalist, employer-employee structure, based on contractual employment, took its place. Mary Lamb, as the daughter of servants, was caught in the maelstrom of this all-encompassing social change. That she should still have retained old ideological loyalties, affecting her ability to conceptualize systematically the injustices of the new order, even as she sought, in writing "On Needle-Work," to defend those disadvantaged by it, cannot be surprising.

Yet Sempronia's letter does challenge, in its arguments if not in its conclusions, the status quo. What is more, contemporary feminist critics have demonstrated that the act of writing as such, when practiced by a woman, in itself constituted a form of social protest in the early nineteenth century, whatever the ideological ambivalences of the texts. Mary Poovey, for example, argues that

> the very act of a woman writing during a period in which self-assertion was considered "unladylike" exposes the contradictions inherent in propriety: just as the inhibitions visible in her writing constitute a record of her historical oppression, so the work itself proclaims her momentary, probably unconscious, but effective, defiance.[43]

In Mary's case, such debilitating inhibitions against creative self-assertion would have been intensified by the fact that, for the potentially insane as a group also, writing, along with imaginative activity generally, was discouraged as a dangerous malpractice, jeopardizing mental balance.[44] A consequence of the unavoidable internalization of such pressures was that Mary did indeed find the practice of writing on all occasions disturbing, experiencing it as a contradiction of her habital attempt to retain a self-obscuring modesty. Her letters often testify to inhibiting fears that her pen will "run away" with her.[45] The composition of "On Needle-Work," during which her sympathies for needlewomen forced her to confront contradictions in her perceptions more directly than elsewhere in her work, aroused particular stress. Her friend Henry Crabb Robinson recorded in his diaries that when he called on her on 11 December 1814 "she had undergone great fatigue from writing an article about needlework for the new *Ladies British Magazine.* She spoke of writing as a most painful occupation, which only necessity could make her attempt."[46] The "necessity" of writing "On Needle-Work" cannot have been substantially a financial one, although Mary may have wished, out of a self-contorting attempt to obscure her need for assertion, to present it as such to herself; Charles's increased earnings, and their father's death, had improved their economic position by this time. But the fact that she permitted herself the writing of it took a heavy toll: the "great fatigue" of its composition brought on a particularly prolonged attack of insanity in mid-December from which she did not recover until the following February.

"On Needle-Work," however, for all the multifaceted pressures upon Lamb as she wrote it, is subversive in more than the statement it makes as an act of women's writing in itself. Its protests may be ambivalent in terms of class relations, and in terms of assessment of the value of the bourgeois marriage, but both of these accommodations can be read as furthering the real goal of the text, that of encouraging the solidarity of women as a group in themselves, across the boundaries of class and marital status. Given her parental background, her insecurity as a potential mental patient, and the gender-role vulnerabilities she shared with all nineteenth-century woman, it would have been in many ways far safer for Mary Lamb to have forgotten that she ever knew at first hand the difficulties of the self-supporting working woman. But in emphasizing in the text the realities of her past experience, she presents her life as a mediating link between one group of women and another, and asks the more affluent women she addresses as her readers to realize, through her, their shared sisterhood with the less privileged sector to which she originally belonged.

The last paragraph of the essay, in particular, challenges middle-class women to demonstrate in practical terms their female allegiance with needlewomen, in a manner that cuts directly across the interests of their husbands. In it she suggests that those of her readers who profess to enjoy their needlework too much to relinquish it, though *"saving"* is not their object, confine themselves to purely ornamental work,

> knitting, knotting, netting carpet working, and the like ingenious pursuit—
> those so-often-praised but tedious works, which are so long in the operation,
> that purchasing the labour has seldom been thought good economy, yet, by
> a certain fascination, they have been found to chain down the great to a self-
> imposed slavery, from which they considerately, or haughtily, excuse the
> needy.

The function of needlework inside a system of upper-class female subordination, fetishized and adopted as such even by the women themselves, is tellingly indicated here. Furthermore, the last sentence of the letter continues:

> But, if those works, more usually denominated useful, yield greater satisfac-
> tion, it might be a laudable scruple of conscience, and no bad test to herself
> of her own motive, if a lady, who had no absolute need, were to give the
> money so saved to poor needle-women belonging to those branches of
> employment from which she has borrowed these shares of pleasurable
> labour. (p. 180)

The significant word here is "borrowed": the lady she addresses is not
asked to give the needlewoman money as a gift of charity, in the conventional noblesse-oblige fashion, but to give it to her as her right, as the
rightful fruits of her labor, "borrowed" from her by the ruling economic
order. The money the gentlewoman is thus to pay back would not, of
course, likely be her own money under nineteenth-century law but that of
her husband, father, brother, or other male protector. At the close of her
essay Mary Lamb enjoys a most revolutionary vision of bourgeois women
busily distributing the fruits of their husbands' capitalist gains amongst the
women exploited by that system, in the name of female solidarity. To what
extent Lamb was writing here with deliberate awareness of the revolutionary implications of her suggestions may, of course, be queried, but the
article's subversive energy is palpable, particularly at its close, though its
author may try deviously to obscure it. The letter as a whole, with its
contradictions and with all the crippling anxieties its composition aroused
in Mary Lamb, may be considered tellingly representative of the struggles
of women of all classes toward female self-respect and autonomy during
the Romantic period.

NOTES

1. *The Morning Chronicle*, 22 September 1796.

2. *The Works of Charles and Mary Lamb*, ed. E. V. Lucas (London: Methuen, 1903–
05), 1:176. All subsequent references in the text to the Lambs' works are taken from
this edition.

3. See, for example, Mary Poovey, *The Proper Lady and the Woman Writer: Ideology
as Style in the Works of Mary Wollstonecraft, Mary Shelley and Jane Austen* (Chicago:
University of Chicago Press, 1984), pp. 35–47; and Sandra M. Gilbert and Susan
Gubar, *The Madwoman in the Attic: The Woman Writer and the Nineteenth-Century
Literary Imagination* (New Haven: Yale University Press, 1979), pp. 45–92.

4. Elaine Showalter, "Feminist Criticism in the Wilderness," in *The New Feminist
Criticism: Essays on Women, Literature and Theory,* ed. Showalter (London: Virago,
1986), p. 264.

5. J. R. Pickmore, "An Address to the Public on the Propriety of Midwives,
instead of Surgeons, practising Midwifery," *The Pamphleteer,* 28 (1827): 115–16;
quoted in Ivy Pinchbeck, *Women Workers and the Industrial Revolution 1750–1850*
(1930; London: Virago, 1981) p. 315.

6. See Pinchbeck, pp. 289 and 309; and Wanda Fraiken Neff, *Victorian Working
Women: An Historical and Literary Study of Women in British Industries and Professions
1832–1850* (London: Allen and Unwin, 1929), pp. 116, 129.

7. "Report on the Society for Bettering the Condition and Increasing the Comforts of the Poor" (1798–1808), 4:182–92; quoted in Pinchbeck, pp. 304–05.

8. See Neff, p 37.

9. *The Letters of Charles and Mary Anne Lamb,* ed. Edwin W. Marrs, Jr. (Ithaca: Cornell University Press, 1975–78), 2:229.

10. Ibid., 1:50.

11. "Written after the Death of Charles Lamb," *The Poetical Works of William Wordsworth,* ed. Ernest de Selincourt and Helen Darbishire (Oxford: Oxford University Press, 1940–49), 4:275.

12. P. G. Patmore, *My Friends and Acquaintances* (London: 1854), 3:200.

13. B. W. Proctor [Barry Cornwall], *Charles Lamb: A Memoir* (London: Edward Moxon, 1866), p. 128.

14. Thomas Noon Talfourd, *Final Memorials of Charles Lamb: consisting chiefly of his letters not before published, with sketches of some of his contemporaries,* (London: Edward Moxon, 1848), 2:123, 126.

15. Thomas de Quincey, "Recollections of Charles Lamb," *The Collected Writings of Thomas de Quincey,* (Edinburgh: Adam and Charles Black, 1889–90), 3:35, 57.

16. Nancy Chodorow, *The Reproduction of Mothering: Psychoanalysis and the Sociology of Gender* (Berkeley and Los Angeles: University of California Press, 1978), pp. 192–93.

17. Dr. John Gregory, *A Father's Legacy to his Daughters* (1774; New York: Garland, 1974), p. 82.

18. Thomas Gisborne, *An Enquiry into the Duties of the Female Sex,* 4th ed. (London: T. Cadell, Jr. and W. Davies, 1799) pp. 122–23; quoted in Poovey, p. 3.

19. Poovey, pp. 44–46.

20. Gilbert and Gubar, pp. 76–78.

21. Talfourd, 2:227–28.

22. *Letters,* ed. Marrs, 2:184–85.

23. Ibid., pp. 185–86.

24. See, for example, her anxiety concerning her letter of August, 1806 to the Wordsworths on Coleridge's marital difficulties, *Letters,* ed. Marrs, 2:238.

25. See Andrew T. Scull, *Museums of Madness: The Social Organization of Insanity in Nineteenth-Century England* (London: Allen Lane, 1979), pp. 18–48.

26. See William F. Bynum, Jr., "Rationales for Therapy in British Psychiatry, 1780–1835," in *Madhouses, Mad-Doctors, and Madmen: The Social History of Psychiatry in the Victorian Era,* ed. Andrew Scull (London: Athlone, 1981), p. 39.

27. For an account of the York Retreat, see Scull, *Museums of Madness,* pp. 67–75.

28. See Elaine Showalter, "Victorian Women and Insanity," in *Madhouses, Mad-Doctors, and Madmen,* ed. Scull, p. 326.

29. Thomas Bakewell, *The Domestic Guide in Cases of Insanity* (London: T. Allbutt, 1805), p. 54.

30. See Lamb's letter to Coleridge, 3 October 1796, *Letters,* ed. Marrs, 1:49.

31. See Scull, *Museums of Madness,* p. 55.

32. See Leslie Joan Friedman, "Mary Lamb: Sister, Seamstress, Murderer, Writer" (Ph.D. diss., Stanford University, 1976), p. 388.

33. R. Paternoster, *The Madhouse System,* (London, 1841); quoted in William Ll. Parry-Jones, *The Trade in Lunacy: A Study of Private Madhouses in England in the Eighteenth and Nineteenth Centuries* (London: Routledge and Kegan Paul, 1972), p. 100.

34. *Letters,* ed. Marrs, 3:60, 2:186.

35. See, for example, Ernest C. Ross, *The Ordeal of Bridget Elia: A Chronicle of the Lambs* (Norman: University of Oklahoma Press, 1940), p. 94.

36. See Scull, *Museums of Madness,* p. 245.

37. Francis Willis, "A Treatise on Mental Derangement" (1823), pp. 157–58; quoted in Parry-Jones, p. 181.

38. For a recent biographical account of the Lambs' childhood, see Winifred F. Courtney, *Young Charles Lamb 1775–1802* (London: Macmillan, 1982), pp. 1–49.

39. See J. Jean Hecht, *The Domestic Servant Class in Eighteenth-Century England* (London: Routledge and Kegan Paul, 1956), p. 61.

40. Procter, p. 119.

41. Quoted in Hecht, p. 37.

42. Ibid., p. 75.

43. Poovey, p. xv.

44. See Norman Dain, *Concepts of Insanity in the United States, 1789–1865* (New Brunswick, N.J.: Rutgers University Press, 1964), p. 16.

45. See, for example, *Letters*, ed. Marrs, 2:252. "I know so well, and often feel so sadly, how irksome writing is."

46. *Henry Crabb Robinson on Books and Their Writers*, ed. Edith J. Morley (London: Dent, 1938), 1:156.

ROMANTIC POETRY

THE I ALTERED

Stuart Curran

Let us suppose they all died young: not just Keats at twenty-five, Shelley at twenty-nine, and Byron at thirty-six, but Coleridge in 1802, Wordsworth in 1807, and Southey on the day in 1813 he became poet laureate. Let us suppose too of the other candidates for fame in verse that Blake was mad, that Campbell and Hunt were journalists, Moore a songster, Rogers a bonvivant, Scott a novelist, and the rest vicars of the church. Let us then suppose a retrospect on British Romanticism just after the death of Byron in the inimitable tones of *Blackwood's,* celebrating this "Age of Genius, only second to that of Elizabeth" and attempting to identify its particular source, "the strong influence in operating the change that has taken place in our poetic literature." It might run along these lines:

> We [are] delighted with the opportunity afforded us of offering our tribute of admiration to one, who, in point of genius, is inferior to no individual on the rolls of modern celebrity—whose labours have given a tone and character to the poetic literature of our nation—whose works were the manuals of our earliest years, and were carried by us, in our school-boy days, to shady nooks, and unfrequented paths, and our most favourite solitudes—whose touching portraitures of the workings of the human soul awakened in us an enthusiasm, to the full as ardent as that which is only inspired in our present youth by the effeminizing sensuality of Moore, or the gloomy and bewildering fascinations of Lord Byron—whose deep and affecting morals, illustrated by the moving examples of her scenes, touched the heart and mind, and improved the understanding by the delightful means of an excited imagination—and whose pages we have never returned to, in our days of more matured judgment, without reviving the fading tints of admiration, and justifying our early estimate of her high intellectual superiority.[1]

Without the pointed pronouns, a modern reader would surely anticipate from this description a contemporary estimate of the greatness of Wordsworth. But, instead, the subject is Joanna Baillie, who, two years before Wordsworth's celebrated preface, had published her own seventy-two-page argument for naturalness of language and situation across all the literary genres. Today, if she appears in modern literary histories, Joanna Baillie is fortunate to be able to duck into a footnote, usually derogatory. And yet, aside from the authority of its preface, her three-volume *Series of Plays: in which it is attempted to delineate the stronger passions of the mind* (1798–1812) was hailed in comparison to Shakespeare and, of all contemporary influences, exerted the most direct practical and theoretical force on serious drama written in the Romantic period. That with the exception of Shelley's *Cenci* we do not read this corpus and almost none of it is revived in the theater is apt testimony to the caprices of history with fame. The caprices of historians with history are quite another matter. Manifest distortions of the record have accrued, and these are the subject of this essay.

If we revert a generation from *Blackwood's* assessment of the contemporary scene, we might focus our perspective at a point midway between Baillie's and Wordsworth's prefaces, which is to say, before Baillie's impact on her culture had taken place. This is how Mary Robinson, a major literary voice of the 1790s, characterized its landscape:

> The best novels that have been written, since those of Smollet, Richardson, and Fielding, have been produced by women: and their pages have not only been embellished with the interesting events of domestic life, portrayed with all the refinement of sentiment, but with forcible and eloquent, political, theological, and philosophical reasoning. To the genius and labours of some enlightened British women posterity will also be indebted for the purest and best translations from the French and German languages. I need not mention Mrs. Dobson, Mrs. Inchbald, Miss Plumptree, &c. &c. Of the more profound researches in the dead languages, we have many female classicks of the first celebrity: Mrs. Carter, Mrs. Thomas, (late Miss Parkhurst;), Mrs. Francis, the Hon. Mrs. Damer, &c. &c.
>
> Of the Drama, the wreath of fame has crowned the brows of Mrs. Cowley, Mrs. Inchbald, Miss Lee, Miss Hannah More, and others of less celebrity. Of Biography, Mrs. Dobson, Mrs. Thickness, Mrs. Piozzi, Mrs. Montagu, Miss Helen Williams, have given specimens highly honourable to their talents. Poetry has unquestionably risen high in British literature from the productions of female pens; for many English women have produced such original and beautiful compositions, that the first critics and scholars of the age have wondered, while they applauded.[2]

Robinson's landscape is then further delineated with a list of thirty-nine exemplary women scholars, artists, and writers, many of whom the modern reader could not have identified before the publication of Janet Todd's *Dictionary*. These thirty-nine articles of faith, as it were, were universally known among the literate of the 1790s and, indeed, could be multiplied several times over. Although our concern is with poetry, the breadth of the list should remind us from the start that by the 1790s in Great Britain there were many more women than men novelists and that the theater was actually dominated by women, all the more so as Joanna Baillie's fame and

influence spread.³ In the arena of poetry, which in the modern world we
have privileged as no other in this age, the place of women was likewise, at
least for a time, predominant, and it is here that the distortions of our
received history are most glaring. Its chronology has been written wholly,
and arbitrarily, along a masculine gender line.

That such distortions started early can be perceived in the midst of
Blackwood's extolling of Joanna Baillie. For the reviewer, identified as
William Harness, implicitly sets Baillie within a nationalistic Scottish milieu
dominated before her entrance by James Beattie, whereas clearly the major
poetic voice in England in the ten years between 1785 and 1795 was that of
William Cowper. But the curious centering of Beattie, who staked his
exaggerated claims on one unfinished poem, should alert us to how difficult
it is for the customary history to center any poet writing in Britain in the
last third of the eighteenth century. After the death of the mercurial and
self-destructive Charles Churchill in 1764, there occurs (according to the
standard account) a remarkable trough in English poetry, which cannot be
filled in by two honored poems each from Oliver Goldsmith and Samuel
Johnson, nor by the inventions of the brilliant Chatterton, an adolescent
suicide, nor by those two antithetical voices of the Scottish Enlightenment,
alike inventors of a spurious past, Macpherson and Beattie. And yet there
was a rush to fill that trough by an entire school of poets—women poets—
who came to maturity in the 1770s out of the intellectual energy of the
bluestocking circle of Elizabeth Carter and Elizabeth Montagu. They were
well aware of one another, sometimes conceiving themselves as rivals of one
another, and found an audience that followed their careers and bought
their books. That they constituted a coterie, however far-flung from its
London origins, is absolutely true, with all the disadvantages we might
associate with it, but with the energy, determination, and staying power to
enforce a transformation in the history of British letters. Aside from
intellectual encouragement, it is important to note, this coterie in its broad-
est manifestation furnished the economic base on which women writers
depended for material support. Thus, while Goldsmith was writing his two
poems and Beattie his one, a succession of women poets came to prominence: Anna Barbauld with five editions of her poems between 1773 and
1777; Hannah More with six sizable volumes of verse between 1773 and
1786; Anna Seward, the Swan of Lichfield, whose *Monody on the Death of
Major Andre* of 1781 went through successive editions and was followed in
1784 by her influential amalgamation of genres, *Louisa, a Poetical Novel,*
making her a literary force to be reckoned with until her death a quarter-
century later; Charlotte Smith, whose *Elegiac Sonnets* of 1784 went through
ten expanding editions in fifteen years; Helen Maria Williams, who cap-
italized on the fame of her first two books of poetry by publishing a
collected *Poems, in Two Volumes* in 1786, when she was yet twenty-four; and
Mary Robinson, whose first poetic volume was published in 1775, and who
the year before her death in 1800 could survey a literary landscape and see
it dominated by women intellectuals.

These six poets, however ignored today or misconceived in their own time, along with Cowper impel the history of poetry in the last quarter of Britain's eighteenth century. They are, as it were, the missing link, all the more missing since, deluged with reprints as the literary academy is today, only Seward's works have shared in that effort; indeed, only two of these six, Anna Barbauld and Hannah More, found their way into Victorian editions. As literary figures, these women poets are by no means isolated; there are dozens of other women of lesser ambition or simply less prominence who emulated them and thereby swelled their ranks into a literary phenomenon without parallel in earlier history. The six had their veritable differences in temperament and ideology—Anna Seward disparaged the propriety of Charlotte Smith's sonnets, for instance, and it is unlikely that Hannah More would have acknowledged the acquaintance of Mary Robinson, though a former student at the Misses More's Bristol academy, once she became celebrated as "Perdita," Mistress of the Prince of Wales—but even so, they could not help being linked in the public mind. They, and their emulators, are the unacknowledged subtext to Mary Wollstonecraft's *Vindication of the Rights of Woman* (1792), their achieved and independent excellence intimating a radical reordering of existing social institutions.

The dates of the six poets are instructive, for only one of them—Mary Robinson—died relatively young; Anna Barbauld lived until 1825, Helen Maria Williams until 1827, and Hannah More until 1833. And they were followed by a second generation of women poets who likewise confound our normative assumptions about the chronology of Romanticism. These are the dates of a handful of the most prominent: Joanna Baillie (1762–1851); Mary Betham (1776–1852); Margaret Hodson (1778–1852)—truly of a second generation, she dedicated her historical epic, *Margaret of Anjou,* in 1816 to her mother Margaret Holford, whose *Gresford Vale* was published in 1798; Mary Russell Mitford (1787–1855); Amelia Opie (1769–1853); Sydney Owenson, afterward Lady Morgan (1783–1859); Caroline Bowles Southey (1786–1854); Jane West (1758–1852). These are not only long-lived women, but for the most part they published far into the Victorian period and it would appear more productively and influentially than any male Romantic contemporary, with the exception of Leigh Hunt. Here, too, were it to be pursued, is a second missing link, only less important than the first because the terms were by this point so firmly set and the energy was so self-fulfilling. Still, in the writings of the two most famous women poets of this generation, Felicia Hemans and Letitia Landon, who died respectively in 1835 and 1838, we can discern what is otherwise almost strikingly absent in the male Romantic universe, an actual transition into the characteristic preoccupations of Victorian verse. Since, moreover, Hemans and Landon were the first women to earn a sizable income from writing only poetry, being accorded recognition in the public mind as professional poets, their success, whatever value we place on it today, testifies to a major transformation in the world of British letters. In fifty years women had come from the margins of that world to an assured, professional place at its center.

Hemans and Landon, to be sure, paid a price for their celebrity, at once fulfilling and defining a literary niche that, however important historically, may explain, if not exactly justify, their later neglect. For the bourgeois public of the 1820s and 1830s their names were synonymous with the notion of a poetess, celebrating hearth and home, God and country in mellifluous verse that relished the sentimental and seldom teased anyone into thought. There are other and darker strains in their voluminous production—a focus on exile and failure, a celebration of female genius frustrated, a haunting omnipresence of death—that seem to subvert the role they claimed and invite a sophisticated reconsideration of their work against the complex background of the transition between Romantic and Victorian poetic modes. But such an analysis must itself depend on our understanding of their principal inheritance, which is not that of the British Romanticism that died young but rather of a half-century of women writers who determinedly invaded a male fiefdom and reconceived its polity. On the surface the interests of these poets seem little different from the dominant poetic genres and modes of thought we associate with their time. They wrote satires as well as sonnets, tragedies along with *vers de société;* a few even wrote epics.[4] But to look with attention and historical discrimination is to realize that some of the genres we associate most closely with British Romanticism, notably the revival of the sonnet and the creation of the metrical tale, were themselves strongly impelled by women poets; that some of the distinctive preoccupations of women poets eventually color the landscape we think of as Romantic; and that others are so decidedly different as to suggest a terra incognita beneath our very feet.

I

We are so accustomed to referring to English Romantic poetry as a poetry of vision that we have numbed ourselves to the paradox that what the word signifies is exactly the opposite of what we mean by it. We mean that it is visionary, borne on what Keats called "the viewless wings of poesy" and obsessed, like Keats's major odes, with imaginative projection as an end in itself. The actual vision might be said to be the province—until late in the careers of Byron and Shelley, even the exclusive province—of women poets, whose fine eyes are occupied continually in discriminating minute objects or assembling a world out of its disjointed particulars. The titles of three of Anna Barbauld's poems, written over a span of forty-five years, are indicative: "Verses Written in an Alcove," " An Inventory of the Furniture in Dr. Priestley's Study," "The First Fire, October 1st, 1815." If a woman's place is in the home, or in the schoolroom as in Anna Barbauld's case, or in the garden, then the particulars of those confined quarters are made the

impetus for verse. Thus a characteristic subgenre of women's poetry in this
period is verse concerned with flowers, and not generally of the Wordsworthian species. Merely to distinguish texture, or scent, or a bouquet of
colors may seem a sufficient end in itself, enforcing a discipline of par-
ticularity and discrimination that is a test of powers. One senses exactly such
a purpose behind Mary Russell Mitford's debut with a collection of her
adolescent *Poems* in 1810, which is virtually a sampler of floral embroidery,
the apprentice work of a literary seamstress. Yet, this category of seemingly
occasional verse, from whose practice men are all but excluded, has the
capacity to encode values, not just of culture but also of perspective, as in a
different medium Georgia O'Keeffe's magnifications have proved to our
century. The world of Charlotte Smith's "Flora" is fantastic, even surreal;
and it is small wonder that so many poems for the nursery or children in
this period, verses like Mrs. Montolieu's *The Enchanted Plants* (1800) or
Alice LeFanu's *The Flowers; or the Sylphid Queen* (1809), invest the garden
with imaginative propensities. It is not, however, merely a "rosy sanctuary,"
like that of Keats in his "Ode to Psyche," built as a retreat "In 'some
untrodden region of [his] mind," which in general parlance might be
considered the quintessential garden of English Romanticism; rather, it
exists for its own sake, for its capacity to refine the vision of the actual. Its
significance is quotidian.

Quotidian values, although present and celebrated in the verse of the
Enlightenment and Victorian periods, have been largely submerged from
our comprehension of Romanticism, with its continual urge for visionary
flight, for an investment in symbols. Even the fragmentary, as in "Kubla
Khan," has served to implicate planes of reality beyond the power of words
to image. Yet obviously the fragmentary can have more mundane and
perhaps less self-congratulatory functions: to suggest a decentered mind or
a society compounded of incongruities, for instance, or, for opposing ends,
to document the sheer energy of life or its resolute thingness. Such are the
ends one discerns from the experiments of Mary Robinson in poetic montage, which at once recall earlier satiric catalogs like Swift's "Description of a
City Shower" and assimilate new and startling cultural elements to the mix.
Although we can discriminate particular elements and even recurring
patterns, the poems resist reduction to thematic uses. They artfully refuse
to reconcile their discords, whether of class, occupation, or mores. The
opening of the eleven-stanza "January 1795" may be taken as an instance:

> Pavement slipp'ry, people sneezing,
> Lords in ermine, beggars freezing;
> Titled gluttons dainties carving,
> Genius in a garret starving.
>
> Lofty mansions, warm and spacious;
> Courtiers cringing and voracious;
> Misers scarce the wretched heeding;
> Gallant soldiers fighting, bleeding.

> Wives who laugh at passive spouses;
> Theatres and meeting-houses;
> Balls, where simp'ring misses languish;
> Hospitals, and groans of anguish.

We are barely conscious here that the backdrop to these clashing juxtaposi-
tions is the war with France, so carefully does Robinson go out of her way to
separate her references. Not until the final two stanzas does she return to
the arena of bleeding soldiers and anguished groans:

> Gallant souls with empty purses;
> Gen'rals only fit for nurses;
> School-boys, smit with martial spirit,
> Taking place of vet'ran merit.

> Honest men who can't get places,
> Knaves who shew unblushing faces;
> Ruin hasten'd, peace retarded;
> Candour spurn'd, and art rewarded.[5]

Peace would be "retarded" for another two decades, with enormous
cultural consequences, while these incongruities played out their attrition
on a world stage to the point of exhaustion. But that is deliberately not the
theater of Robinson's poem; rather, it is merely one aspect of the universal
pursuit of mundane and amoral self-aggrandizement.

What had already become the longest war of modern history is also the
backdrop to Robinson's even more remarkable "Winkfield Plain; or, a
Description of a Camp in the Year 1800," an evocation of sheer energy
continually reverting to its sexual base.[6]

> Tents, *marquees*, and baggage-waggons;
> Suttling-houses, beer in flagons;
> Drums and trumpets, singing, firing;
> Girls seducing, beaux admiring;
> Country lasses gay and smiling,
> City lads their hearts beguiling;
> Dusty roads, and horses frisky,
> Many an *Eton boy* in whisky;
> Tax'd carts full of farmers' daughters;
> Brutes condemn'd, and man who slaughters!
> Public-houses, booths, and castles,
> *Belles* of fashion, serving vassals;
> Lordly gen'rals fiercely staring,
> Weary soldiers, sighing, swearing!
> *Petit-maitres* always dressing,
> In the glass themselves caressing;
> Perfum'd, painted, patch'd, and blooming
> Ladies—manly airs assuming!
> Dowagers of fifty, simp'ring,
> Misses for their lovers whimp'ring;

Husbands drill'd to household tameness;
Dames heart sick of wedded sameness.
Princes setting girls a-madding,
Wives for ever fond of gadding;
Princesses with lovely faces,
Beauteous children of the Graces!
Britain's pride and virtue's treasure,
Fair and gracious beyond measure!
Aids-de-camps and youthful pages,
Prudes and vestals of all ages!
Old coquets and matrons surly,
Sounds of distant hurly-burly!
Mingled voices, uncouth singing,
Carts full laden, forage bringing;
Sociables and horses weary,
Houses warm, and dresses airy;
Loads of fatten'd poultry; pleasure
Serv'd (to nobles) without measure;
Doxies, who the waggons follow;
Beer, for thirsty hinds to swallow;
Washerwomen, fruit-girls cheerful,
Ancient ladies—*chaste* and *fearful*!!
Tradesmen leaving shops, and seeming
More of *war* than profit dreaming;
Martial sounds and braying asses,
Noise, that ev'ry noise surpasses!
All confusion, din, and riot,
Nothing clean—and nothing quiet.

"Winkfield Plain" is a tour-de-force in more ways than one, for no man could have written this poem so conscious of the place of women within the economy of war and no woman in English society but an inhabitant of the demi-monde like Robinson, would have dared to. As realistic genre-painting it is years ahead of its time: its vision of the actual is penetrating. It may be true that little of Mary Robinson's copious oeuvre falls into the genre of realistic montage; but a quick comparison with the major realist among the male poets of the 1790s, Robert Southey, would suggest what literary victories are implicit in her refusal to categorize by class or politics or morality. The quotidian is absolute.

Morality is, on the other hand, the true subject of the brilliant *Essays in Rhyme on Morals and Manners* that Jane Taylor published in 1806. But the moral vantage point is only attained through the accumulation of minute detail, each piece precisely calibrated to ground morality in quotidian life. Taylor, who is the only woman poet in England during the Romantic period to have been honored with a twentieth-century selection, immediately reminds us, with her fine irony, of Jane Austen; but there are obvious differences in perspective. A devout Methodist, she is the analyst of its bourgeois underpinnings, and, like many Dissenting women, she is

not to be dismayed by squalor. Above all, she understands what it is to
work—or, in the case of the mayor and mayoress in "Prejudice" to *have*
worked until the spirit is a mere extension of materiality:[7]

> In yonder red-brick mansion, tight and square,
> Just at the town's commencement, lives the mayor.
> Some yards of shining gravel, fenc'd with box,
> Lead to the painted portal—where one knocks:
> There, in the left-hand parlour, all in state,
> Sit he and she, on either side the grate.
> But though their goods and chattels, sound and new,
> Bespeak the owners *very well to do,*
> His worship's wig and morning suit betray
> Slight indications of an humbler day.
>
> That long, low shop, where still the name appears,
> Some doors below, they kept for forty years:
> And there, with various fortunes, smooth and rough,
> They sold tobacco, coffee, tea, and snuff.
> There labell'd drawers display their spicy row,—
> Clove, mace, and nutmeg: from the ceiling low
> Dangle long *twelves* and *eights,* and slender rush,
> Mix'd with the varied forms of *genus brush;*
> Cask, firkin, bag, and barrel, crowd the floor,
> And piles of country cheeses guard the door.
> The frugal dames came in from far and near,
> To buy their ounces and their quarterns here.
> Hard was the toil, the profits slow to count,
> And yet the mole-hill was at last a mount;
>
> Those petty gains were hoarded day by day,
> With little cost, for not a child had they;
> Till, long proceeding on the saving plan,
> He found himself a *warm, fore-handed man:*
> And being now arrived at life's decline,
> Both he and she, they formed the bold design.
> (Although it touch'd their prudence to the quick)
> To turn their savings into stone and brick.
> How many an ounce of tea and ounce of snuff,
> There must have been consumed to make enough!
>
> At length, with paint and paper, bright and gay,
> The box was finish'd, and they went away.
> But when their faces were no longer seen
> Amongst the canisters of *black* and *green,*
> —Those well known faces, all the country round—
> 'Twas said that had they levell'd to the ground
> The two old walnut trees before the door,
> The customers would not have missed *them* more.
> Now, like a pair of parrots in a cage,
> They live, and civic honours crown their age:

Thrice, since the Whitsuntide they settled there,
Seven years ago, has he been chosen mayor;
And now you'd scarcely know they were the same;
Conscious he struts, of power, and wealth, and fame,
Proud in official dignity, the dame:
And extra stateliness of dress and mien,
During the mayoralty, is plainly seen;
With nicer care bestow'd to puff and pin
The august lappet that contains her chin.

   Such is her life; and like the wise and great,
The mind has journey'd hand in hand with fate
Her thoughts, unused to take a longer flight
Than from the left-hand counter to the right,
With little change, are vacillating still,
Between his worship's glory and the till.
The few ideas moving, slow and dull,
Across the sandy desert of her skull,
Still the same course must follow, to and fro,
As first they travers'd three-score years ago;
From whence, not all the world could turn them back,
Or lead them out upon another track.
What once was right or wrong, or high or low
In her opinion, always must be so:—
You might, perhaps, with reasons new and pat,
Have made *Columbus* think the world was flat;
There might be times of energy worn out,
When his own theory would *Sir Isaac* doubt;
But not the powers of argument combin'd,
Could make this dear good woman change her mind,
Or give her intellect the slightest clue
To that vast world of things she never knew.
Were but her brain dissected, it would show
Her stiff opinions fastened in a row,
Rang'd duly, side by side, without a gap,
Much like the plaiting on her Sunday cap.

Taylor's capacity to reveal the inner life as a thing is, it could be asserted, unrivaled in English literature before Dickens; and she possesses what for the ends of comedy he often sacrificed, a quiet compassion for its cost. That we feel for those who cannot is the impetus for the moral bond Taylor would establish with her reader. Taylor's moralizing is deeply embedded in the Dissenting aesthetic that we have wished away from the Romantic period, but that is nonetheless present as a crucial link between Enlightenment moral satire and Victorian concerns with social- and self-improvement.[8] To ignore it is in effect to marginalize both the burgeoning role of women as social teachers in early nineteenth-century culture and the literary interests of the increasingly educated lower classes.

   If the quotidian has its view, it also has its sound. The timbre that can be discerned in these poems by Robinson and Taylor is that of the vernacular, what we are accustomed to call, following Wordsworth, "the real language of men." It was even more so, with fine irony, the language of women—not to say also, of Dissenting culture and of the lower classes. Not only is a vernacular not confined to men, but it is at least arguable that women poets, with their relative freedom from establishment conventions and their investment in the quotidian, are those who explored most deliberately the extent to which its language could be incorporated in poetry. If it could describe, if it could moralize, it could also incite. Perhaps the bridge that spans the long distance from the pastoral drama and tragedy with which Hannah More began her career to the evangelical agitation for which she is now known is simply a woman's voice and a woman's professional experience. From the theater she had learned how to know her audience and how to command its attention, as is exemplified in this stanza from a piece called "The Bad Bargain":

> But the great gift, the mighty bribe,
> Which Satan pours amid the tribe,
> Which millions seize with eager haste,
> And all desire at least to taste,
> Is—plodding reader! what d'ye think?
> Alas!—'tis money—money—chink![9]

The importance of More for the future directions of British fiction has recently been admirably charted by Mitzi Myers.[10] But the ease of such verse, its dramatic involvement of the reader, and the introduction of everyday slang had equal consequences for poetry, the poetry of the leveling Romanticism first enunciated by Joanna Baillie.

II

If women tended to see differently from men, it was axiomatic in the eighteenth century that they felt differently too. A singular phenomenon, suddenly appearing in mid-century and not only coinciding with the rise of women poets but also its very hallmark, was the cult of sensibility, which, despite Rousseau's impact on this culture, was largely a female creation. It was unquestionably a central concern in writing by women, whether in the ubiquitous romances or in poetry. The relative fame accorded Henry Mackenzie's novella of 1771, *The Man of Feeling,* should not blind us to the crucial fact foregrounded in his title: that men, too, can feel. The obvious literary struggle on the part of women authors was to convince those men that women, too, can *think;* but precisely because of the powerful shibboleth against the learned woman, an ideological control of remarkable intensity, sensibility was all the more to be cultivated, even celebrated. Hannah More's tribute to the bluestockings of 1782 entitled "Sensibility: An Epistle to the Honourable Mrs. Boscawen" centers its world of learned exchange within an ambience of refined fellow-feeling, suggesting that this is the natural atmosphere in which intellectual development is fostered and shaped. What had been widely considered the defect of a female mind is there shrewdly reclaimed as its distinguishing virtue.

In the culture of sensibility it was relatively easy for women to assert their superiority by the very act of writing. A decade before More's celebration of a collective endeavor, Anna Barbauld had illustrated the process in "The Mouse's Petition, Found in the TRAP where he had been confin'd all Night [by Dr. Priestley]," a poem whose considerable charm masks a studied self-reflexiveness.[11]

O HEAR a pensive prisoner's prayer,
   For liberty that sighs;
And never let thine heart be shut
   Against the wretch's cries!

For here forlorn and sad I sit,
   Within the wiry grate;
And tremble at the' approaching morn,
   Which brings impending fate.

If e'er thy breast with freedom glowed,
   And spurned a tyrant's chain,
Let not thy strong oppressive force
   A free-born mouse detain!

O do not stain with guiltless blood
   Thy hospitable hearth!
Nor triumph that thy wiles betrayed
   A prize so little worth.

The scattered gleanings of a feast
   My frugal meals supply;
But if thine unrelenting heart
   That slender boon deny,—

The cheerful light, the vital air,
   Are blessings widely given;
Let Nature's commoners enjoy
   The common gifts of Heaven.

The well-taught philosophic mind
   To all compassion gives;
Casts round the world an equal eye,
   and feels for all that lives.

If mind,—as ancient sages taught,—
   A never dying flame,
Still shifts through matter's varying forms,
   In every form the same;

Beware, lest in the worm you crush,
   A brother's soul you find;

> And tremble lest thy luckless hand
>   Dislodge a kindred mind.
>
> Or, if this transient gleam of day
>   Be *all* of life we share,
> Let pity plead within thy breast
>   That little *all* to spare.
>
> So may thy hospitable board
>   With health and peace be crowned
> And every charm of heartfelt ease
>   Beneath thy roof be found.
>
> So when destruction lurks unseen,
>   Which men, like mice, may share
> May some kind angel clear thy path
>   And break the hidden snare.

Like all fables, "The Mouse's Petition" has its interior shades of meaning. Even if addressed with youthful affection to an admired family associate, the poem is a direct assertion of the claims of feminine sensibility against male rationality. Making a virtue out of the necessities of feminine existence, its winning style enacts the claim of its underlying metaphor, a release from prison. And in this "The Mouse's Petition" is of a piece with the collection in which Barbauld first published it in 1773, an act of liberation through, not from, femininity. In the clarity and delicacy of its style, it challenges the male universe exemplified by Priestley's scientific experiments. If it is not itself weighty, it embodies as it reflects the tensile strength of a cultural movement gathering momentum.

The poetry of sensibility is at base a literature of psychological exploration, and it is the foundation on which Romanticism was reared. From within the bluestocking circle itself arose a lively debate between the claims of sensibility and those of stoicism, the latter being centered in Elizabeth Carter's 1758 translation of Epictetus and Mrs. Greville's "Ode to Indifference." The debate broadened in the poetry of the later eighteenth century into an entire subgenre written by women, who represented the contrary currents either within the same poem (as in Helen Maria Williams) or in companion pieces in which "To Sensibility" would be countered with the title "To Apathy" (as in Mary Robinson) or "To Indifference" (as in Hannah Cowley and Ann Yearsley). The existence of such a feminized "L'Allegro" and "Il Penseroso" is much more than simply a curiosity. It is the mark of the formation of an independent and shared woman's poetic, and the paradox of its analytical exposition of fine feeling should suggest as well its suitability as a locus for an encoded treatment of the female condition. Ann Yearsley, known as the Milkwoman of Clifton, near Bristol, and a protégé of Elizabeth Montagu and Hannah More, is a case in point. She is not, by and large, a poet of lasting claims, being an example of the proletarian genius that the late Enlightenment, with its humanitarian principles, promoted. But precisely because of those credentials her rendering of the complex reveals the values that underlie these conventions, what they encode. The poem she chooses to introduce her *Poems on Various Subjects* of 1787, the expanded fourth edition of the *Poems on Several Occasions* published a few years earlier, is "Addressed to Sensibility." It ends with this passage:

> . . . ye who boast
> Of bliss *I* n'er must reach, ye, who can fix
> A rule for sentiment, if rules there are,
> (For much I doubt, my friends, if rule e'er held
> Capacious sentiment) ye sure can point
> My mind to joys that never touch'd the heart.
> What is this joy? Where does its essence rest?
> Ah! self-confounding sophists, will ye dare
> Pronounce *that* joy which never touch'd the heart?
> Does Education give the transport keen,
> Or swell your vaunted grief? No, Nature feels
> Most poignant, undefended; hails with me
> The Pow'rs of Sensibility untaught.[12]

Crude as this blank verse is, it embodies a defense of the right of women, with no capacity for education beyond that offered by boarding school or indulgent parents, to literary status, and, beyond that, a claim for an underlying affinity with maternal nature and through it to those elements that are essentially, fundamentally human. In other words, once again to recall Wordsworth's phrase, and here with an exact propriety, it is women who truly do speak "the real language of men."[13]

Yet even as such an analytical mode as verses to one's own sensibility may implicate serious social concerns, its primary impulse was introspective, and the far-reaching consequence was to create the first sustained literary exercise in women's self-reflexiveness. And in turn, that mode slowly permeated the whole of English Romanticism. Likewise, we can trace into the mainstream of Romanticism the dialectical counterpoint between emotional extremes that is the subject and substance of the poems on female sensibility. Yet also the very extremity of this self-reflexive dialectic continually verges on a feminine version of Romantic irony. In the orchestrated emotional abandon of Mary Robinson's sonnet sequence, *Sappho and Phaon,* lies a fictionalized embrace of psychological self-destruction that is virtually a *Liebestod.* Again, the comparative lack of sophistication of the Milkwoman of Clifton, Ann Yearsley, allows her complementary ode "To Indifference" to reveal the darker fears that are at work across a broad spectrum of women poets:

> . . . INDIFF'RENCE come! thy torpid juices shed
> On my keen sense: plunge deep my wounded heart,
> In thickest apathy, till it congeal,
> Or mix with thee incorp'rate. Come, thou foe

To sharp sensation, in thy cold embrace
A death-like slumber shall a respite give
To my long restless soul, tost on extreme,
From bliss to pointed woe. . . .
      Then leave me, Sensibility! begone,
Thou chequer'd angel! Seek the soul refin'd:
I hate thee! and thy long progressive brood
Of joys and mis'ries. Soft Indiff'rence, come!
In this low cottage thou shalt be my guest,
Till Death shuts out the hour: here down I'll sink
With thee upon my couch of homely rush,
Which fading forms of Friendship, Love, or Hope
Must ne'er approach. Ah!—quickly hide, thou pow'r,
Those dear intruding images! Oh, seal
The lids of mental sight, lest I adjure
My freezing supplication.—All is still.
IDEA, smother'd, leave my mind a waste,
Where SENSIBILITY must lose her prey.[14]

Behind Yearsley's histrionic posturing is an innocence that is culturally revelatory, which by no means is merely to suggest, even as it reminds us of future avatars of sensibility, that a Shelley curling up like a child by the Mediterranean or Keats "half in love with easeful death" will make great art from the pains of too acute a sensibility. For this is pointedly a woman's voice, a prey to victimization, resonant with psychological entropy, in retreat to mindless domesticity—"leave my mind a waste"—and its timbres are echoed by every prominent woman poet of this period. Among the women poets of the 1780s and 1790s, this is the particular tonality of Mary Robinson and Charlotte Smith and the reason why they are perhaps the crucial poets of these decades.

Charlotte Smith made a virtual career out of self-pity. She rises from it in her novels, but it is the obsession of her poetry and, to judge by her letters, of her life. But, in sober fact, she had ample justification. In 1783 she joined her wastrel husband, to whom she had been forcibly married in mid-adolescence, in debtors' prison, surrounded with a veritable brood of their children. In effect, from that point on they were her sole responsibility, and her recourse was to write—and write. The first edition of her *Elegiac Sonnets* in 1784 brought her sudden fame and opportunity, but for her the profession of letters was not an indulgence in feminine liberation nor in middle-class mobility; it was an absolute necessity. By 1787 she had separated from Benjamin Smith with responsibility for nine children but no legal freedom. Instead, her husband could comfortably pursue his ways with the insurance of a new and more secure source of income to relieve his chronically dire straits, that guaranteed by his wife's publishing contracts. There was no escaping him, nor was there any legal means, though Smith pursued them all, of independently attaching money left from his father to set up trusts for her children. So it went until her last year, when during her own decline, in a cruel irony, she received news of her husband's death.

Although Smith is virtually an archetype of the female condition of the late eighteenth century, and in her wide influence a promulgator of its values, her situation in the abstract is replicated by the history of Mary Robinson. Left fatherless in adolescence, she was married off by an Austenesque mother to a man who spent on women what he did not lose in gambling or in the assumption of loans at exorbitant rates of interest, a style of living that also lodged her, with their infant daughter, in debtors' prison. Her way out by economic necessity was through the stage, where she became a star before she was twenty. Attracting the attention of the young Prince of Wales, she resisted but at last stepped into the demi monde of his promises, which within a year dissolved in scandal. Left to herself, unable to return to the stage, Robinson contracted rheumatic fever at the age of twenty-three and was thereafter invalided for the rest of her life. A small annuity was finally procured from the prince, and she found a rather more stable, if not always steady, lover, with whom she traversed European spas in a futile search for a cure. There at least she could exist in society, from which she was almost rigidly excluded in England. But with the declaration of war in 1792 she was forced to return to London, where for the next eight years she wrote for a living. Hers was an unsatisfying, lonely existence, especially after she was again jilted in 1796, and it is reflected constantly in her poetry. If one adds her voice to Charlotte Smith's, the result is something beyond merely somber tones. It is veritably existential.

The constant theme of Charlotte Smith's *Elegiac Sonnets* is of rootless exile. Permanence is situated in the external phenomena of nature; even the most impermanent objects—the moon, storm clouds, the ocean, a shipwrecked denizen of a desert island—have an integrity that recoils on the speaker's sense of emptiness. The grotesque forty-fourth sonnet, "Written in the Churchyard at Middleton in Sussex," is astonishing in its trope, the interior life being first compared with a seaside cemetery washed away by a tidal wave—"their bones whiten in the frequent wave . . . With shells and sea-weed mingled"—and then contrasted; for the living woman cannot attain the entropic nonmeaning of dissolution she desires: "I am doom'd— by life's long storm opprest, / To gaze with envy on their gloomy rest."[15] But if extreme, the sonnet is of a piece with the collection that surrounds it, the whole portraying a disembodied sensibility at the mercy of an alien universe and without discernible exit from its condition. The entire sonnet revival of the Romantic period was impelled into existence by this vision, and, even where (as with Wordsworth) the tonalities are reversed, the underlying dynamic of an isolated sensibility informs all the sonnets written in Smith's wake.

Her most finished poem, beyond the collection of *Elegiac Sonnets,* is *The Emigrants* of 1793. Its dedication to William Cowper is forthright in acknowledging his desultory meditation of *The Task* as her model. But his is ultimately a poem of ringing optimism—at least it aspires to that end— whereas the underlying metaphorical strategy of *The Emigrants* is to connect Charlotte Smith as center of perception to the exiles from France's Terror, wandering the Kent shore cut off by but a dozen miles from their home-land, which is as present and as inexplicable to them as the suddenness of their reduction from opulence to penury. Their compounded loss of lan-guage, country, and means threatens their very sense of cultural and personal identity, and as the poem increasingly focuses on them as emblems of alienated humanity, the greater becomes their correspondence to the solitary figure observing them. In an uncanny way Charlotte Smith creates her own identity in the poem by absorbing their emptiness. In the process the details of her own vicissitudes are inflated to mythic status, and the intrusion of her legal frustrations as an embryonic version of the nightmare Dickens was to depict in Chancery seems justified by the abuses of state power from which these exiles have fled. The opening of book 2 is repre-sentative of the overall design of *The Emigrants:*[16]

> Long wintry months are past; the Moon that now
> Lights her pale cresent even at noon, has made
> Four times her revolution; since with step,
> Mournful and slow, along the wave-worn cliff,
> Pensive I took my solitary way,
> Lost in despondence, while contemplating
> Not my own wayward destiny alone,
> (Hard as it is, and difficult to bear!)
> But in beholding the unhappy lot
> Of the lorn Exiles; who, amid the storms
> Of wild disastrous Anarchy, are thrown,
> Like shipwreck'd sufferers, on England's coast,
> To see, perhaps, no more their native land,
> Where Desolation riots: They, like me,
> From fairer hopes and happier prospects driven,
> Shrink from the future, and regret the past.
> But on this Upland scene, while April comes,
> With fragrant airs, to fan my throbbing breast,
> Fain would I snatch an interval from Care,
> That weighs my wearied spirit down to earth;
> Courting, once more, the influence of Hope
> (For "Hope" still waits upon the flowery prime)
> As here I mark Spring's humid hand unfold
> The early leaves that fear capricious winds,
> While, even on shelter'd banks, the timid flowers
> Give, half reluctantly, their warmer hues
> To mingle with the primroses' pale stars.
> No shade the leafless copses yet afford,
> Nor hide the mossy labours of the Thrush,
> That, startled, darts across the narrow path;
> But quickly re-assur'd, resumes his task,
> Or adds his louder notes to those that rise
> From yonder tufted brake; where the white buds
> Of the first thorn are mingled with the leaves
> Of that which blossoms on the brow of May.

Smith gambles daringly in *The Emigrants,* and perhaps she does not wholly succeed, for the stakes are too large for the table on which she plays. But by the end of the poem we have before us a wholly recast model. Cowper is willing to allow the world to flow through his centering consciousness, but he is characteristically self-effacing rather than absorbent. In "The Emigrants," most fully of Charlotte Smith's poems, one understands the deep impulse behind Wordsworth's generous praise of her in 1833 as "a lady to whom English verse is under greater obligations than are likely to be either acknowledged or remembered." In his tribute he singled out her "true feeling for rural nature," which is accurate enough, but perhaps the least of what he could have learned from her.[17] The year *The Emigrants* was published, 1793, was also the year of the twenty-three-year-old Wordsworth's debut with *Descriptive Sketches* and *An Evening Walk,* poems manifestly in search of a style and subject matter. A cursory glance at the above passage will suggest how charged is Charlotte Smith's poem with features that in a few years were to become identifiably Wordsworth's: in style, the long, sinuous verse paragraphs, the weighted monosyllables, the quick evocation of natural detail; in matter, the absorbing and self-mythicizing voice and the creatures of its contemplation—the aged, the idiots, the female vagrants, the exiled and alienated.

These are figures with which we have been long familiar, in Coleridge's, as well as Wordsworth's, contributions to *Lyrical Ballads,* perhaps less so in Southey's *Botany-Bay* and *English Eclogues,* which are cut from the same bolt. In Southey's hands, in particular, they are instruments of a leveling political program. But their ubiquity, and their continuation, transcend the limited environment in which we now locate them, for they are the legitimate offspring of this first generation of self-reflecting women poets. In the year of her death, 1800, Mary Robinson published her last and best volume of verse, with the firm of Longman's, bearing an advertising sheet that featured their second edition of *Lyrical Ballads,* and poems by Southey and Cottle. But to read the titles of her *Lyrical Tales,* as well as poems not published there, is to recognize more than her affinity with Wordsworth and Coleridge. "The Alien Boy," "All Alone," "The Deserted Cottage," "The Exile," "The Fugitive," "The Maniac," "The Savage of Aveyron"— these are the displacements of feminine consciousness, the victims of sensibility, mice in the trap. And though we can locate their genesis in the later years of the eighteenth century, they are still discernibly the characteristics of women's poetry throughout the first quarter of the nineteenth century. As an instance we might take Margaret Hodgson's large historical poems in the meter and after the manner of Scott. The first, *Wallace; or, the Fight of Falkirk* (1809), after building up our sympathy for the Scottish patriots, records their utter annihilation, capping the grisly record by the betrayal and capture of Wallace: his death is left to the last footnote. That Hodgson's is not simply an unintentional misfocusing is clear from her even longer Epic romance of seven years later, *Margaret of Anjou,* which concludes with the Battle of Tewkesbury in 1471. All our sympathy is placed on the legitimate pretender to the English throne, Prince Edward, and even his imperious and unlikeable mother, the title figure, is elevated to heroic stature; then he and his forces are slaughtered and her great heart breaks. As late as Felicia Hemans's *The Forest Sanctuary* of 1825, the poem she is said to have thought her best (and certainly its Spenserian stanzas are of a high finish), we witness a retreat into the savage interior of South America by a father and son—a displacement as evident as it is endemic in poetry by women—escaping the manifold persecutions of European civilization. At the end they are alienated and alone, with such integrity as still carries meaning. Even as both Hemans and Landon moved away from such hard-minded realism into the realms of piety and sentimentality, their heroines still regularly perished. Contrary to what one might conventionally expect, in poetry at least, the unhappy ending is the norm of women writers of the Romantic period.

III

The two features of women's poetry we have been examining, an invest-ment in quotidian tones and details and a portrayal of alienated sensibility, are not as isolated as this analysis would make them appear. Often they are present in tandem, with an effect that presages much later poetry and casts an oblique light on our customary expectations of the literature of British Romanticism—as will be evident if we return to the oeuvre of Jane Taylor. What follows is the second part of a poem blankly titled "A Pair," in which she simply contrasts the empty life of a rich youth with the world of the urban proletariat. In both cases the moral meaning is wholly invested in quotidian detail; and the lacuna between the startling contrasts is, as with Robinson, left to the reader to fill, if any reader has the capacity, or mental temerity, to bridge such cultural polarities. The London of this poem is closer to Dickens, not born for another six years, than to Blake; and, though it is beyond proof, it is nonetheless the case that the young Dickens was far more likely to know Taylor, well-recognized in her time, than Blake. So, for that matter, was the later poet whose tones are most reminiscent of Taylor's excruciatingly compassionate calm, Thomas Hardy.[18]

> Down a close street, whose darksome shops display
> Old clothes and iron on both sides the way;
> Loathsome and wretched, whence the eye in pain,
> Averted turns, nor seeks to view again;
> Where lowest dregs of human nature dwell,
> More loathsome than the rags and rust they sell;—
> A pale mechanic rents an attic floor,
> By many a shatter'd stair you gain the door:
> 'Tis one poor room, whose blacken'd walls are hung
> With dust that settled there when he was young.
> The rusty grate two massy bricks displays,

To fill the sides and make a frugal blaze.
The door unhing'd, the window patch'd and broke,
The panes obscur'd by half a century's smoke:
There stands the bench at which his life is spent,
Worn, groov'd, and bor'd, and worm-devour'd, and bent,
Where daily, undisturb'd by foes or friends,
In one unvaried attitude he bends.
His tools, long practis'd, seem to understand
Scarce less their functions, than his own right hand.
With these he drives his craft with patient skill;
Year after year would find him at it still:
The noisy world around is changing all,
War follows peace, and kingdoms rise and fall;
France rages now, and Spain, and now the Turk;
Now victory sounds;—but there he sits at work!
A man might see him so, then bid adieu,—
Make a long voyage to China or Peru;
There traffic, settle, build; at length might come,
Alter'd, and old, and weather-beaten home,
And find him on the same square foot of floor
On which he left him twenty years before.
—The self same bench, and attitude, and stool,
The same quick movement of his cunning tool;
The very distance 'twixt his knees and chin,
As though he had but stepp'd just out and in.

Such is his fate—and yet you might descry
A latent spark of meaning in his eye.
—That crowded shelf, beside his bench, contains
One old, worn, volume that employs his brains:
With algebraic lore its page is spread,
Where *a* and *b* contend with *x* and *z:*
Sold by some *student* from an Oxford hall,
—Bought by the pound upon a broker's stall.
On this it is his sole delight to pore,
Early and late, when working time is o'er:
But oft he stops, bewilder'd and perplex'd,
At some hard problem in the learned text;
Pressing his hand upon his puzzled brain,
At what the dullest school-boy could explain.

From needful sleep the precious hour he saves,
To give his thirsty mind the stream it craves:
There, with his slender rush beside him plac'd,
He drinks the knowledge in with greedy haste.
At early morning, when the frosty air
Brightens Orion and the northern Bear,
His distant window mid the dusky row,
Holds a dim light to passenger below.
—A light more dim is flashing on his mind,
That shows its darkness, and its views confin'd.

> Had science shone around his early days,
> How had his soul expanded in the blaze!
> But penury bound him, and his mind in vain
> Struggles and writhes beneath her iron chain.
>
> —At length the taper fades, and distant cry
> Of early sweep bespeaks the morning nigh;
> Slowly it breaks,—and that rejoicing ray
> That wakes the healthful country into day,
> Tips the green hills, slants o'er the level plain,
> Reddens the pool, and stream, and cottage pane,
> And field, and garden, park, and stately hall,—
> Now darts obliquely on his wretched wall.
> He knows the wonted signal; shuts his book,
> Slowly consigns it to its dusty nook;
> Looks out awhile, with fixt and absent stare,
> On crowded roofs, seen through the foggy air;
> Stirs up the embers, takes his sickly draught,
> Sighs at his fortunes, and resumes his craft.

There is a further aspect to Taylor's poem, which suggests how a concern for absolute detail links dialectically with sensibility, even with the sublime of sensibility, in which all detail is swallowed in a gulf of longing. Take away the moral thrust implicit in Taylor's portrait of this unaccommodated man, or simply take away the algebra text in which he absurdly invests meaning, and you have a stark portrait of an existential condition. Look without prejudice at the uncompromising materiality of her "Prejudice" and again you encounter a void of signification. Or if a reader cannot center the disconnected fragments of Mary Robinson's montage, who can? The humanitarianism of the Dissenting tradition makes women poets sympathetic to distress and victimization, but the void at the center of sensibility should alert us to a profound awareness among these poets of being themselves dispossessed, figured through details they do not control, uniting an unstructurable longing of sensibility with the hard-earned sense of thingness.

That the threat of a collapse into this void is generally averted is, however, as significant as its presence. Even as we extract patterns from historical retrospect, it is essential to recognize that Smith's sonnets or Taylor's moral essays are the elaboration of a literary formula as much as are the *Lyrical Ballads*. A collapse in such circumstances would have been a contradiction of premises. What saves Charlotte Smith from the inanition she inscribes is quite simply its inscription. Edition after edition of the *Elegiac Sonnets* testified to a success that cannot be undervalued, success within a traditional male preserve. And her experience is paradigmatic. Even where the perspective of the poet seems radically self-denying, it is balanced by the self-confidence of its art. Where isolation seems most acute, there is the knowledge that a community is being built in its stead. The achievement of these women poets was to create literature from perspectives necessarily limited by the hegemony of male values. And that those perspectives should enter the cultural mainstream was, in the large sense, the foremost view they had in mind, even though they could not from their contemporary recognition have anticipated the effacement they suffered from history. Poets, they might well have told us, even if confined to the domestic circle, are still the unacknowledged legislators of the world.

NOTES

The research and writing of this essay were made possible by a fellowship, sponsored by the National Endowment for the Humanities, from the Henry E. Huntington Library, San Marino, California.

1. [William Harness], *Blackwood's*, 16 (1824); 162.

2. *Thoughts on the Condition of Women, and on the Injustice of Mental Subordination*, 2nd ed. (London: Longman's, 1799), pp. 95–96. The first edition of this work was published under the pseudonymn Anne Frances Randall: although conclusive proof of Mary Robinson's authorship has not been advanced, the attribution is venerable. For the identities of the writers cited, consult *A Dictionary of British and American Women Writers: 1660–1800*, ed. Janet Todd (Totowa, N.J.: Rowman and Allenheld, 1985).

3. On the novelists, see Katherine M. Rogers, *Feminism in Eighteenth-Century England* (Urbana: University of Illinois Press, 1982), pp. 22ff. After the withdrawal of Sheridan, the backbone of the London theater was supplied by such women as Frances Brooke, Hannah Parkhurst Cowley, Elizabeth Inchbald, and Hannah More, not to ignore the signal contribution of Sarah Siddons in giving professional and social respectability to a theatrical career.

4. Although this list is probably incomplete, the following ten poets, ranging from the mid-1780s to the mid-1820s, were authors of poems of epic ambition: Elizabeth Barrett, Sophia Burrell, Hannah Cowley, Charlotte Elizabeth Dixon, Elizabeth Hands, Margaret Hodson, Mary Linwood, Eleanor Ann Porden, Elizabeth Smith (of Birmingham), and Helen Maria Williams.

5. *The Poetical Works of Mary E. Robinson* (London: Richard Phillips, 1806), 3: 274–76.

6. This poem was published in the *Morning Post* and reprinted after Robinson's death in an anthology edited by her daughter: *The Wild Wreath*, ed Mary E. Robinson (London: Richard Phillips, 1804), pp. 160–62. It was not included in the *Poetical Works* of 1806, presumably on grounds of decorum.

7. Jane Taylor, *Poetry and Prose*, ed. F. V. Barry (London: Humphrey Milford, 1924), pp. 87–89.

8. On religious verse during the eighteenth century, consult David Morris, *The Religious Sublime: Christian Poetry and Critical Tradition in Eighteenth-Century England* (Lexington: University Press of Kentucky, 1972); for a survey of women's hymnody during this period, see Margaret Maison's essay, "'Thine, Only Thine!' Women Hymn Writers in Britain, 1760–1835," in *Religion in the Lives of English Women, 1760–1930*, ed. Gail Malmgreen (Bloomington: Indiana University Press, 1986), pp. 11–40.

9. *Poems* (London: Cadell and Davies, 1816), p. 286.

10. See "Hannah More's Tracts for the Times: Social Fiction and Female Ideology," in *Fettered or Free? British Women Novelists 1670–1815*, ed. Mary Anne Schofield and Cecilia Macheski (Athens: Ohio University Press, 1985), pp. 264–84.

11. *The Works of Anna Laetitia Barbauld* (London: Longman's, 1825), I: 35–38.

12. *Poems on Various Subjects* (London: G. G. J. and J. Robinson, 1787), p. 6.

13. Yearsley continually reiterates her proletarian access to human truth, for instance in "To Mr ****, an Unlettered Poet, on Genius Improved" ("Deep in the soul live ever tuneful springs, / Waiting the touch of Ecstasy, which strikes / Most pow'rful on defenceless, untaught Minds," p. 81). In her best, or at least her most self-assertive, poem she goes on the attack: see "Addressed to Ignorance, Occasioned by a Gentleman's desiring the Author never to assume a Knowledge of the Ancients" (pp. 93–99), where, with considerable effect, Yearsley reduces major figures of classical myth and literature to their contemporary, vernacular British equivalents.

14. *Poems on Various Subjects,* pp. 49, 52–53.

15. *Elegiac Sonnets,* 6th ed. (London: Cadell and Davies, 1792), p. 44.

16. Charlotte Smith, *The Emigrants* (London: Thomas Cadell, 1793), pp. 39–41.

17. See William Wordsworth, *Poetical Works,* ed. Ernest De Selincourt and Helen Darbishire (Oxford: Clarendon Press, 1952–59), 4: 403.

18. *Poetry and Prose,* pp. 106–08.

AN EARLY ROMANCE

MOTHERHOOD AND WOMEN'S WRITING IN MARY WOLLSTONECRAFT'S NOVELS

Laurie Langbauer

I'd like to begin with a gossipy anecdote about Matthew Gregory Lewis that Mrs. Oliphant tells in her *Literary History*. Lewis, you remember, was the author of that scandalous romance, *The Monk* (1795). Yet the scandal Mrs. Oliphant recounts is not about *The Monk* at all, but quite other. After *The Monk* was published:

> The family history of the Lewises [she writes] was . . . disturbed by an incident which plunged them into unimaginable terror. . . . [The mother] wrote a novel! When this terrible fact was known, her son with a panic almost beyond words, rushed to pen and ink to implore her to suppress it.[1]

Lewis warns his mother of the injuries her novel's publication would cause: his father would be shattered, his unmarried sister left an old maid, his married sister disgraced in her husband's family, and Lewis himself would have to flee to the Continent. Mrs. Oliphant suggests that Lewis objects to his mother's authorship because he fears it would coopt his own. He hears rumors that *she* has written *The Monk*, and writes "This goes more to put me out of humour with the book than" the critics' fury over it.[2] But authorship is not alone at risk; Lewis fears his mother's writing would threaten her identity as a mother, and his own as her son (Oliphant depicts Lewis, in fact, as a mama's boy, whose relationship to his mother is central to his life). "I always consider a female author as a sort of half-man,"[3] Lewis writes to his mother, and his attempt to suppress her novel becomes an effort to avoid the gender uncertainties into which her writing would cast him: what would it mean if one's mother were half-man?

I present Monk Lewis here as an extreme example of a pervasive attitude. Although he is contemporary with Mary Wollstonecraft, he represents a view that is more than just locally and historically bound—more than the quaint prejudice of a certain class of the eighteenth century that Mrs. Oliphant, herself a famous nineteenth-century writing mother, attempts (but too determinedly) to argue that it is. Rather, this view points us to the enduring structures of the unconscious and writing. That the greatest horror Monk Lewis could imagine was his mother writing provides the background for my own discussion of motherhood and women's writing. I'll first consider the intersection of mothers and writing through the example of a woman novelist—Mary Wollstonecraft. Then I'd like briefly to consider the role of the mother in terms of feminist theory. What I want to bring us back to is the horror of the mother writing, the horror of uncertainty.

How do motherhood and women's writing figure in Mary Wollstonecraft's work? Certainly in her novels—*Mary, a Fiction* (published in 1788) and *The Wrongs of Woman; or Maria, a Fragment* (1798), Wollstonecraft presents those two rarities of fiction—mothers and women writers—side by side. *Mary* opens with the story of the title-character's mother; *The Wrongs of Woman* tells of Maria's mother, among others, and Maria's own motherhood is the focus of its story. Mary and Maria both write, and their lyrical prose effusions, as well as Maria's extended auto-biographical narrative, are included for us in the texts.

I suggest that we can get at the relation of motherhood and women's writing through Wollstonecraft's treatment of romance. Mary Poovey argues that Mary Wollstonecraft's novels set out to critique "romantic expectations,"[4] but get caught up in romance themselves. Poovey condemns this collapse of Wollstonecraft's novels into romance because of its ultimate effect: by succumbing to romance, her novels merely fall into the patriarchal traps she is able to escape in her *Vindication of the Rights of Woman* (published in 1792, it falls in between the two novels). "Finally," Poovey writes, "[in her novels] . . . what Wollstonecraft really wants is to achieve a new position of dependence within a paternal order of her own choosing."[5]

I read Wollstonecraft's treatment of romance differently: I see romance aligned not with the paternal but with the maternal. Wollstonecraft explicitly thematizes this association in *The Wrongs of Woman*. She moves us literally from what we've come to call the Name of the Father to the Name of the Mother by repeating, but significantly altering, a scene. Midway through her story, Maria, whose husband has stolen her baby, recounts the separation of a parent and child—in this case, an infant son, who lisps "papa" to an absent father.[6] Yet one ending of the unfinished *Wrongs of Woman* closes Maria's story with the restoration of her baby daughter, who utters instead "the word 'Mamma!'" (*Wrongs:* Conclusion.203). In Wollstonecraft's fiction, mothers and daughters supplant fathers and sons. In this romantic ending (romantic in the traditional sense that it unrealistically fulfills a wish) mothers and daughters enjoy a union and happiness denied the men. Wollstonecraft goes on in her novels to link the maternal with romance even more securely, drawing on more senses of romance than just this traditional one. Yet we still need to ask whether doing so makes any difference at all, especially for the woman writer.

In order to answer that question, I'd like to consider the other senses of the word "romance" that inform Wollstonecraft's collusion of the maternal and women's writing. Women as writers are linked to romance in another traditional sense of the term. We are all familiar, I think, with a common usage of the word romance: immature writing, lacking the novel's complexity of form and sophistication of content—in its most generous usage, pure, artless, simple, naive writing. Traditional—especially eighteenth-century—constructions of *women* sound very similar to this sense of romance: women are immature too, which makes them at best pure, artless, simple, and naive. Because of this similarity, romance as a form is usually considered proper to women; it is all that they are fitted to read or write.

On one level, Wollstonecraft seems to accept this equation between women and romance, and the derision it implies. Writing anonymously as a novel-critic—presumably a male novel-critic—for the *Analytic Review,* she several times accounts for books that are "romantic unnatural fabrication[s]," as she calls them, marred both by bad writing and inexperience of life, by attributing them to the pen of "a very young lady."[7] She distinguishes between such romances and a different, better form, the novel, writing tongue in cheek of one "insipid, harmless production" that "we would have termed this a romance, if it had not proclaimed itself a Novel in the title page."[8]

Yet Wollstonecraft does not consistently accept the traditional definition of women, or of romance. In her *Vindication of the Rights of Woman,* she radically redefines women, especially in relation to traditional assumptions about their maturity. Men treat women as if "they were in a state of perpetual childhood,"[9] and confuse that state with "innocence" (*Vindication:* 4.153). Yet innocence is a "specious name" for ignorance, an enforced ignorance that is the cause of women's ills (*Vindication:* 2.100): they are not naturally childish; they are kept that way to bar them from a better state. After exposing this male sophistry that confuses and enslaves them, Wollstonecraft offers women a way to redefine themselves. She substitutes for the innocence they have been urged to cultivate its very opposite—"the treasure of life, experience" (*Vindication:* 2.114).

For Wollstonecraft, experience in general means education and exposure to the vicissitudes of life, a position of knowledge if not of mastery. But, more than that, the experience she values—the experience that the male authorities she criticizes in the *Vindication* think is implied in any other, which is why they feel women must be kept innocent/ignorant—that experience is especially sexual experience. In *The Wrongs of Woman,* Wollstonecraft suggests that "freedom of conduct has emancipated many women's minds" (*Wrongs:* 10.156), and it is her advocacy of women's sexual experience that immediately made her an anathema to an enduring critical tradition. Wollstonecraft argues that ignorance never equals sexual innocence:

women barred from direct experience are actually the most corrupt—they debauch their minds reading romances (as Mary's mother is in danger of doing[10]), while a maid who falls can still remain mentally pure (*Vindication:* 8.241). Granting women sexual—bodily—experience is a way of protecting them from imaginative impurity, from the contagion of romance. In this interest, Wollstonecraft dispels the myth of woman's essential ignorance and immaturity so that her seemingly natural connection to ignorant, immature romance can dissolve.

And in the development of her own fiction Wollstonecraft seems deliberately to move beyond romance. In its very opening, *The Wrongs of Woman*— meant as a novelistic continuation of the *Vindication*[11]—proclaims itself an antiromance: Maria is in a madhouse, a place that is really horrible, not some silly haunted castle of "romantic fancy" (*Wrongs:* 1.75). This comparison is particularly telling, for Wollstonecraft's own less experienced work, her first novel, *Mary,* written before the *Vindication,* has just such a castle, where its heroine loves to go and muse (*Mary:* 4.9). Wollstonecraft seems aware that this first work is immature, naive—traditionally romantic. Although in her preface to *The Wrongs of Woman* she deliberately calls it a novel (*Wrongs:* Preface.73), the editors of the Oxford edition of *Mary* point out that "both the title and preface [of that book] . . . carefully avoid the word novel,"[12] —no proclaiming a romance a novel in the title page for Wollstonecraft. While writing *The Wrongs of Woman,* Wollstonecraft admits in a letter that *Mary* is "a crude production . . . an imperfect sketch,"[13] and Emily Sunstein, in her biography of Wollstonecraft, *A Different Face,* speaks for the majority of critics who indeed find *Mary* a "sentimental romance."[14]

As a novel, *The Wrongs of Woman* seems to take up where the romance, *Mary,* leaves off; Maria's situation critiques the deluded naiveté of the earlier heroine. Whereas *Mary* ends with the heroine living with her husband, *The Wrongs of Woman* opens with a heroine who has broken away from hers. Maria is older, savvy, and worldly wise in a way Mary never is: Mary never sleeps with her lover, for instance, while Maria does. Wollstonecraft inscribes experience's triumph over romance into the very plot of *The Wrongs of Woman.* As a wife, Maria has been treated as an "idiot, or perpetual minor" (*Wrongs:* 11.159) to the extent that her husband has wrongly imprisoned her in the madhouse, kidnapped their daughter, and stolen her inheritance. In order to oppose the view of women that makes this treatment seem right and natural, Wollstonecraft has Maria write a narrative of her life, a story of her own painful road to experience, to the shedding of traditional—"romantic," as she calls them (*Wrongs:* 7.128)— notions of her duties and abilities as a woman. Maria writes in order to aid and instruct her daughter, to help her also "gain experience—ah! gain it—" (*Wrongs:* 7.124).

Maria's book takes the place of—in fact, becomes—the experience she wishes to hand on to her daughter. By making Maria a writer, and collapsing her text and her experience, Wollstonecraft underscores her new— unromantic—view of the possibilities for women's writing. The depiction of

Maria necessarily reflects on Wollstonecraft as a woman writer: through Maria, she bolsters her own position as experienced—a position she certainly takes in the *Vindication*—passing that legacy through her writing on to her readers, who fill in the place of Maria's lost daughter.

Where does motherhood fit into all this? For Wollstonecraft, maternity is crucially linked to women's sexual experience—maternity is especially sexuality's sign, what makes it manifest: the sexually experienced Maria is definitely a mother, though Mary never is. And Maria's (sexual) experience, which leads to her maternity, collapses into it, and becomes what enables her writing. Maria is a much more experienced and accomplished writer than Mary (she can give us a complete narrative rather than just Mary's fragments) partly becaue she is a mother. Maria's maternity provides the ability and occasion for writing: she writes to pass along her experience. But she also writes to maintain her very identity as a mother: she dedicates her narrative to her daughter, apostrophizing her in it, as an attempt to secure her (for that daughter may actually be dead, and Maria no longer a mother). Motherhood is not only the emblem of the woman writer in Wollstonecraft; Maria may only be a mother *while* she is writing.

Yet the mother, through her connection with writing, does not only move beyond romance in Wollstonecraft's fiction. The titles of her novels, by their repetition of variants of "Mary" (Wollstonecraft's own name, of course, as well as the name of our culture's most renowned mother), suggest a continuity as well as a contrast between the books. While writing *The Wrongs of Woman*, Wollstonecraft, responding to her lover William Godwin's accusation of a "radical defect" in her writing,[15] acknowledges an "original defect" in her mind, a sort of mother defect—a tendency toward romance.[16]

Romance does invade *The Wrongs of Woman* as much as it invades *Mary*. Maria, like Mary, is romantic: she confesses to her daughter peculiarities of temperament—"which by the world are indefinitely termed romantic" (*Wrongs:* 7.128). In *The Wrongs of Woman*, it is the world surrounding Maria, particularly her husband, who more often than the narrative itself denounces Maria's romance (*Wrongs:* 11.161; 12.167, 169). Because it is Maria's brutish husband who dismisses as romantic all of her best qualities—Maria tells us "romantic sentiments . . . was the indiscriminate epithet he gave to every mode of conduct or thinking superior to his own" (*Wrongs:* 12.167)—romance also becomes a sign of the narrative's approbation.

This instability in the attitude toward romance in Wollstonecraft's writing grows out of an instability within the term itself. Wollstonecraft elsewhere writes of "romantic wavering feelings"; she collapses the "romantic and inconstant" (*Vindication:* 4.169). Romance takes on a new meaning, aligned with those qualities of indeterminacy; it comes to stand for instability itself, and hence becomes what Wollstonecraft calls "tantamount to nonsensical."[17] Romance as nonsense becomes a valorized term in Wollstonecraft's novels, one associated, as is its more traditional and derisive meaning, with the maternal: Wollstonecraft directly connects the romantic and nonsensical, for example, in her own paean to the imagination—the "mother of sentiment."[18] While, as we have seen, romance and motherhood can stand opposed—the mother, through her experience, breaking away from the romantic—within this second sense the two are inseparable. And this connection leads away again from experience: Wollstonecraft insisted on keeping her inexperienced "romantic" feelings in the face of her first lover's—Gilbert Imlay's—wiser experience and "judgment" because "they resemble the mother more than the father"[19]—that is, they come more from the imagination, the province of romance she has earlier criticized.

Romance, nonsense, motherhood, and immaturity: to understand their connection in Wollstonecraft's writing we need for a moment to consider these terms in another context, for they also demarcate the category of the semiotic in the early writings of the psychoanalytic theorist Julia Kristeva. The semiotic is Kristeva's own move from the Name of the Father to the Mother; as Mary Jacobus argues, Kristeva substitutes the pre-oedipal mother for the oedipal father in terms of their relation to the origins of discourse.[20] In *Desire in Language,* Kristeva yokes and opposes the semiotic to the symbolic. Kristeva's symbolic we can understand largely in Lacan's terms; she links it to meaning, signification, representation, the location of sense and of the subject, the entry into language brought about through the agency of the father and the threat of castration. The semiotic is impossibly, but necessarily, outside meaning and subjectivity, calling them into question (it is heterogeneous to signification, operates "through, despite, and in excess of it," and comes before or is outside of "the operating consciousness" of the subject created by the symbolic order[21]). Kristeva gestures to the impossible place of the semiotic by aligning it with (fantasies of) the pre-oedipal—with immature archaic expression, "uncertain and indeterminate articulation," with the utterances of infants, and particularly with what she calls the maternal chora, the maternal body and its responses to the infant, which embody this antirepresentational, disruptive dimension[22] (a dimension in which the literary critic Dianne Sadoff places that formless and undifferentiated realm that we call "in narrative terminology, the romance"[23]).

Jane Gallop does a canny, perverse, and, I think, sometimes incorrect reading of the problems of Kristeva's semiotic, the dangers of collapsing it with the maternal, of believing the mother controls it.[24] Richard Klein, on the other hand, suggests—and I agree with him—that Kristeva actually constructs the maternal precisely around the very splitting, the doubleness of identity that Gallop argues it totalizes.[25] Perhaps this doubleness will become clearer in a moment, for I would like us now to consider the relation of semiotic forces with the maternal in Wollstonecraft's writing expressly to consider it as just one aspect of the mother, who is at the same time opposed to that character of herself as well.

Motherhood is associated with semiotic forces in *The Wrongs of Woman* from the opening of the book, in which we find Maria confined within the madhouse. Her confinement there figures that other confinement, childbirth: Maria's imprisonment in the madhouse is the direct result of the birth of her daughter, heir to the fortune her husband wishes to possess. Similarly, another inmate, and fellow female artist, the "lovely warbler" whose songs Maria admires, underscores this interrelation of meanings: she has gone mad "during her first lying-in" (*Wrongs:* 2.88) as Wollstonecraft's own sister may have done. The madhouse figures the nonsense of the maternal chora, quite literally in the babble of the mad, "the burden of . . . incessant ravings" (*Wrongs:* 2.84) that is the constant background to Maria's story. The narrator likens Maria's situation to being "in a strange land, where the human voice conveys no information to the eager ear" (*Wrongs:* 2.86), and Maria's ordering of her life in her autobiography is in reaction to, but called into question by, the linguistic chaos surrounding her. When the novel directly associates the breakdown of language and shattering of meaning with the maternal, its effects remain disruptive of order, but can be rapturous as well as threatening: Maria's fervent observations on maternity "interrupt" her narrative (*Wrongs:* 10.154), and those observations are so fervent because her pleasure in being a mother is "unutterable" (*Wrongs:* 10.154).

And the mother is marked within Wollstonecraft's fiction not just through her presence, but also through her absence. For, although Wollstonecraft gestures to the mother more than is usual, the maternal space remains curiously vacant too. In describing Mary's mother, the narrator refers to her as a "mere nothing," one of the female "noughts" (*Mary:* 1.2), and that is the position mothers occupy throughout Wollstonecraft's work: Maria's mother becomes important when she dies, and Maria's own motherhood is posited but never realized in her novel—her daughter almost immediately disappears and their time together is only a blank in the text. The mother is shadowy, not completely represented, because her place is outside the signifying order, unrepresentable.

Interruption, partial representation, becomes a narrative principle in the novel; *The Wrongs of Woman* is itself nonsensical, interrupted by violence as well as rapture, especially at its end, which is particularly fragmented, almost meaningless. In place of closure, Wollstonecraft presents competing and contradictory versions of Maria's response to a new pregnancy (Wollstonecraft was herself pregnant again at the time and died shortly after giving birth). Such semiotic forces would indeed represent for a male critic a romantic "defect" in the woman writer, and in two senses: *defect's* sense of lack—her writing's lack of sense, the nonsense of its language (Godwin particularly criticized Wollstonecraft's lack of control over language, her problems with grammar) playing upon what a man would see as Wollstonecraft's own essential lack as a woman writer—and also *defect's* sense of desertion—the woman writer leaving the rank and file of the male (symbolic) order. In her preface to *The Wrongs of Woman*, Wollstonecraft emphasizes that the situation of maternity is the vehicle for such writing: she contrasts her book to ones in which maternity is bypassed altogether— male writing, books (perhaps by Richardson and Rousseau, from whom she distinguishes herself in the advertisement to *Mary*) that treat their heroines as if they had "just come forth highly finished Minervas from the head of Jove" (*Wrongs:* Preface.73). Wollstonecraft's novel, on the other hand, is the product of a woman, and one that she suggests is fully formed in the rather formless state we receive it—she warns her readers against dismissing it as a mere sketch, as "the abortion of a distempered fancy" (*Wrongs:* Preface.73).

In Wollstonecraft's writing, then, the mother is double. She is both outside and inside romance: in command of language even to speaking new terms for her own self-definition, to breaking with romance's ignorance and immaturity, and at the same time subverting language's order and meaning, partaking of the romance of the infantile and unutterable.

At the beginning of this paper, I questioned whether it made any difference for the woman writer to write under the Name of the Father or the Mother, to relocate the romantic with the maternal. The terms of my question, I think, provide for its answer, for *difference* is what is crucial, the mother's difference from herself; through her connection with romance, we see the mother in Wollstonecraft as both experienced and of a realm in which experience is meaningless. She is both the one who knows—what Gallop calls the phallic mother—and the one outside of and undercutting knowledge—the maternal chora.

This self-division extends and dissolves the very category of Name: of language, and of writing. By moving from the father to the mother, we emphasize that naming, language, is not just the function of the transcendental signifier, the phallus, but also of the undertones and side effects of signification—its babble and noise—that won't leave it alone, that call it into question. And the category of the mother, alternately fixed and undercutting itself, is created by and reflects this very movement. The mother actually is what Monk Lewis fears—she is half-man, partially constituted as a subject, within mastery and language. Maria's desire "to be a father, as well as a mother" (*Wrongs:* 13.180) to her daughter suggests Wollstonecraft's recognition of her double role. Locating the woman writer with motherhood, difference, and division allows her to make sense—and nonsense—within the paternal order, to work within it without completely accepting its rule. And that, I think, makes all the difference.

Directing my argument about the mother is what has become a standard critical move: the maternal is that which threatens a system of power—patriarchy or representation—and is cast out accordingly, her absence shoring it up. And yet that system can never dispatch her because she is really part of it. Or, rather, I've made that system part of the maternal, relocating this play of difference within the mother—she is what is subverted as well as what subverts. But I'd like to push my argument a little further by asking, "why the mother?" What might be involved in using her as an emblem of difference, and what might be the problems of doing so? One objection might be that locating difference within the mother is a regressive fantasy of plenitude that actually collapses difference: she be-

comes the Mother who is—and therefore has—everything, a new appearance of an old friend, the Phallic Mother, and once again gets aligned
with sameness, with the phallus. I'm intrigued by the collapse of difference
implied in conjuring it, and would like to follow it, to get to the same place
along a different route by raising another objection we could make to the
use of the maternal.

For isn't examining a text in terms of the category of the mother also a
regression to a dangerous essentialism that feminist critics have been trying
hard to avoid? Doesn't recourse to the mother simply collapse the woman
with the body in the worst way—reduce her to the reproduction that has
always entrapped her? And isn't that especially risky when discussing
women writers, since traditionally maternity has been the only type of
experience they've been thought able to depict? I might respond to that
objection by saying that motherhood means something more than experience as I've been using the term. But one answer to whether the category of
the mother sheers off into essentialism would have to be "yes." And yet—
why?—and does that pose a problem?

We can examine this collapse into the body and biology by turning again
to Mary Wollstonecraft's writing. Writing about the body is particularly
attractive to Wollstonecraft: Godwin quotes an introduction of hers to an
early conduct-book, in which she wishes that her audience were ready for
stories about "the organs of generation."[26] Wollstonecraft's display of the
body within her writing seems to be the offense for which her most
vehement critic, Rev. Richard Polwhele, attacked her. In his poem, *The
Unsex'd Females* (1797), he objects to that very conduct-book piece: "Mary
Wollstonecraft does not blush to say . . . that 'in order to lay the axe at the
root of corruption . . . it would be right to speak of the organs of generation.'"[27] Polwhele, however, only seems to be objecting to Wollstonecraft's
attention to the body; what actually bothers him is how much she ignores it,
how much she bucks the essentialism in which he grounds his attack. What
is horrifying to him about what he calls Wollstonecraft's "new philosophical
system" is that it "confounds the distinction of the sexes"[28]—and
Wollstonecraft does, in fact, write in the *Vindication* that "the sexual distinction that men have so warmly insisted upon, is arbitrary" (*Vindication:*
13.318). For Polwhele, the difference between men's and women's bodies
determines the difference between their minds: woman's weaker physique
ensures what he calls her "comparative imbecility"[29] and "inferiority . . . in
the scale of intelligence."[30] For Polwhele, Wollstonecraft's "philosophy" is
what unsexes her—makes it impossible to tell that she is female. Moreover,
the implications of Wollstonecraft's system unsexes men as well: Polwhele
misquotes Wollstonecraft—according to Godwin's version of the text, she
writes only that she is trying to "root out this dreadful evil," not that she
wishes to "lay the axe at the root of corruption." Polwhele's misquotation
shows that what bothers him about Wollstonecraft's system is the threat of
castration. Rather than displaying the organs of generation in a way that

shows clearly who's who, Wollstonecraft wants to mix up the boys and the girls. Polwhele goes on to write:

> I shudder at the new unpictur'd scene,
> Where unsex'd woman vaunts the imperious mien;
> Where girls, affecting to dismiss the heart,
> Invoke the Proteus of petrific Art.[31]

Representation and essentialism go hand in hand: to depict something is to place it within sexual difference. What horrifies Polwhele is that Wollstonecraft refuses to do this; she aligns herself instead with the "unpictur'd" and "protean" rather than the "petrific."

Critics like Laura Mulvey and Mary Jacobus have continued the argument that any representation inscribes essentialist distinctions:[32] given this argument, the maternal as sign—even as sign for the unsignifiable—is only the extension of representation's logic. For this very reason, French feminists collapse woman with her body, her maternity; by flaunting the maternal body, they expose the built-in essentialism of any structure of knowledge, disrupting its smooth and secret workings.

But another approach is to refuse maternity's essentialism, to argue that representation—even the representation of the body—is just that: figurative, not literal. What distinguishes Mary Wollstonecraft's treatment of the body is that it is not about the body at all; it points us, through Polwhele's reaction to it, to how the body becomes just another figure, a metaphor, in Polwhele's case an impossible fantasy of some clear-cut ground of reference—a fantasy Wollstonecraft refuses. The body is a metaphor for something else for Wollstonecraft, as we can see in the shift from the literal to the figurative in her advertisement to *Mary:*

> In an artless tale, without episodes, the mind of a woman, who has thinking powers is displayed. The female organs have been thought too weak for this arduous employment. . . . Without arguing physically about *possibilities*—in a fiction, such a being may be allowed to exist; whose grandeur is . . . drawn by the individual from the original source. (*Mary:* Advertisement)

In *Mary,* Wollstonecraft finally gives us a tale of organs—female organs. But the mother, the "original source," of which they're an extension, is not the womb but the mind, and these organs produce thought—and stories—rather than children. The body becomes a metaphor for writing; the physical leads us to the fictional.

The oscillation between the literal and figurative is important, for, with them, we end with another pair of differences—like the novel and romance, men and women, or the two aspects of the maternal—that can't quite be kept apart, that keep collapsing into each other. My first conclusion about the importance of the maternal for women's writing emphasized difference. I'd like now to propose a different conclusion that emphasizes sameness. A move to the maternal is also a move to the same, a move that undercuts the distinctions between mother and father, literature and life, other and self. And Monk Lewis's and Polwhele's need for difference, their horror when it breaks down, are instructive: we become no different from them if we don't recognize our similarity to them—our own insistence on difference is, like theirs, to stave off a threat, the threat of undeterminability, which undoes genre, gender, even identity, which, at least on one level, implicates us in categories from which we wish to distinguish ourselves. The category of women's writing, for example, although a useful fiction, in its reliance on supposedly clear-cut gender distinctions must be recognized *as* a fiction, a difference we impose for our own purposes. So, I would also say that the move from the paternal to the maternal actually makes no difference, if we keep in mind the ways they inhabit each other. But, in saying that, I'm really not disagreeing with my earlier conclusion: I'm just saying the same thing.

NOTES

1. Margaret Oliphant, *The Literary History of England* (London: Macmillan, 1886), 3:139–40. Inga-Stina Ewbank also quotes this passage in the first chapter of her book on the Brontës, perhaps suggesting Mrs. Oliphant's role as a point of origin for female critics, a kind of mother-critic.

2. Oliphant, 3:141.

3. Oliphant, 3:140.

4. Mary Poovey, *The Proper Lady and the Woman Writer* (Chicago: University of Chicago Press, 1984), p. 98. Almost all the women to whom I refer in this paper are named some variant of Mary: a coincidence or a consequence of a paper about mothers?

5. Poovey, p. 67.

6. Mary Wollstonecraft, *The Wrongs of Woman; or Maria, a Fragment*, in *Mary and The Wrongs of Woman*, ed. James Kinsley and Gary Kelly (New York: Oxford University Press, 1980), chap. 7, p. 131. All further references to this novel (abbreviated *Wrongs*) will appear in parenthesis in the text.

7. Quoted in *A Wollstonecraft Anthology*, ed. Janet Todd (Bloomington: Indiana University Press, 1977), p. 223; see also pp. 221, 224–25.

8. Todd, p. 224.

9. Mary Wollstonecraft, *A Vindication of the Rights of Woman* (New York: Penguin, 1975), Introduction, p. 81. All further references to this book (abbreviated *Vindication*) will appear in parentheses in the text.

10. Mary Wollstonecraft, *Mary, A Fiction* in *Mary and the Wrongs of Woman*, ed. Kinsley and Kelly, chap. 1, pp. 2–3. All further references to this novel (abbreviated *Mary*) will appear in parentheses in the text according to chapter and page number.

11. Kinsley and Kelly, "Introduction," to *Mary and The Wrongs of Woman*, p. xvi.

12. Kinsley and Kelly, "Introduction," p. ix.

13. "To Everina Wollstonecraft," March 22d [1797], *Collected Letters of Mary Wollstonecraft*, ed. Ralph Wardle (Ithaca: Cornell University Press, 1979), p. 385.

14. Emily W. Sunstein, *A Different Face: the Life of Mary Wollstonecraft* (New York: Harper and Row, 1975), p. 153.

15. "To William Godwin," [September 4, 1796], *Letters*, p. 345.

16. "To William Godwin," [May 21, 1797], *Letters*, p. 394.

17. "To Gilbert Imlay," September 22 [1794], *Letters*, p. 263.

18. "To Gilbert Imlay," September 22 [1794], *Letters*, p. 263.

19. "To Gilbert Imlay," August 17 [1794], *Letters*, p. 258.

20. Mary Jacobus, *Reading Woman: Essays in Feminist Criticism* (New York: Columbia University Press, 1986), p. 145.

21. Julia Kristeva, "From One Identity to Another," in her *Desire in Language*, ed. Leon S. Roudiez, trans. Thomas Gora, Alice Jardine, and Leon S. Roudiez (New York: Columbia University Press, 1980), p. 133.

22. Kristeva, p. 133. Jane Gallop (cited below) may be right in implying that the pre-oedipal position is not just a fantasy for Kristeva but always *risks* becoming a developmental "fact" that seems to offer the mother as a "solution" to gender problems, as it does in the object-relations psychology on which Kristeva sometimes relies. For a discussion of the political effects of this and related confusions in Kristeva's thought, see Ann Rosalind Jones, "Julia Kristeva on Femininity: The Limits of a Semiotic Politics," *Feminist Review* 18 (Nov. 1984): 56–73; and Donna C. Stanton, "Difference on Trial: A Critique of the Maternal Metaphor in Cixous, Irigary, and Kristeva," in *The Poetics of Gender*, ed. Nancy K. Miller (New York: Columbia University Press, 1986), pp. 157–82.

23. Dianne F. Sadoff, *Monsters of Affection* (Baltimore: Johns Hopkins University Press, 1982), p. 124.

24. Jane Gallop, "The Phallic Mother: Fraudian Analysis," in her *The Daughter's Seduction: Feminism and Psychoanalysis* (Ithaca: Cornell University Press, 1982), pp. 113–31.

25. Richard Klein, "In the Body of the Mother," *Enclitic* 7 (Spring 1983): 70.

26. William Godwin, *Memoirs of Mary Wollstonecraft*, ed. with a Preface, a Supplement, . . . and a Biographical Note by W. Clark Durant (New York: Greenberg, 1927), Supplement, p. 200. Godwin is quoting here from Wollstonecraft's "Introductory Address to Parents," in her *Elements of Morality*. The passage he quotes reads:

> I would willingly have said something of chastity and impurity; for impurity is now spread so far, that even children are infected; and by it the seeds of every virtue, as well as the germ of their posterity, which the Creator has implanted in them for wise purposes, are weakened or destroyed. I am thoroughly persuaded that the most efficacious method to root out this dreadful evil, would be to speak to children of the organs of generation as freely as we speak of the other parts of the body, and explain to them the noble use which they were designed for, and how they may be injured . . . [but] many people would have been shocked at tales, which might early in life have accustomed their children to see the dreadful consequences of incontinence; I have therefore been induced to leave them out. (pp. 200–01)

27. Richard Polwhele, *The Unsex'd Females* (New York: Cobbett, 1797) 11n.

28. Polwhele, 27n.

29. Polwhele, 20n.

30. Polwhele, 19n.

31. Polwhele, 19n.

32. Laura Mulvey, "Visual Pleasure and the Narrative Cinema," *Screen* 16 (1975): 6–18; and Jacobus, pp. 110–36.

POSSESSING NATURE

THE FEMALE IN *FRANKENSTEIN*

Anne K. Mellor

When Victor Frankenstein identifies Nature as female—"I pursued nature to *her* hiding places"[1]—he participates in a gendered construction of the universe whose ramifications are everywhere apparent in *Frankenstein*. His scientific penetration and technological exploitation of female nature, which I have discussed elsewhere,[2] is only one dimension of a more general cultural encoding of the female as passive and possessable, the willing receptacle of male desire. The destruction of the female implicit in Frankenstein's usurpation of the natural mode of human reproduction symbolically erupts in his nightmare following the animation of his creature, in which his bride-to-be is transformed in his arms into the corpse of his dead mother—"a shroud enveloped her form, and I saw the grave-worms crawling in the folds of the flannel" (p. 53). By stealing the female's control over reproduction, Frankenstein has eliminated the female's primary biological function and source of cultural power. Indeed, for the simple purpose of human survival, Frankenstein has eliminated the necessity to have females at all. One of the deepest horrors of this novel is Frankenstein's implicit goal of creating a society for men only: his creature is male; he refuses to create a female; there is no reason that the race of immortal beings he hoped to propagate should not be exclusively male.[3]

On the cultural level, Frankenstein's scientific project—to become the sole creator of a human being—supports a patriarchal denial of the value of women and of female sexuality. Mary Shelley, doubtless inspired by her mother's *A Vindication of the Rights of Woman*, specifically portrays the consequences of a social construction of gender that values the male above the female. Victor Frankenstein's nineteenth-century Genevan society is founded on a rigid division of sex roles: the male inhabits the public sphere, the female is relegated to the private or domestic sphere.[4] The men in Frankenstein's world all work outside the home, as public servants (Alphonse Frankenstein), as scientists (Victor), as merchants (Clerval and his father), or as explorers (Walton). The women are confined to the home; Elizabeth, for instance, is not permitted to travel with Victor and "regretted that she had not the same opportunities of enlarging her experience and cultivating her understanding" (151). Inside the home, women are either kept as a kind of pet (Victor "loved to tend" on Elizabeth "as I should on a favorite animal" [p. 30]); or they work as house wives, childcare providers, and nurses (Caroline Beaufort Frankenstein, Elizabeth Lavenza, Margaret Saville) or as servants (Justine Moritz).

As a consequence of this sexual division of labor, masculine work is kept outside of the domestic realm; hence intellectual activity is segregated from emotional activity. Victor Frankenstein cannot do scientific research and think lovingly of Elizabeth and his family at the same time. His obsession with his experiment has caused him "to forget those friends who were so many miles absent, and whom I had not seen for so long a time" (p. 50). This separation of masculine work from the domestic affections leads directly to Frankenstein's downfall. Because Frankenstein cannot work and love at the same time, he fails to feel empathy for the creature he is constructing and callously makes him eight feet tall simply because "the minuteness of the parts formed a great hindrance to my speed" (p. 49). He then fails to love or feel any parental responsibility for the freak he has created. And he remains so fixated on himself that he cannot imagine his monster might threaten someone else when he swears to be with Victor "on his wedding-night."

This separation of the sphere of public (masculine) power from the sphere of private (feminine) affection also causes the destruction of many of the women in the novel. Caroline Beaufort dies unnecessarily because she feels obligated to nurse her favorite Elizabeth during a smallpox epidemic; she thus incarnates a patriarchal ideal of female self-sacrifice (this suggestion is strengthened in the 1831 revisions where she eagerly risks her life to save Elizabeth). She is a woman who is devoted to her father in wealth and in poverty, who nurses him until his death, and then marries her father's best friend to whom she is equally devoted.

The division of public man from private woman also means that women cannot function effectively in the public realm. Despite her innocence of the crime for which she is accused, Justine Moritz is executed for the murder of William Frankenstein (and is even half-persuaded by her male confessor that she is responsible for William's death). And Elizabeth, fully convinced of Justine's innocence, is unable to save her: the impassioned defense she gives of Justine arouses public approbation of Elizabeth's generosity but does nothing to help Justine, "on whom the public indignation was turned with renewed violence, charging her with the blackest ingratitude" (p. 80). Nor can Elizabeth save herself on her wedding night. Both these deaths are of course directly attributable to Victor Frankenstein's self-devoted concern for his own suffering (the creature will attack only him) and his own reputation (people would think him mad if he told them his own monster had killed his brother).

Mary Shelley underlines the mutual deprivation inherent in a family and social structure based on rigid and hierarchical gender divisions by portraying an alternative social organization in the novel: the De Lacey family. The political situation of the De Lacey family, exiled from their native France by the manipulations of an ungrateful Turkish merchant and a draconian legal system, points up the injustice that prevails in a nation where masculine values of competition and chauvinism reign. Mary Shelley's political critique of a society founded on the unequal distribution of power and possessions is conveyed not only through the manifest injustice of Justine's execution and of France's treatment first of the alien Turkish merchant and then of the De Lacey family, but also through the readings in political history that she assigns to the creature. From Plutarch's *Parallel Lives of the Greeks and Romans* and from Volney's *Ruins, or Meditations on the Revolutions of Empires,* the creature learns both of masculine virtue and of masculine cruelty and injustice. "I heard of the division of property, of immense wealth and squalid poverty; . . . I learned that the possessions most esteemed . . . were high and unsullied descent united with riches" (p. 115). "Was man, indeed, at once so powerful, so virtuous, and magnificent, yet so vicious and base?" the creature asks incredulously. Implicit in Mary Shelley's attack on the social injustice of established political systems is the suggestion that the separation from the public realm of feminine affections and compassion has caused much of this social evil. Had Elizabeth Lavenza's plea for mercy for Justine, based on her intuitively correct knowledge of Justine's character, been heeded, Justine would not have been wrongly murdered by the courts. As Elizabeth exclaims,

> how I hate [the] shews and mockeries [of this world]! when one creature is murdered, another is immediately deprived of life in a slow torturing manner; then the executioners, their hands yet reeking with the blood of innocence, believe that they have done a great deed. They call this *retribution.* Hateful name! when the word is pronounced, I know greater and more horrid punishments are going to be inflicted than the gloomiest tyrant has ever invented to satiate his utmost revenge. (p. 83)

In contrast to this pattern of political inequality and injustice, the De Lacey family represents an alternative ideology: a vision of a social group based on justice, equality, and mutual affection. Felix willingly sacrificed his own welfare to ensure that justice was done to the Turkish merchant. More important, the structure of the De Lacey family constitutes Mary Shelley's ideal, an ideal derived from her mother's *A Vindication of the Rights of Woman.* In the impoverished De Lacey household, all work is shared equally in an atmosphere of rational companionship, mutual concern, and love. As their symbolic names suggest, Felix embodies happiness, Agatha goodness. They are then joined by Safie (*sophia* or wisdom). Safie, the daughter of the Turkish merchant, is appalled both by her father's betrayal of Felix and by the Islamic oppression of women he endorses; she has therefore fled from Turkey to Switzerland, seeking Felix. Having reached the De Lacey household, she promptly becomes Felix's beloved companion and is taught to read and write French. Safie, whose Christian mother instructed her "to aspire to higher powers of intellect, and an independence of spirit, forbidden to the female followers of Mahomet" (p. 119), is the incarnation of Mary Wollstonecraft in the novel. Wollstonecraft too traveled alone through Europe and Scandinavia; more important, she advocated in *A Vindication* that women be educated to be the "companions" of men and be permitted to participate in the public realm by voting, working outside the home, and holding political office.

But this alternative female role-model of an independent, well-educated, self-supporting, and loving companion, and this alternative nuclear family structure based on sexual equality and mutual affection, is lost in the novel, perhaps because the De Lacey family lacks the mother who might have been able to welcome the pleading, pitiable creature. When Safie flees with the De Lacey family, we as readers are deprived of the novel's only alternative to a rigidly patriarchal construction of gender and sex roles, just as Mary Shelley herself was deprived of a feminist role-model when her mother died and was subsequently denounced in the popular British press as a harlot, atheist, and anarchist. Safie's disappearance from the novel reflects Mary Shelley's own predicament. Like Frankenstein's creature, she has no positive prototype she can imitate, no place in history. That unique phenomenon envisioned by Mary Wollstonecraft, the wife as the lifelong intellectual equal and companion of her husband, does not exist in the world of nineteenth-century Europe experienced by Mary Shelley.

The doctrine of the separate spheres that Victor Frankenstein endorses encodes a particular attitude to female sexuality that Mary Shelley subtly exposes in her novel. This attitude is manifested most vividly in Victor's response to the creature's request for a female companion, an Eve to comfort and embrace him. After hearing his creature's autobiographical account of his sufferings and aspirations, Frankenstein is moved by an awakened conscience to do justice toward his Adam and promises to create a female creature, on condition that both leave forever the neighborhood of mankind. After numerous delays, Frankenstein finally gathers the necessary instruments and materials together into an isolated cottage on one of the Orkney Islands off Scotland and proceeds to create a female being. Once again he becomes ill: "my heart often sickened at the work of my hands. . . . my spirits became unequal; I grew restless and nervous" (p. 162).

Disgusted by his enterprise, Frankenstein finally determines to stop his work, rationalizing his decision to deprive his creature of a female companion in terms that repay careful examination. Here is Frankenstein's meditation:

> I was now about to form another being, of whose dispositions I was alike ignorant; she might become ten thousand times more malignant than her mate, and delight, for its own sake, in murder and wretchedness. He had sworn to quit the neighborhood of man, and hide himself in deserts; but she had not; and she, who in all probability was to become a thinking and reasoning animal, might refuse to comply with a compact made before her creation. They might even hate each other; the creature who already lived

loathed his own deformity, and might he not conceive a greater abhorrence
for it when it came before his eyes in the female form? She also might turn
with disgust from him to the superior beauty of man; she might quit him,
and he be again alone, exasperated by the fresh provocation of being
deserted by one of his own species.

Even if they were to leave Europe, and inhabit the deserts of the new
world, yet one of the first results of those sympathies for which the daemon
thirsted would be children, and a race of devils would be propagated upon
the earth, who might make the very existence of the species of man a
condition precarious and full of terror. Had I a right, for my own benefit, to
inflict this curse upon everlasting generations? . . . I shuddered to think that
future ages might curse me as their pest, whose selfishness had not hesitated
to buy its own peace at the price perhaps of the existence of the whole
human race. (p. 163)

What does Victor Frankenstein truly fear, which causes him to end his
creation of a female? First, he is afraid of an independent female will,
afraid that his female creature will have desires and opinions that cannot be
controlled by his male creature. Like Rousseau's natural man, she might
refuse to comply with a social contract made before her birth by another
person; she might assert her own integrity and the revolutionary right to
determine her own existence. Moreover, those uninhibited female desires
might be sadistic: Frankenstein imagines a female "ten thousand times"
more evil than her mate, who would "delight" in murder for its own sake.
Third, he fears that his female creature will be more ugly than his male
creature, so much so that even the male will turn from her in disgust.
Fourth, he fears that she will prefer to mate with ordinary males; implicit
here is Frankenstein's horror that, given the gigantic strength of this
female, she would have the power to seize and even rape the male she
might choose. And finally, he is afraid of her reproductive powers, her
capacity to generate an entire race of similar creatures. What Victor
Frankenstein truly fears is female sexuality as such. A woman who is
sexually liberated, free to choose her own life, her own sexual partner (by
force, if necessary). And to propagate at will can appear only monstrously
ugly to Victor Frankenstein, for she defies that sexist aesthetic that insists
that women be small, delicate, modest, passive, and sexually pleasing—but
available only to their lawful husbands.

Horrified by this image of uninhibited female sexuality, Victor Frankenstein violently reasserts a male control over the female body, penetrating
and mutilating the female creature at his feet in an image that suggests a
violent rape: "trembling with passion, [I] tore to pieces the thing on which I
was engaged" (p. 164). The morning after, when he returns to the scene,
"The remains of the half-finished creature, whom I had destroyed, lay
scattered on the floor, and I almost felt as if I had mangled the living flesh
of a human being" (p. 167). However he has rationalized his decision to
murder the female creature, Frankenstein's "passion" is here revealed as a

fusion of fear, lust, and hostility, a desire to control and even destroy female sexuality.

Frankenstein's fear of female sexuality is endemic to a patriarchal construction of gender. Uninhibited female sexual experience threatens the very foundation of patriarchal power: the establishment of patrilineal kinship networks together with the transmission of both status and property by inheritance entailed upon a male line. Significantly, in the patriarchal world of Geneva in the novel, female sexuality is strikingly repressed. All the women are presented as sexless: Caroline Beaufort is a devoted daughter and chaste wife while Elizabeth Lavenza's relationship with Victor is that of a sister.

In this context, the murder of Elizabeth Lavenza on her wedding night becomes doubly significant. The scene of her death is based on a painting Mary Shelley knew well, Henry Fuseli's famous "The Nightmare." The corpse of Elizabeth lies in the very attitude in which Fuseli placed his succubus-ridden woman: "She was there, lifeless and inanimate, thrown across the bed, her head hanging down, and her pale and distorted features half covered by her hair" (p. 193). Fuseli's woman is an image of female erotic desire, both lusting for and frightened of the incubus (or male demon) that rides upon her, brought to her bed-chamber by the stallion that leers at her from the foot of her bed; both the presence of this incubus and the woman's posture of open sexual acceptance leave Fuseli's intentions in no doubt.[5] Evoking this image, Mary Shelley alerted us to what Victor fears most: his bride's sexuality.[6] Significantly, Elizabeth would not have been killed had Victor not sent her into their wedding bedroom *alone*. Returning to the body of the murdered Elizabeth, Victor "embraced her with ardour; but the deathly languor and coldness of the limbs told me, that what I now held in my arms had ceased to be the Elizabeth whom I had loved and cherished" (p. 193). Victor most ardently desires his bride when he knows she is dead; the conflation with his earlier dream, when he thought to embrace the living Elizabeth but instead held in his arms the corpse of his mother, signals Victor's most profound erotic desire, a necrophiliac and incestuous desire to possess the dead female, the lost mother.

To put this point another way, we might observe that Victor Frankenstein's most passionate relationships are with men rather than with women. He sees Clerval as "the image of my former self" (p. 155), as his "friend and dearest companion" (p. 181), as his true soul mate. His description of Clerval's haunting eyes—"languishing in death, the dark orbs covered by the lids, and the long black lashes that fringed them" (p. 179)—verges on the erotic. Similarly, Walton responds to Frankenstein with an ardor that borders on the homoerotic. Having desired "the company of a man who could sympathize with me; whose eyes would reply to mine" (p. 13), Walton eagerly embraces Frankenstein as "a celestial spirit" (p. 23) whose death leaves him inarticulate with grief: "what can I say," Walton writes to his sister, "that will enable you to understand the depth of my sorrow?" (p. 216)

Finally, Frankenstein dedicates himself to his scientific experiment with a passion that can be described only as erotic: as Mary Shelley originally described Frankenstein's obsession, "I wished, as it were, to procrastinate my feelings of affection, until the great object of my affection was compleated." Frankenstein's homoerotic fixation upon his creature, whose features he had selected as "beautiful" (p. 52) in a parody of Pygmalion and Galatea, was underlined by Mary Shelley in a revision she made in the Thomas copy of *Frankenstein*. Describing his anxious enslavement to his task, Frankenstein confesses: "my voice became broken, my trembling hands almost refused to accomplish their task; I became as timid as a lovesick girl, and alternate tremor and passionate ardour took the place of wholesome sensation and regulated ambition" (51:31–35). In place of a normal heterosexual attachment to Elizabeth, Victor Frankenstein has substituted a homosexual obsession with his creature,[7] an obsession that in his case is energized by a profound desire to reunite with his dead mother, by becoming himself a mother.

To sum up, at every level Victor Frankenstein is engaged upon a rape of nature, a violent penetration and usurpation of the female's "hiding places," of the womb. Terrified of female sexuality and the power of human reproduction it enables, both he and the patriarchal society he represents use the technologies of science and the laws of the polis to manipulate, control, and repress women. Thinking back on Elizabeth Lavenza strangled on her bridal bier and on Fuseli's image of female erotic desire that she replicates, we can now see that at this level Victor's creature, his monster, realizes his own most potent lust. The monster, like Fuseli's incubus, leers over Elizabeth, enacting Victor's own repressed desire to rape, possess, and destroy the female. Victor's creature here becomes just that, his "creature," the instrument of his most potent desire: to destroy female reproductive power so that only men may rule.

However, in Mary Shelley's feminist novel, Victor Frankenstein's desire is portrayed not only as horrible and finally unattainable but also as self-destructive. For Nature is not the passive, inert, or "dead" matter that Frankenstein imagines.[8] Frankenstein assumes that he can violate Nature and pursue her to her hiding places with impunity. But Nature both resists and revenges herself upon his attempts. During his research, Nature denies to Victor Frankenstein both mental and physical health: "my enthusiasm was checked by my anxiety, and I appeared rather like one doomed by slavery to toil in the mines, or any other unwholesome trade, than an artist occupied by his favourite employment. Every night I was oppressed by a slow fever, and I became nervous to a most painful degree" (p. 51). When his experiment is completed, Victor has a fit that renders him "lifeless" for "a long, long time" and that marks the onset of a "nervous fever" that confines him for many months (p. 57). Victor continues to be tormented by anxiety attacks, bouts of delirium, periods of distraction and madness. As soon as he determines to blaspheme against Nature a second time, by creating a female human being, Nature punishes him: "the eternal twinkling of the stars weighed upon me, and . . . I listened to every blast of wind, as if it were a dull ugly siroc on its way to consume me" (p. 145). His mental illness returns: "Every thought that was devoted to it was an extreme anguish, and every word that I spoke in allusion to it caused my lips to quiver and my heart to palpitate" (p. 156); "my spirits became unequal; I grew restless and nervous" (p. 162). Finally, Frankenstein's obsession with destroying his creature exposes him to such mental and physical fatigue that he dies at the age of twenty-five.

Appropriately, Nature prevents Frankenstein from constructing a normal human being: an unnatural method of reproduction produces an unnatural being, in this case a freak of gigantic stature, watery eyes, a shriveled complexion, and straight black lips. This physiognomy causes Frankenstein's instinctive withdrawal from his child, and sets in motion the series of events that produces the monster who destroys Frankenstein's family, friends, and self.

Moreover, Nature pursues Victor Frankenstein with the very electricity he has stolen: lightning, thunder, and rain rage around him. The November night on which he steals the "spark of being" from Nature is dreary, dismal, and wet: "the rain . . . poured from a black and comfortless sky" (p. 54). He next glimpses his creature during a flash of lightning as a violent storm plays over his head at Plainpalais (p. 71); significantly, the almighty Alps, and in particular Mont Blanc, are represented in this novel as female, as an image of omnipotent fertility[9]—on his wedding day, Victor admires "the beautiful Mont Blanc, and the assemblage of snowy mountains that in vain endeavour to emulate *her*" (p. 190; my italics). Before Frankenstein's first encounter with his creature among the Alps, "the rain poured down in torrents, and thick mists hid the summits of the mountains" (p. 91). Setting sail from the Orkney island where he has destroyed his female creature, planning to throw her mangled remains into the sea, Frankenstein wakes to find his skiff threatened by a fierce wind and high waves that portend his own death: "I might be driven into the wide Atlantic, and feel all the tortures of starvation, or be swallowed up in the immeasurable waters that roared and buffetted around me. I . . . felt the torment of a burning thirst; . . . I looked upon the sea, it was to be my grave" (p. 169). Frankenstein ends his life and his pursuit of the monster he has made in the arctic regions, surrounded by the aurora borealis, the electromagnetic field of the North Pole. The atmospheric effects of the novel, which most readers have dismissed as little more than the traditional trappings of Gothic fiction, in fact manifest the power of Nature to punish those who transgress her boundaries. The elemental forces that Victor has released pursue him to his hiding places, raging round him like avenging Furies.

Finally, Nature punishes Victor Frankenstein the life-stealer most justly by denying him the capacity for natural procreation. His bride is killed on their wedding night, cutting off his chance to engender his own children. His creature—that "great object, which swallowed up every habit of my nature" (50)—turns against him, destroying not only his brother William, his soul mate Clerval, his loyal servant Justine, his grief-stricken father, and his wife, but finally pursuing Victor himself to his death, leaving Frankenstein entirely without progeny. Nature's revenge is absolute: he who violates her sacred hiding places is destroyed.

Mary Shelley's novel thus portrays the penalties of raping Nature. But it also celebrates an all-creating Nature loved and revered by human beings. Those characters capable of deeply feeling the beauties of Nature are rewarded with physical and mental health. Even Frankenstein in his moments of tranquillity or youthful innocence can respond powerfully to the glory of Nature. As Walton notes, "the starry sky, the sea, and every sight afforded by these wonderful regions, seems still to have the power of elevating his soul from earth" (p. 23). In Clerval's company Victor becomes again

> the same happy creature who, a few years ago, loving and beloved by all, had no sorrow or care. When happy, inanimate nature had the power of bestowing on me the most delightful sensations. A serene sky and verdant fields filled me with ecstacy. (p. 65)

Clerval's relationship to Nature represents one moral touchstone of the novel: since he "loved with ardour . . . the scenery of external nature" (p. 154), Nature endows him with a generous sympathy, a vivid imagination, a sensitive intelligence and an unbounded capacity for devoted friendship. His death annihilates the possibility that Victor Frankenstein might regain a positive relationship with Nature.

Mary Shelley envisions Nature as a sacred life-force in which human beings ought to participate in conscious harmony. Elizabeth Lavenza gives voice to this ideal in her choice of profession for Ernest Frankenstein:

> I proposed that he should be a farmer. . . . A farmer's is a very healthy happy life; and the least hurtful, or rather the most beneficial profession of any. My uncle [wanted him] educated as an advocate . . . but . . . it is certainly more creditable to cultivate the earth for the sustenance of man, than to be the confidant, and sometimes the accomplice, of his vices. (p. 59)

Nature nurtures those who cultivate her; perhaps this is why, of all the members of Frankenstein's family, only Ernest survives. Mary Shelley shares Wordsworth's concept of a beneficial bond between the natural and the human world, which is broken only at man's peril. Had Victor Frankenstein's eyes not become "insensible to the charms of nature" (p. 50) and the affections of family and friends, he would not have defied Mary Shelley's moral credo:

> A human being in perfection ought always to preserve a calm and peaceful mind, and never to allow passion or a transitory desire to disturb his tranquillity. I do not think that the pursuit of knowledge is an exception to this rule. If the study to which you apply yourself has a tendency to weaken your affections, and to destroy your taste for those simple pleasures in

which no alloy can possibly mix [e.g., the "beautiful season"], then that study is certainly unlawful, that is to say, not befitting the human mind. (p. 51)

As an ecological system of interdependent organisms, Nature requires the submission of the individual ego to the welfare of the family and the larger community. Like George Eliot after her, Mary Shelley is profoundly committed to an ethic of cooperation, mutual dependence, and self-sacrifice. The Russian sea-master willingly sacrifices his own desires that his beloved and her lover may marry; Clerval immediately gives up his desire to attend university in order to nurse his dear friend Victor back to health; Elizabeth offers to release her beloved Victor from his engagement should he now love another. Mary Shelley's moral vision thus falls into that category of ethical thinking which Carol Gilligan has recently identified as more typically female than male. Where men have tended to identify moral laws as abstract principles that clearly differentiate right from wrong, women have tended to see moral choice as imbedded in an ongoing shared life. As Gilligan contrasts them, a male "ethic of justice proceeds from the premise of equality—that everyone should be treated the same" while a female "ethic of care rests on the premise of nonviolence—that no one should be hurt."[10] This traditional female morality can probably be traced to what Nancy Chodorow and Dorothy Dinnerstein have shown to be the daughter's greater identification with the mother.[11] Whereas the son has learned to assert his separateness from the mother (and the process of mothering), the daughter has learned to represent that gendered role and thus has felt more tightly (and ambivalently) bound to the mother. Less certain of her ego boundaries, the daughter has been more likely to engage in moral thinking which gives priority to the good of the family and the community rather than to the rights of the individual.

Insofar as the family is the basic social unit, it has historically represented the system of morality practiced by the culture at large. The hierarchical structure of the Frankenstein family embodies a masculine ethic of justice in which the rights of the individual are privileged: Frankenstein pursues his own interests in alchemy and chemistry, cheerfully ignoring his family obligations as he engages "heart and soul" in his research, and is moreover encouraged to leave his family and fiancée for two years ("for a more indulgent and less dictatorial parent did not exist upon earth" [p. 130]). In contrast, the egalitarian and interdependent structure of the De Lacey family ideologically encodes a female ethic of care in which the bonding of the family unit is primary. Felix blames himself most because his self-sacrificing action on behalf of the Turkish merchant involved his family in his suffering. Agatha and Felix perform toward their father "every little office of affection and duty with gentleness; and he rewarded them by his benevolent smiles"; they willingly starve themselves that their father may eat (106). Safie's arrival particularly delighted Felix but also "diffused gladness through the cottage, dispelling their sorrow as the sun dissipates the morning mists" (112). In portraying the De Laceys as an archetype of the egalitarian, benevolent, and mutually loving nuclear family, Mary Shelley clearly displayed her own moral purpose, which Percy Shelley rightly if somewhat vaguely described in his Preface as "the exhibition of the amiableness of domestic affection, and the excellence of universal virtue" (7).

Mary Shelley's grounding of moral virtue in the preservation of familial bonds (against which Frankenstein, in his failure to parent his own child, entirely transgresses) entails an aesthetic credo as well. While such romantic descendants as Walter Pater and Oscar Wilde would later argue that aesthetics and morality, art and life, are distinct, Mary Shelley endorsed a traditional mimetic aesthetic that exhorted literature to imitate ideal Nature and defined the role of the writer as a moral educator. Her novel purposefully identifies moral virtue, based on self-sacrifice, moderation, and domestic affection, with aesthetic beauty. Even in poverty, the image of the blind old man listening to the sweetly singing Agatha is "a lovely sight, even to me, poor wretch! who had never beheld aught beautiful before" (103). In contrast, Frankenstein's and Walton's dream of breaking boundaries is explicitly identified as both evil and ugly. As Walton acknowledges, "my day dreams are . . . extended and magnificent; but they want (as the painters call it) *keeping*" (p. 14). "Keeping," in painting, means "the maintenance of the proper relation between the representations of nearer and more distant objects in a picture; hence, in a more general sense, "the proper subserviency of tone and colour in every part of a picture, so that the general effect is harmonious to the eye" (*OED*). Walton thus introduces Mary Shelley's ethical norm as an aesthetic norm; both in life and in art, her ideal is a balance or golden mean between conflicting demands, specifically here between large and small objects. In ethical terms, this means that Walton must balance his dreams of geographical discovery and fame against the reality of an already existing set of obligations (to his family, his crew, and the sacredness of Nature). Similarly, Frankenstein should have better balanced the obligations of great and small, of parent and child, of creator and creature. Frankenstein's failure to maintain *keeping*, to preserve "a calm and peaceful mind" (p. 51), is thus in Mary Shelley's eyes both a moral and an aesthetic failure, resulting directly in the creation of a hideous monster.

NOTES

1. Mary W. Shelley, *Frankenstein, or The Modern Prometheus* (London: Lackington, Hughes, Harding, Mavor and Jones, 1818); all further references to *Frankenstein* will be to the only modern reprint of this first edition, edited by James Rieger (New York: Bobbs-Merrill, 1974; reprinted, Chicago: University of Chicago Press, 1982), and will be cited by page number only in the text. This phrase occurs on page 49.

2. Anne K. Mellor, *"Frankenstein*: A Feminist Critique of Science," in *One Culture: Essays on Literature and Science*, ed. George Levine (Madison: University of Wisconsin Press, 1988), pp. 287–312.

3. Mary Shelley thus heralds a tradition of literary utopias and dystopias that depict single-sex societies, a tradition most recently appropriated by feminist writers

to celebrate exclusively female societies. For an analysis of the strengths and weaknesses of such feminist utopian writing, in which female societies are reproduced by parthenogenesis, see my "On Feminist Utopias," *Women's Studies* (1982): 241–62. Leading examples of this genre include Charlotte Perkins Gilman's *Herland,* Sally Miller Gearhart's *The Wanderground,* Joanna Russ's *The Female Man,* James Tiptree, Jr.'s "Houston, Houston Do You Read?" and Suzy McKee Charnas's trilogy *The Vampire Tapestry.*

4. On the gender division of nineteenth-century European culture, see Jean Elshtain, *Public Man, Private Woman: Women in Social and Political Thought* (Oxford: Robertson, 1981); and *Victorian Women: A Documentary Account of Women's Lives in Nineteenth-Century England, France, and the United States,* ed. E. Hellerstein, L. Hume, and K. Offen (Stanford: Stanford University Press, 1981). For a study of sex roles in *Frankenstein,* see Kate Ellis, "Monsters in the Family: Mary Shelley and the Bourgeois Family," in *The Endurance of Frankenstein,* ed. George Levine and U. C. Knoepflmacher (Berkeley, Los Angeles, London: University of California Press, 1979), pp. 123–42; and Anca Vlasopolos, "*Frankenstein*'s Hidden Skeleton: The Psycho-Politics of Oppression," *Science-Fiction Studies* 10 (1983): 125–36.

William Veeder, in his insightful but occasionally reductive psychological study of Mary and Percy Shelley and *Frankenstein, Mary Shelley and Frankenstein: The Fate of Androgyny* (1986), wishes to define masculinity and femininity as the complementary halves of an ideally balanced androgynous or agapic personality that is destroyed or bifurcated by erotic self-love; his book traces the reasons why Mary Shelley's fictional characters realize or fail to achieve her androgynous ideal. While he is right to argue that Mary Shelley believed in balancing "masculine" and "feminine" characteristics, he consistently defines as innate psychological characteristics those patterns of learned behavior (masculinity, femininity) that I prefer to see as socially constructed gender roles. His readings thus unintentionally reinforce an oppressive biological determinism and sex-stereotyping, even as they call attention to the dangers of extreme masculine and feminine behaviors.

5. Henry Fuseli, *The Nightmare,* first version, 1781; The Detroit Institute of Art. This famous painting was widely reproduced throughout the early nineteenth century and was of particular interest to Mary Shelley, who knew of her mother's early passionate love for Fuseli. H. W. Janson has suggested that Fuseli's representation of the nightmare is a projection of his unfulfilled passion for Anna Landolt, whose portrait is drawn on the reverse side (H. W. Janson, "Fuseli's *Nightmare,*" *Arts and Sciences* 2 [1963]: 23–28). When Fuseli learned that Anna Landolt had married, he wrote to her uncle and his good friend Johann Lavater from London on 16 June 1779 that he had dreamed of lying in her bed and fusing "her body and soul" together with his own. Fuseli's painting is thus a deliberate allusion to traditional images of Cupid and Psyche meeting in her bedroom at night; here the welcomed god of love has been transformed into a demonic incubus of erotic lust (see also Peter Tomory, *The Life and Art of Henry Fuseli,* London: 1972, pp. 92ff.; and the Catalogue Raisonnée by Gert Schiff, *Johann Heinrich Fussli,* Zurich: 1973, pp. 757–59).

Gerhard Joseph first noted the allusion to Fuseli's painting, "Frankenstein's Dream: The Child Is Father of the Monster," *Hartford Studies in Literature* 7 (1975): 97–115, 109. William Veeder denies the association (*Mary Shelley and Frankenstein,* 192–93) on the grounds that Elizabeth's hair half-covers her face; in this regard, it may be significant that Fuseli's woman's face is half-covered in shadow.

6. Paul A. Cantor has discussed Frankenstein's rejections both of normal sexuality and of the bourgeois lifestyle, in *Creature and Creator: Myth-making and English Romanticism* (New York: Cambridge University Press, 1984), pp. 109–15.

7. William Veeder has emphasized the homosexual bond between Frankenstein and his monster (*Mary Shelley and Frankenstein,* pp. 89–92). Eve Kosofsky Sedgwick arrives at this conclusion from a different direction. In her *Between Men: English*

Literature and Male Homosocial Desire (New York: Columbia University Press, 1985), she observes in passing that *Frankenstein,* like William Godwin's *Caleb Williams,* is "about one or more males who not only is persecuted by, but considers himself transparent to and often under the compulsion of, another male. If we follow Freud [in the case of Dr. Schreber] in hypothesizing that such a sense of persecution represents the fearful, phantasmic rejection by recasting of an original homosexual (or even merely homosocial) desire, then it would make sense to think of this group of novels as embodying strongly homophobic mechanisms" (pp. 91–92).

8. While I largely agree with Mary Poovey's intelligent and sensitive analysis of Frankenstein's egotistic desire (in *The Proper Lady and the Woman Writer,* pp. 123–33), I do not share her view that the nature we see in the novel is "fatal to human beings and human relationships." Poovey fails to distinguish between Frankenstein's view of nature and the author's and between the first and second editions of the novel in this regard.

9. On Mary Shelley's subversive representation of the traditionally masculinized Alps as female, see Fred V. Randel, "*Frankenstein,* Feminism, and the Intertextuality of Mountains," *Studies in Romanticism* 23 (Winter, 1984): 515–33.

10. Carol Gilligan, *In a Different Voice: Psychological Theory and Women's Development* (Cambridge, Mass: Harvard University Press, 1982), p. 174.

11. See Nancy Chodorow, *The Reproduction of Mothering: Psychoanalysis and the Sociology of Gender* (Berkeley and Los Angeles: University of California Press, 1978); Dorothy Dinnerstein, *The Mermaid and the Minotaur: Sexual Arrangements and Human Malaise* (New York: Harper and Row, 1976); cf. Nancy Friday, *My Mother/My Self: The Daughter's Search for Identity* (New York: Dell, 1977).

CONTRIBUTORS

Jane Aaron is a Lecturer in English at the University of Leicester, England. She has published essays on the Lambs and on Dickens and is currently completing a book on Charles and Mary Lamb.

Stuart Curran is Professor of English at the University of Pennsylvania and editor of the *Keats-Shelley Journal*. His most recent book is *Poetic Form and British Romanticism* (1986). He is currently writing a critical study of women poets of the Romantic period.

Nancy Moore Goslee, Associate Professor of English at the University of Tennessee, is the author of *Uriel's Eye: Miltonic Stationing and Statuary in Blake, Keats, and Shelley* (1986). Her essay on Shelley's sketches in his *Prometheus* notebooks received the Keats-Shelley Association award in 1986. She is completing a book on Scott's poetry.

Kurt Heinzelman is Associate Professor of English at the University of Texas at Austin and the author of *The Economics of the Imagination* (1980) as well as articles on Milton, British Romanticism, and modern poetry.

Sonia Hofkosh is a doctoral candidate in the Department of English at the University of California, Berkeley. She is working on a feminist interpretation of literary professionalism in the early nineteenth century.

Laurie Langbauer is Assistant Professor of English at Swarthmore College. Her work has appeared in *Novel* and *ELH,* and she is completing a book entitled *Women and Romance.*

Anne K. Mellor, Professor of English at UCLA, is the author of *Blake's Human Form Divine* (1974), *English Romantic Irony* (1980), and *Mary Shelley* (1988). She chaired the English Romantic Period Division meeting of the Modern Language Association in December, 1985, from which this volume of essays originated.

Alan Richardson, Assistant Professor of English at Boston College, is the author of the forthcoming *A Mental Theater: Poetic Drama and Consciousness in the Romantic Age.* He is presently writing a book on educational theory, ideology, and literary representations of childhood and schooling in the Romantic period.

Marlon B. Ross is Assistant Professor of English at the State University of New York at Stony Brook. He is completing a book to be entitled *Romanticism and the Contours of Masculine Desire* and beginning another on Romantic historicism and the ideology of metrical romance.

Karen Swann, Assistant Professor of English at Williams College, has published articles on Coleridge's romance narratives and is now working on a longer study of the English Romantic poets' experiments in romance.

Susan J. Wolfson is Associate Professor of English at Rutgers University and the author of *The Questioning Presence: Wordsworth, Keats, and the Interrogative Mode in Romantic Poetry* (1986). Her articles on Romanticism have appeared in *PMLA, ELH, JEGP, Criticism,* and *Keats-Shelley Journal.* The essay in this collection is part of a book in progress entitled *The Romantic Feminine: Figures on the Margin.*

INDEX

Aaron, Jane, 7
Abel, and Cain, 103
Adam, and Eve, 59, 61–62, 66, 148
Androgyny, 7; Romantic, 19–21, 24
Anger, 4, 8
Art: criticism, 14; and sensibility, in Keats, 199
Ashburner, Peggy, 60
Auerbach, Nina, 116
Austen, Jane, 4, 21, 115, 134, 192

Baillie, Joanna, 185–87, 188, 195
Bakewell, Thomas, 177
Barbauld, Anna, 187, 188, 189–90, 196–97
Barthes, Roland, 109
Beattie, James, 187
Betham, Mary, 188
Bettelheim, Bruno, 125
Blackstone, William, 20
Blake, William, 3, 203; childhood in, 16; emanation as feminine in, 20–21; "female form" in, 15; God as artistic imagination in, 7
Blanchot, Maurice, 110
Bloom, Harold, 27–28, 30, 41
Body, the, 15, 211, 216–17
Brawne, Fanny, 106–108
Brönte, Charlotte, 4
Brönte, Emily, 28, 174–75
Burton, Mary, 21
Byron, Lord, 3, 6, 19, 48–49, 93–110; on poetry, 34–40, 93–94; and Scott, 99–104; self-possession in, 45–46

Cain, and Abel, 103
Capitalism, 32–33
Carter, Elizabeth, 187, 197
Castration, threat of, 213
Chaos, as liberating, 5
Chartier, Alain, 90
Chateaubriand, Francois-René de, 14
Childhood, in Blake and Wordsworth, 16
Chodorow, Nancy, 14–15, 55, 229
Chora, 5, 215
Christ, 18, 122
Christianity, 122–23
Churchill, Charles, 187
Cixous, Hélène, 6
Coleridge, Samuel P., 3, 7, 47, 202; androgyny in, 20; and Wordsworth, 59, 64, 68, 74

Connection, and selfhood, 13–14
Consciousness, self-, 26
Cornwall, Barry, 173
Cowley, Hannah, 197
Cowper, William, 187, 188, 200, 202
Culler, Jonathan, 149
Curran, Stuart, 7

Derrida, Jacques, 5
Desire, 8, 97–98
Dickens, Charles, 194, 201, 203
Dickinson, Emily, 28
Difference, 215; sexual, 3, 5, 217–18
Dinnerstein, Dorothy, 229
Discourse, patriarchal, 6
Domesticity, 52–76, 133–34, 221
Douglas, W.W., 54
Dryden, John, 36
Dualism, in Western thought, 5

Ecriture féminine, 6
Ego, 6, 15
Eliot, George, 4, 229
Emotion, 15, 34–44
Empathy: in art criticism, 14; in Blake, 16; and selfhood, in Chodorow, 13, 14–15
Empiricism, 14
Enlightenment, the, 8
Ethics, 14
Experience, as textual, 71
Eyre, Jane, 72

Feeling, Man of, 15, 16
Felman, Shoshana, 81–82, 83
Female, the: death of, and figurative language, 6; denial of, and language, 6; labor, 59–62, 66, 69; language of (écriture féminine), 6; and male psychological development, 174; and the Romantic ego, 7
Feminine: depiction of the, 21; devaluation of, in the English Augustan period, 14; emanation as, in Blake, 20–21; emotion, and masculine power, 37; empathy, in Chodorow, 14–15; male incorporation of the, 16–22; power, and powerlessness, 98; sensibility, in Rousseau, 15–16
Femininity, 14, 16–17
Feminist theory, French, 3, 5–6
Fetterley, Judith, 4
Fisher, John, 70
Foucault, Michel, 94

235